# THE LION BOOK OF
# CHRISTIAN
# POETRY

*For J.J.*

**Thanks**
My warm thanks to Pat Alexander,
my original editor, and to Catherine Giddings
who has prepared this edition for publication;
also to my husband, Alan, and my daughter,
Pauline Shelton, for their generous help.

# THE LION BOOK OF
# CHRISTIAN POETRY

## MARY BATCHELOR

A LION BOOK

A Lion Book
an imprint of
**Lion Hudson plc**
Mayfield House, 256 Banbury Road,
Oxford OX2 7DH, England
www.lionhudson.com
ISBN 0 7459 5183 X

First published in 1995 under the title
*The Lion Christian Poetry Collection*

This abridged edition published 2005
10 9 8 7 6 5 4 3 2 1 0

A catalogue record for this book is available
from the British Library

Typeset in 10/12pt Berkeley Old Style
Printed and bound in Great Britain by
Cox & Wyman Ltd, Reading

# Contents

INTRODUCTION   7

IN TOUCH WITH GOD   9
The Search   10
God's Mercy and Forgiveness   27
Thankfulness and Praise   37
God Is Near   48
Love and Trust   57

THE WORLD WE LIVE IN   69
Nature and Landscape   70
Water and Seascape   83
Town and City   87
All God's Creatures   90
Times and Seasons   110

THE PILGRIM'S WAY   125
The Journey   126
Faith and Doubt   134
The Struggle of Good and Evil   154
Sickness and Suffering   164

JESUS THE CHRIST   189
Christ the Child: Christmas Nativity   190
Christ the Man: Easter Death and Resurrection   221

THE HOLY SPIRIT AND THE CHURCH   239
The Holy Spirit: Pentecost   240
The Church – and Churches   244

## DAILY LIFE   255

Work   256

Home   270

Morning and Night   276

Who Cares? The Voice of Protest   284


## PERSON TO PERSON   300

Love   301

Introspective   313

Parents and Children   318

Youth and Age   326

Grandparents   335


## TIME AND ETERNITY   338

The Passing Beat of Time   339

Death and Beyond   345

Death   347

On the Death of Others   358

Hereafter   363

Presences Unseen   366

Heaven   370

The Return of Christ and the Last Judgment   376


## PEN PORTRAITS   382

Bible Characters   383

Saints Official – and Saints in the Making   394


Biographies of Authors   408

Index of Authors   420

Index of First Lines   423

Acknowledgments   430

# Introduction

I do hope that this anthology will give great pleasure –
that is its main purpose – and that it will be enjoyed by
everyone who at some time or other has had a taste for
poetry, witty or romantic, humorous or sad. The poet's
gift is to put into memorable forms and words the joys,
sorrows and humour that we all experience and to help
us to see life in a fresh way.

This is a 'Christian' poetry anthology, so many of the
poems have been written by poets who are Christian,
but not all of them are writing within the usual Christian
traditions. The poet, like the prophet, opens our eyes
to the truth and often exposes the falseness or staleness
of accepted beliefs and ideas. Some of these poems cut
across accepted patterns of Christian thinking and give us
new insights into what God is like and into our ways of
responding to him. By exposing what is shallow or false
they will help us to see more clearly and, in the end,
strengthen faith.

I have included verses that we usually think of as hymns
in the hope that setting them among other poems will
make them easier to read as poems in their own right.
I have also limited my choice to English-speaking poetry
rather than use translations. The only translated poems
are those from medieval Latin, beautifully crafted by the
medieval scholar and poet Helen Waddell. In the case
of poems in Anglo-Saxon (King Alfred's time) or Middle
English (the English of Chaucer), I have sometimes
done no more than replace obscure words with better
understood modern ones. But in the case of Langland –
a contemporary of Chaucer – I have used the splendid
translations made by Ronald Tamplin, who has created
brilliant and vivid poems that splendidly reflect their
colourful originals. I am also especially grateful to
Professor Tamplin for providing a translation of *Love in
Action* especially for this anthology.

As well as using different words and styles, poets from
different centuries have different preoccupations. In the
Middle Ages, when life was short and harsh, death and

judgment were much thought and written about. In Victorian times, too, the death of babies and young people was only too common and the poetry of the time echoes the tragedy of grief and loss. Modern poets have less to say about death but plenty about the new moral choices that face our society at a time of rapid medical and scientific research and the threat of weapons of mass destruction.

The poems are arranged in sections according to their subject. This is to help readers find the right poems to meet their choice or requirements, but a by-product of this arrangement is the delightful mix that results from putting the works of different times and styles alongside one another. I hope that this mix-and-match adds spice and texture to what could otherwise be a more monotonous diet. I suspect, too, that if the poems were in chronological order, most of us would skip those from earlier times. Old and new together create a balanced fare. For readers who wish to read all the poems by a particular author there is an index that lists them. There are also brief biographies of the poets in a separate index.

Readers may think that some of the poems are not particularly 'religious'. But, as one poet put it, 'I think that if the mind is directed in faith, then all poetry, as all action, is religious'.

Poetry brings us a wake-up call to the best, the most important matters in life; it also lights up the ordinary and mundane with spiritual insight and significance. So, in the words of the greatest of all Prophets and Poets (as proof, read his words in the Gospels), 'If you have ears to hear, listen!'

*Mary Batchelor*

# In Touch With God

## Presence

Expecting him, my door was open wide:
    Then I looked round
    If any lack of service might be found,
And saw him at my side:
    How entered, by what secret stair,
    I know not, knowing only he was there.

*T.E. Brown*
*1830–97*

# The Search

## Apparition

How shall I find him, who can be my guide?
  Wears he a human form, a tear-marred face,
By blood-red raiment may he be descried,
  Or broods he far withdrawn through stellar space?
Perchance, informing all, his coils entwine
  And bind the monstrous fabric cell to cell,
Or, veiled in service, 'neath this Bread and Wine
  A homely God, he deigns with men to dwell.
Lo! just beyond the skyline he may stand,
  Speak just without the waftage of mine ear,
I all but touch him with my outstretched hand,
  Clear to my senses he may straight appear.

I hush my drumming heart, I stay my breath
To catch his step, to hearken what he saith.

*Eugene Mason*
*1862–1935*

## Lost and Found

I missed him when the sun began to bend;
I found him not when I had lost his rim;
With many tears I went in search of him,
Climbing high mountains which did still ascend,
And gave me echoes when I called my friend;
Through cities vast and charnel-houses grim,
And high cathedrals where the light was dim,
Through books and arts and works without an end,
But found him not – the friend whom I had lost.
And yet I found him – as I found the lark,
A sound in fields I heard but could not mark;
I found him nearest when I missed him most;
I found him in my heart, a life in frost,
A light I knew not till my soul was dark.

*George MacDonald*
*1824–1905*

# A New Hymn for Solitude

I found thee in my heart, O Lord,
    As in some secret shrine;
I knelt, I waited for thy word,
    I joyed to name thee mine.

I feared to give myself away
    To that or this; beside
Thy altar on my face I lay,
    And in strong need I cried.

Those hours are past. Thou art not mine,
    And therefore I rejoice,
I wait within no holy shrine,
    I faint not for the voice.

In thee we live; and every wind
    Of heaven is thine; blown free
To west, to east, the God unshrined
    Is still discovering me.

*Edward Dowden*
*1843–1913*

# Wait a Little

Lord, thou clepedest* me,
And I nought ne answerèd thee
But wordès slow and sleepy:
'Thole* yet! Thole a little!'
But 'yet' and 'yet' was endèless,
And 'thole a little' a long way is.

*Anonymous*
*Medieval*

\* *clepedest:* you called me; *thole:* wait

# Come in at My Door

Who is at my window? Who? Who?
Go from my window! Go! Go!
Who calls there, like a stranger,
Go from my window! Go!

– Lord, I am here, a wretched mortal,
That for thy mercy doth cry and call
Unto thee, my lord celestiàl,
See who is at thy window, who? –

Remember thy sin, remember thy smart,
And also for thee what was my part,
Remember the spear that pierced my heart,
And in at my door thou shalt go.

I ask no thing of thee therefore,
But love for love, to lay in store.
Give me thy heart; I ask no more,
And in at my door thou shalt go.

Who is at my window? Who?
Go from my window! Go!
Cry no more there like a stranger,
But in at my door thou go!

*Anonymous*
*about 1500*

# No Coming to God without Christ

Good and great God! How should I fear
To come to thee, if Christ not there!
Could I but think, he would not be
Present, to plead my cause for me;
To Hell I'd rather run, than I
Would see thy face, and he not by.

*Robert Herrick*
*1591–1674*

# Divine Possession

He fumbles at your soul
As players at the keys
Before they drop full music on.
He stuns you by degrees,
Prepares your brittle nature
For the ethereal blow
By fainter hammers further heard,
Then nearer, then so slow
Your breath has time to straighten,
Your brain to bubble cool,
Deals one imperial thunderbolt
That scalps your naked soul.

When winds take forests in their paws
The universe is still.

*Emily Dickinson*
*1830–86*

# Disclosure

Prayer is like watching for the
Kingfisher. All you can do is
Be where he is likely to appear, and
Wait.
Often, nothing much happens;
There is space, silence and
Expectancy.
No visible sign, only the
Knowledge that he's been there
And may come again.
Seeing or not seeing cease to matter,
You have been prepared.
But when you've almost stopped
Expecting it, a flash of brightness
Gives encouragement.

*Anne Lewin*
*20th century*

# None Other Lamb

None other Lamb, none other Name,
  None other Hope in heaven or earth or sea,
None other Hiding-place from guilt and shame,
    None beside thee.

My faith burns low, my hope burns low
  Only my heart's desire cries out in me
By the deep thunder of its want and woe
    Cries out to thee.

Lord, thou art Life tho' I be dead,
  Love's Fire thou art, however cold I be:
Nor heaven have I, nor place to lay my head,
    Nor home, but thee.

*Christina Rossetti*
*1830–94*

# A Stranger in this Land

Lord, I am lonely
And the sun is shining,
Listless, while the wind
Shakes the ageing leaves.
The harvest has been gathered
All is bagged and barned,
Silos burst with grain.
  Why, Lord, must I still stand
Dropping blind seeds
On to a barren soil?

Come, sweet Jesus, cut me down
With the sickle of your mercy,
For I am lonely
And a stranger in this land.

*Cliff Ashby*
*20th century*

# The Prayer

Wilt thou not visit me?
The plant beside me feels thy gentle dew,
   And every blade of grass I see
From thy deep earth its quickening moisture drew.

   Wilt thou not visit me?
Thy morning calls on me with cheering tone;
   And every hill and tree
Lend but one voice – the voice of thee alone.

   Come, for I need thy love,
More than the flower the dew or grass the rain;
   Come, gently as thy holy dove;
And let me in thy sight rejoice to live again.

   I will not hide from them
When thy storms come, though fierce may be their wrath,
   But bow with leafy stem,
And strengthened follow on thy chosen path.

   Yes, thou wilt visit me:
Nor plant nor tree thine eye delights so well,
   As, when from sin set free,
My spirit loves with thine in peace to dwell.

*Jones Very*
*1813–80*

15

# The Great Intruder

It is exasperating
to be called
so persistently
when the last thing
we want to do
is get up
and go
but God
elects
to keep on haunting
like some
holy ghost.

*Thomas John Carlisle*
*20th century*

# The Divine Guest

My spirit longeth for thee
  Within my troubled breast;
Although I be unworthy
  Of so divine a Guest.

Of so divine a Guest,
  Unworthy though I be;
Yet has my heart no rest,
  Unless it comes from thee.

Unless it comes from thee,
  In vain I look around:
In all that I can see,
  No rest is to be found.

No rest is to be found,
  But in thy blessed love;
O, let my wish be crowned,
  And send it from above.

*John Byrom*
*1692–1763*

# Lord of the Winds

Lord of the winds, I cry to thee,
  I that am dust,
And blown about by every gust
  I fly to thee.

Lord of the waters, unto thee I call,
  I that am weed upon the waters borne,
    And by the waters torn,
Tossed by the waters, at thy feet I fall.

*Mary Coleridge*
*1861–1907*

# An Invocation

To God, the everlasting, who abides,
One Life within things infinite that die:
To him whose unity no thought divides
Whose breath is breathèd through immensity.

Him neither eye hath seen, nor ear hath heard;
Nor reason, seated in the souls of men,
Though pondering oft on the mysterious word,
Hath e'er revealed his being to mortal ken.

Earth changes, and the starry wheels roll round;
The seasons come and go, moons wax and wane;
The nations rise and fall, and fill the ground,
Storing the sure results of joy and pain:

Slow knowledge widens towards a perfect whole,
From that first man who named the name of heaven,
To him who weighs the planets as they roll,
And knows what laws to every life are given.

Yet he appears not. Round the extreme sphere
Of science still thin ether floats unseen:
Darkness still wraps him round; and ignorant fear
Remains of what we are, and what have been.

Only we feel him; and in aching dreams,
Swift intuitions, pangs of keen delight,
The sudden vision of his glory seems
To sear our souls, dividing the dull night.

O God, unknown, invisible, secure,
Whose being by dim resemblances we guess,
Who in man's fear and love abidest sure,
Whose power we feel in darkness and confess!

Without thee nothing is, and thou art nought
When on thy substance we gaze curiously:
By thee impalpable, named force and thought,
The solid world still ceases not to be.

Lead thou me, God, law, reason, duty, life!
All names for thee alike are vain and hollow –
Lead me, for I will follow without strife;
Or, if I strive, still must I blindly follow.

*John Addington Symonds*
*1840–93*

# Beyond the Headlines

Then I saw the wild geese flying
In fair formation to their bases in Inchicore
And I knew that these wings would outwear the wings of war
And a man's simple thoughts outlive the day's loud lying.
Don't fear, don't fear, I said to my soul.
The Bedlam of Time is an empty bucket rattled,
'Tis you who will say in the end who best battles.
Only they who fly home to God have flown at all.

*Patrick Kavanagh*
*20th century*

# *From:* The Hound of Heaven

I fled him, down the nights and down the days;
  I fled him, down the arches of the years;
I fled him, down the labyrinthine ways
  Of my own mind; and in the mist of tears
I hid from him, and under running laughter.
    Up vistaed hopes I sped;
    And shot, precipitated,
Adown Titanic glooms of chasmed fears,
  From those strong Feet that followed, followed after.
    But with unhurrying chase,
    And unperturbèd pace,
  Deliberate speed, majestic instancy,
    They beat – and a Voice beat
    More instant than the Feet –
'All things betray thee, who betrayest me.'.

    Halts by me that footfall:
    Is my gloom, after all,
Shade of his hand, outstretched caressingly?
    'Ah, fondest, blindest, weakest,
    I am he whom thou seekest!
Thou dravest love from thee, who dravest me.'

*Francis Thompson*
*1859–1907*

# *From:* Wrestling Jacob

(GENESIS 32)

Come, O thou Traveller unknown,
   Whom still I hold, but cannot see,
My company before is gone,
   And I am left alone with thee,
With thee all night I mean to stay,
And wrestle till the break of day.

I need not tell thee who I am,
   My misery, or sin declare,
Thyself has called me by my name,
   Look on thy hands, and read it there,
But who, I ask thee, who art thou?
Tell me thy name, and tell me now.

In vain thou strugglest to get free,
   I never will unloose my hold:
Art thou the Man who died for me?
   The secret of thy love unfold.
Wrestling I will not let thee go,
Till I thy name, thy nature know...

What though my shrinking flesh complain,
   And murmur to contend so long,
I rise superior to my pain,
   When I am weak then I am strong,
And when my all of strength shall fail,
I shall with the God-Man prevail...

I know thee, Saviour, who thou art,
   Jesus, the feeble sinner's friend;
Nor wilt thou with the night depart,
   But stay, and love me to the end;
Thy mercies never shall remove,
Thy nature and thy name is Love.

*Charles Wesley*
*1707–88*

# Resurrection

Each time you go, I'm buried and I hear
seething with honest worms, the truthful loam.
But coming again, you riddle at my ear
with promises of being in air, at home.
I'm comfortable enough, cupboarded in earth –
Oh, I would take the idiom of air:
sirens and chimes and mother's shrieks in birth
and silence in perpetual repair.
But repeated resurrection I can't bear.
Let me grow into death the way of a stone
or let me wear the wind against my ear
eternally. I'm worried like a bone.
Above, I hear your footsteps: in your mouth
promises raucous as the sky when geese fly south.

*Jeanne Murray Walker*
*20th century*

# Surrender

Batter my heart, three-personed God, for you
As yet but knock, breathe, shine, and seek to mend;
That I may rise and stand, o'erthrow me and bend
Your force to break, blow, burn, and make me new.
I, like an usurped town, to another due,
Labour to admit you, but O, to no end.
Reason, your viceroy in me, me should defend,
But is captived and proves weak or untrue.
Yet dearly I love you and would be loved fain,
But am betrothed unto your enemy.
Divorce me, untie, or break that knot again,
Take me to you, imprison me, for I,
Except you enthrall me, never shall be free,
Nor ever chaste, except you ravish me.

*John Donne*
*1572–1631*

# Hymn

Thou hidden love of God, whose height,
   Whose depth unfathomed no man knows,
I see from far thy beauteous light,
   Inly I sigh for thy repose;
My heart is pained, nor can it be
At rest, till it finds rest in thee.

Thy secret voice invites me still,
   The sweetness of thy yoke to prove:
And fain I would: but though my will
   Seems fixed, yet wide my passions rove;
Yet hindrances strew all the way;
I aim at thee, yet from thee stray.

'Tis mercy all, that thou hast brought
   My mind to seek her peace in thee;
Yet while I seek, but find thee not,
   No peace my wandering soul shall see;
O when shall all my wanderings end,
And all my steps to thee-ward tend!...

O Love, thy sovereign aid impart,
   To save me from low-thoughted care:
Chase this self-will through all my heart,
   Through all its latent mazes there:
Make me thy duteous child, that I
Ceaseless may Abba, Father, cry!...

Each moment draw from earth away
   My heart that lowly waits thy call:
Speak to my inmost soul, and say,
   I am thy love, thy God, thy all!
To feel thy power, to hear thy voice,
To taste thy love, be all my choice.

*John Wesley*
*1703–91*

# The Invitation

Lord, what unvalued pleasures crowned
   The days of old;
When thou wert so familiar found,
   Those days were gold; –

When Abram wished thou couldst afford
   With him to feast;
When Lot but said, 'Turn in, my Lord,'
   Thou wert his guest.

But, ah! this heart of mine doth pant,
   And beat for thee;
Yet thou art strange, and wilt not grant
   Thyself to me.

What, shall thy people be so dear
   To thee no more?
Or is not heaven to earth as near
   As heretofore?

The famished raven's hoarser cry
   Finds out thine ear;
My soul is famished, and I die
   Unless thou hear.

O thou great ALPHA! King of kings
   Or bow to me,
Or lend my soul seraphic wings,
   To get to thee.

*Anonymous*
*17th century*

## From: The Task

I was a stricken deer, that left the herd
Long since; with many an arrow deep infixt
My panting side was charged, when I withdrew
To seek a tranquil death in distant shades.
There was I found by one who had himself
Been hurt by th'archers. In his side he bore,
And in his hands and feet, the cruel scars.
With gentle force soliciting the darts,
He drew them forth, and healed, and bade me live.
Since then, with few associates, in remote
And silent woods I wander, far from those
My former partners of the peopled scene;
With few associates, and not wishing more.

*William Cowper*
*1731–1800*


## God our Refuge

If there had anywhere appeared in space
   Another place of refuge where to flee,
Our hearts had taken refuge in that place,
      And not with thee.

For we against creation's bars had beat
   Like prisoned eagles, through great worlds had sought
Though but a foot of ground to plant our feet,
      Where thou wert not.

And only when we found in earth and air,
   In heaven or hell, that such might nowhere be –
That we could not flee from thee anywhere,
      We fled to thee.

*Richard Chenevix Trench*
*1807–86*

# A Dig through Dust

I dream a dig through dust:
a pit I cannot tell how deep,
Sheol, the grave perhaps,
timber long since riddled to ash.
I scratch and sieve for goods;
ornaments, spindle-whorls and bones.

Find none. A post-hole then
whose tree and cross-tree raised a roof;
I comb the flinty ground
for sherds, grain, signs of the sacred
or profane, black layers
of occupation; and find none.

But for three Roman nails,
rust-cankered. Post-hole then, and grave.
Out of the dig's raised dust
a man – a gardener – appears
to set a seed in it.
Water, he says. I wake in tears.

*Paul Hyland*
*20th century*

# That Holy Thing

They were all looking for a king
    To slay their foes and lift them high:
Thou cam'st, a little baby thing
        That made a woman cry.

O Son of Man, to right my lot
    Naught but thy presence can avail;
Yet on the road thy wheels are not,
        Nor on the sea thy sail!

My how or when thou wilt not heed,
    But come down thine own secret stair,
That thou mayst answer all my need –
        Yea, every bygone prayer.

*George MacDonald*
*1824–1905*

# Christ my All-in-all

I've found the pearl of greatest price,
　My heart doth sing for joy;
And sing I must, for Christ is mine,
　Christ shall my song employ.

Christ is my Prophet, Priest, and King:
　My Prophet full of light,
My great High Priest before the throne,
　My King of heavenly might.

For he indeed is Lord of lords,
　And he the King of kings;
He is the Sun of Righteousness,
　With healing in his wings.

Christ is my peace; he died for me,
　For me he gave his blood;
And as my wondrous sacrifice
　Offered himself to God.

Christ Jesus is my All-in-all,
　My comfort and my love;
My life below; and he shall be
　My glory-crown above.

*John Mason*
*about 1645–94*

# Prayer

I asked for Peace –
   My sins arose,
    And bound me close,
I could not find release.

I asked for Truth –
   My doubts came in,
    And with their din
They wearied all my youth.

I asked for Love –
   My lovers failed,
    and griefs assailed
Around, beneath, above.

I asked for thee –
   And thou didst come
    To take me home
Within thy heart to be.

*Digby Mackworth Dolben*
*1848–67*

# The Search

Pilgrim remember
For all your pain
The Master you seek abroad
You will find at home –
Or walk in vain.

*Anonymous*
*7th century*

# God's Mercy and Forgiveness

## God's mercy

God's boundless mercy is (to sinful man)
Like to the ever-wealthy ocean:
Which though it sends forth thousand streams, 'tis ne'er
Known, or else seen, to be the emptier;
And though it takes all in, 'tis yet no more
Full, and filled full, than when full filled before.

*Robert Herrick*
*1591–1674*

## 'Neither Shadow of Turning'

I could not name a single blessing
   That came to me in disguise;
The gifts I asked arrived unmasked
   Under broad day's honest skies.

God does not play a senile game
   That wraps his mercies round
With a leprous sheet, a scabbed deceit:
   His good, from the start, is sound.

There is no heaven disguised as hell,
   No jail by which we're freed;
A twist that mocks is no paradox –
   It's the devil's twist indeed.

'Deliver us from evil' – why,
   If the evil has good inside?
God's war is grim – we are bruised with him:
   HIS gifts never mystified.

*Jack Clemo*
*20th century*

# Saul Kane's Conversion

FROM: THE EVERLASTING MERCY

All earthly things that blessed morning
Were everlasting joy and warning.
The gate was Jesus' way made plain,
The mole was Satan foiled again,
Black blinded Satan snouting way
Along the red of Adam's clay;
The mist was error and damnation,
The lane the road unto salvation,
Out of the mist into the light;
O blessed gift of inner sight.
The past was fading like a dream;
There come the jingling of a team,
A ploughman's voice, a clink of chain,
Slow hoofs, and harness under strain.
Up the slow slope a team came bowing,
Old Callow at his autumn ploughing,
Old Callow, stooped above the hales,
Ploughing the stubble into wales;
His grave eyes looking straight ahead,
Shearing a long straight furrow red;
His plough-foot high to give it earth
To bring new food for men to birth.

O wet red swathe of earth laid bare,
O truth, O strength, O gleaming share,
O patient eyes that watch the goal,
O ploughman of the sinner's soul.
O Jesus, drive the coulter deep
To plough my living man from sleep...

O Christ who holds the open gate,
O Christ who drives the furrow straight,
O Christ, the plough, O Christ, the laughter
Of holy white birds flying after,
Lo, all my heart's field red and torn,
And thou wilt bring the young green corn,
The young green corn divinely springing,
The young green corn for ever singing;
And when the field is fresh and fair

Thy blessèd feet shall glitter there.
And we will walk the weeded field,
And tell the golden harvest's yield,
The corn that makes the holy bread
By which the soul of man is fed,
The holy bread, the food unpriced,
Thy everlasting mercy, Christ

*John Masefield*
*1878–1967*

## Christian Arrives at the Cross and Sepulchre

(FROM: THE PILGRIM'S PROGRESS)

Thus far did I come loaden with my sin,
Nor could aught ease the grief that I was in
Till I came hither. What a place is this!
Must here be the beginning of my bliss?
Must here the burden fall from off my back?
Blessed Cross! Blessed Sepulchre! Blessed rather be
The man that there was put to shame for me.

*John Bunyan*
*1622–88*

# CONFESSION AND FORGIVENESS

## Forgive the Prodigal Heart

Behold the prodigal! To thee I come,
To hail my Father and to seek my home.
Nor refuge could I find, nor friend abroad,
Straying in vice and destitute of God.

O let thy terrors and my anguish end!
Be thou my refuge and be thou my friend:
Receive the son thou didst so long reprove,
   Thou that art the God of love!

*Matthew Prior*
*1664–1721*

# A Hymn

Drop, drop, slow tears
  and bathe those beauteous feet,
Which brought from heaven
  the news and Prince of peace:
Cease not, wet eyes,
  his mercy to entreat;
To cry for vengeance
  sin doth never cease:
In your deep floods
  drown all my faults and fears;
Nor let his eye
  see sin, but through my tears.

*Phineas Fletcher*
*1582–1650*

# Holy Sonnets

2

At the round earth's imagined corners blow
Your trumpets, angels, and arise, arise
From death, you numberless infinities
Of souls, and to your scattered bodies go:
All whom the flood did, and fire shall o'erthrow,
All whom war, dearth, age, agues, tyrannies,
Despair, law, chance hath slain, and you whose eyes
Shall behold God and never taste death's woe.
But let them sleep, Lord, and me mourn a space,
For if above all these my sins abound,
'Tis late to ask abundance of thy grace
When we are there. Here on this holy ground
Teach me how to repent; for that's as good
As if thou hadst sealed my pardon with thy blood.

*John Donne*
*1572–1631*

# Mercy

Mercy is hendest* where sin is most,
Mercy is slower where sin is least;
Mercy abideth and looketh all day
When man from sin will turn away;
Mercy saveth that law would spill:*
Mercy asketh but God's will.

*Anonymous*
Medieval

* *hendest*: readiest; *spill*: destroy

# Conscience

If I could shut the gate against my thoughts
  And keep out sorrow from this room within,
Or memory could cancel all the notes
  Of my misdeeds, and I unthink my sin:
How free, how clear, how clean my soul should lie
Discharged of such a loathsome company!

Or were there other rooms within my heart
  That did not to my conscience join so near,
Where I might lodge the thoughts of sin apart
  That I might not their clamorous crying hear;
What peace, what joy, what ease should I possess,
Freed from their horrors that my soul oppress!

But, O my Saviour, who my refuge art,
  Let thy dear mercies stand 'twixt them and me
And be the wall to separate my heart
  So that I may at length repose me free;
That peace, and joy, and rest may be within,
And I remain divided from my sin.

*Anonymous*
17th century

## Second Lazarus

O come, dear Lord, unbind: like Lazarus, I
lie wrapped in stifling grave clothes of self-will.
Come give me life that I to death may die.
I stink: the grave of sin is worm-filled still
despite our turning from its rottenness,
unwilling to admit that we are bound,
too proud to mention our begottenness.
Come, open sin's sarcophagus. I'm wound
in selfishness, self-satisfaction, pride,
fear of change, demands of love, greed,
self-hate, sweet sins that come in fair disguise.
Help me accept this death and open wide
the tight-closed tomb. If pain comes as we're freed,
Your daylight must have hurt first Lazarus's eyes.

*Madeleine L'Engle*
*20th century*

## Frailty

Fain would I say, 'Forgive my foul offence!'
   Fain promise never more to disobey;
But, should my Author health again dispense,
   Again I might desert fair virtue's way;
Again in folly's path might go astray;
   Again exalt the brute and sink the man;
Then how should I for heavenly mercy pray,
   Who act so counter heavenly mercy's plan?
Who sin so oft have mourned, yet to temptation ran?

*Robert Burns*
*1759–96*

# Little Prayer for Samson and Delilah

When all virtue
like Samson's Rastafarian locks
lies strewn about us,
have mercy, Lord,
on those who sleep in weakness
and those who have shorn us of strength.

Like the growing stubble on Samson's head,
let us be renewed to undertake
the phenomenal as matter of course
when we awaken
from the lap of philistine ease.

*Diane Karay Tripp*
*20th century*

# Times without Number

Times without number have I prayed
   'This only once forgive';
Relapsing, when thy hand was stayed,
   And suffered me to live: –

Yet now the kingdom of thy peace,
   Lord, to my heart restore;
Forgive my vain repentance,
   And bid me sin no more.

*Charles Wesley*
*1707–88*

# A Hymn to God the Father

Wilt thou forgive that sin where I begun,
  Which is my sin, though it were done before?
Wilt thou forgive those sins through which I run,
  And do them still, though still I do deplore?
    When thou hast done, thou hast not done,
      For I have more.

Wilt thou forgive that sin by which I won
  Others to sin, and made my sin their door?
Wilt thou forgive that sin which I did shun
  A year or two, but wallowed in a score?
    When thou hast done, thou hast not done,
      For I have more.

I have a sin of fear, that when I've spun
  My last thread, I shall perish on the shore;
Swear by thyself that at my death thy sun
  Shall shine as it shines now, and heretofore;
    And having done that, thou hast done,
      I have no more.

*John Donne*
*1572–1631*

# A Hymn to God the Father

Hear me, O God!
  A broken heart
  Is my best part:
Use still thy rod
  That I may prove
  Therein thy love.

If thou hadst not
  Been stern to me,
  But left me free,
I had forgot
  Myself and thee.

For sin's so sweet,
  As minds ill bent
  Rarely repent
Until they meet
  Their punishment.

Who more can crave
  Than thou hast done,
  That gav'st a son
To free a slave,
  First made of nought,
  With all since bought?

Sin, Death, and Hell
  His glorious Name
  Quite overcame,
Yet I rebel,
  And slight the same.

But I'll come in,
  Before my loss
  Me farther toss,
As sure to win
  Under his cross.

*Ben Jonson*
1572–1637

# Heaven's Sun Shining on my Soul

But, ah, our sins, our clouds benight the air;
Lord, drain the fens of this my boggy soul,
Whose grosser vapours make my day so foul;
The Son hath strength to chase away
These rising fogs, and make a glorious day:
Rise, and shine always clear; but, most of all
Let me behold thy glory, in thy fall;
That being set, poor I (my flesh being hurled
From this) may meet thee, in another world.

*Francis Quarles*
*1592–1644*

# A Prayer for Grace

View me, Lord, a work of thine:
Shall I then lie drowned in night?
Might thy grace in me but shine,
I should seem made all of light.

But my soul still surfeits so
On the poisoned baits of sin,
That I strange and ugly grow,
All is dark and foul within.

Cleanse me, Lord, that I may kneel
At thine altar, pure and white:
They that once thy mercies feel,
Gaze no more on earth's delight.

Worldly joys like shadows fade,
When the heavenly light appears;
But the cov'nants thou hast made,
Endless, know nor days, nor years.

In thy word, Lord, is my trust,
To thy mercies fast I fly;
Though I am but clay and dust,
Yet thy grace can lift me high.

*Thomas Campion*
*1567–1620*

# Thankfulness and Praise

## From: Providence

Of all the creatures both in sea and land,
Only to man thou hast made known thy ways,
And put the pen alone into his hand,
And made him secretary of thy praise.

*George Herbert*
*1593–1633*

## Non Nobis Domine

*Non nobis Domine!* –
  Not unto us, O Lord!
The praise or glory be
  Of any deed or word;
For in thy judgement lies
  To crown or bring to nought
All knowledge or device
  That man has reached or wrought.

And we confess our blame –
  How all too high we hold
That noise which men call fame,
  That dross which men call gold.
For these we undergo
  Our hot and godless days,
But in our hearts we know
  Not unto us the praise.

O Power by whom we live –
  Creator, Judge, and Friend,
Upholdingly forgive
  Nor fail us at the end:
But grant us well to see
  In all our piteous ways –
*Non nobis Domine!* –
  Not unto us the praise!

*Rudyard Kipling*
*1865–1936*

# Fill the World with Praise

From all that dwell below the skies
Let the Creator's praise arise;
Let the Redeemer's name be sung
Through every land by every tongue.

Eternal are thy mercies, Lord;
Eternal truth attends thy word;
Thy praise shall sound from shore to shore,
Till suns shall rise and set no more.

In every land begin the song;
To every land the strains belong:
In cheerful sounds all voices raise
And fill the world with loudest praise.

*Isaac Watts*
*1674–1748*

# Antiphon

Let all the world in ev'ry corner sing,
   My God and King!
 The heavens are not too high,
 His praise may thither fly;
 The earth is not too low,
 His praises there may grow.

Let all the world in ev'ry corner sing,
   My God and King!
 The church with psalms must shout,
 No door can keep them out;
 But above all, the heart
 Must bear the longest part.

Let all the world in ev'ry corner sing,
   My God and King!

*George Herbert*
*1593–1633*

## *From:* A Song to David

Praise above all – for praise prevails;
Heap up the measure, load the scales,
   And good to goodness add:
The generous soul her Saviour aids,
But peevish obloquy degrades;
   The Lord is great and glad...

Glorious the sun in mid career;
Glorious the assembled fires appear;
   Glorious the comet's train:
Glorious the trumpet and alarm;
Glorious the Almighty's stretched-out arm;
   Glorious the enraptured main:

Glorious the northern lights a-stream;
Glorious the song, when God's the theme;
   Glorious the thunder's roar:
Glorious Hosanna from the den;
Glorious the catholic Amen;
   Glorious the martyr's gore:

Glorious – more glorious is the crown
Of him that brought salvation down
   By meekness, called the Son;
Thou that stupendous truth believed,
And now the matchless deed's achieved
   Determined, dared and done.

*Christopher Smart*
*1722–71*

## Song of Creation

Now we must praise the Guardian of Heaven,
the might of the Lord and his purpose of mind,
the work of the Glorious Father; for he,
God eternal, established each wonder,
he, Holy Creator, first fashioned
heaven as a roof for the sons of men.
Then the Guardian of Mankind adorned
this middle-earth below, the world for men,
Everlasting Lord, Almighty King.

*Caedmon's Song*
*late 7th century?*

# All Praise

To God, ye choir above, begin
  A hymn so loud and strong
That all the universe may hear
  And join the grateful song.

Praise him, thou sun, who dwells unseen
  Amidst transcendent light,
Where thy refulgent beam would seem
  A spot, as dark as night.

Thou silver moon, ye host of stars,
  The universal song
Through the serene and silent night
  To listening worlds prolong.

Sing him, ye distant worlds and suns,
  From whence no travelling ray
Hath yet to us, through ages past,
  Had time to make its way.

Assist, ye raging storms, and bear
  On rapid wings his praise,
From north to south, from east to west,
  Through heaven, and earth, and seas.

Exert your voice, ye furious fires
  That rend the watery cloud,
And thunder to this nether world
  Your Maker's words aloud.

Ye works of God, that dwell unknown
  Beneath the rolling main;
Ye birds, that sing among the groves,
  And sweep the azure plain;

Ye stately hills, that rear your heads,
  And towering pierce the sky;
Ye clouds, that with an awful pace
  Majestic roll on high;

Ye insects small, to which one leaf
  Within its narrow sides
A vast extended world displays,
  And spacious realms provides;

Ye race, still less than these, with which
　　The stagnant water teems,
To which one drop, however small,
　　A boundless ocean seems;

—Whate'er ye are, where'er ye dwell,
　　Ye creatures great or small,
Adore the wisdom, praise the power,
　　That made and governs all.

*Philip Skelton*
*1707–87*

## O Rex Gentium

O King! thou art the wall-stone
which of old the workmen
from their work rejected!
Well it thee beseemeth
that thou hold the headship
of this Hall of glory,
and should'st join together
with a fastening firm
the broad-spaced walls
of the flint unbreakable
all fitly framed together;
that among the earth's dwellers
all with sight of eyes
may for ever wonder.
O Prince of glory!
now through skill and wisdom
manifest thy handiwork,
true-fast and firm-set
in sovereign splendour.

*From Cynewulf,*
*based upon the antiphon 'O Rex Gentium' about 820*

# Jesus Christ the Apple Tree

The tree of life my soul hath seen,
Laden with fruit, and always green:
The trees of nature fruitless be
Compared with Christ the apple tree.

His beauty doth all things excel:
By faith I know, but ne'er can tell
The glory which I now can see
In Jesus Christ the apple tree.

For happiness I long have sought,
And pleasure dearly I have bought:
I missed of all; but now I see
'Tis found in Christ the apple tree.

I'm weary with my former toil,
Here I will sit and rest awhile:
Under the shadow I will be,
Of Jesus Christ the apple tree.

This fruit doth make my soul to thrive,
It keeps my dying faith alive;
Which makes my soul in haste to be
With Jesus Christ the apple tree.

*From Divine Hymns or Spiritual Songs,*
*compiled by Joshua Smith, New Hampshire 1784*

# *From:* The Christian Year

IN CHOIRS AND PLACES WHERE THEY SING,
HERE FOLLOWETH THE ANTHEM.

Lord, make my heart a place where angels sing!
   For surely thoughts low-breathed by thee
Are angels gliding near on noiseless wing;
   And where a home they see

Swept clean, and garnished with adoring joy,
   They enter in and dwell,
   And teach that heart to swell
With heavenly melody, their own untired employ.

*John Keble*
*1792–1866*

# Bermudas – Song of the Emigrants

Where the remote Bermudas ride
In the ocean's bosom unespied,
From a small boat that rowed along,
The listening winds received this song.
  'What should we do but sing his praise
That led us through the watery maze,
Unto an isle so long unknown
And yet far kinder than our own?
Where he the huge sea-monsters wracks,
That lift the deep upon their backs.
He lands us on a grassy stage,
Safe from the storm's and prelates' rage.
He gave us this eternal spring,
Which here enamels everything;
And sends the fowls to us in care,
On daily visits through the air.
He hangs in shades the orange bright,
Like golden lamps in a green night,
And does in the pom'granates close
Jewels more rich than Ormus shows.
He makes the figs our mouths to meet,
And throws the melons at our feet;
But apples* plants of such a price
No tree could ever bear them twice.
With cedars, chosen by his hand,
From Lebanon, he stores the land;
And makes the hollow seas that roar
Proclaim the ambergris on shore.
He cast (of which we rather boast)
The Gospel's pearl upon our coast,
And in these rocks for us did frame
A temple, where to sound his name.
Oh let our voice his praise exalt,
Till it arrive at heaven's vault,
Which thence, perhaps, rebounding may
Echo beyond the Mexique Bay.'
  Thus sang they in the English boat,
An holy and a cheerful note,
And all the way, to guide their chime,
With falling oars they kept the time.

*Andrew Marvell*
1621–78

* *apples*: pineapples

# *From:* The Dream of Gerontius

Praise to the Holiest in the height,
    And in the depth be praise,
In all his words most wonderful,
    Most sure in all his ways.

Oh loving wisdom of our God!
    When all was sin and shame,
A second Adam to the fight
    And to the rescue came.

Oh wisest love! that flesh and blood,
    Which did in Adam fail,
Should strive afresh against the foe,
    Should strive and should prevail.

And that a higher gift than grace
    Should flesh and blood refine,
God's presence and his very self,
    And essence all-divine.

Oh generous love! that he who smote
    In man for man the foe,
The double agony in man
    For man should undergo;

And in the garden secretly,
    And on the cross on high,
Should teach his brethren, and inspire
    To suffer and to die.

Praise to the Holiest in the height,
    And in the depth be praise,
In all his words most wonderful,
    Most sure in all his ways.

*John Henry Newman*
*1801–90*

# King of Glory

King of glory, King of peace,
  I will love thee;
And that love may never cease,
  I will move thee.

Thou hast granted my request,
  Thou hast heard me:
Thou didst note my working breast,
  Thou hast spared me.

Wherefore with my utmost art
  I will sing thee,
And the cream of all my heart
  I will bring thee.

Though my sins against me cried
  Thou didst clear me;
And alone, when they replied,
  Thou didst hear me.

Seven whole days, not one in seven,
  I will praise thee.
In my heart, though not in heaven,
  I can raise thee.

Thou grew'st soft and moist with tears,
  Thou relentedst:
And when Justice called for fears,
  Thou dissentedst.

Small it is in this poor sort
  To enrol thee:
Ev'n eternity is too short
  To extol thee.

*George Herbert*
*1593–1633*

# God's Unending Mercies

When all thy mercies, O my God,
   My rising soul surveys;
Transported with the view, I'm lost
   In wonder, love and praise.

O how shall words with equal warmth
   Thy gratitude declare,
That glows within my ravished heart!
   But thou canst read it there.

Thy providence my life sustained
   And all my wants redressed,
When in the silent womb I lay,
   And hung upon the breast.

To all my weak complaints and cries,
   Thy mercy lent an ear,
Ere yet my feeble thoughts had learnt
   To form themselves in prayer.

Unnumbered comforts to my soul
   Thy tender care bestowed,
Before my infant heart conceived
   From whom these comforts flowed.

When in the slippery path of youth
   With heedless steps I ran.
Thine arm unseen conveyed me safe
   And led me up to man.

Through every period of my life
   Thy goodness I'll pursue,
And after death, in distant worlds,
   The glorious theme renew.

Through all eternity to thee
   A joyful song I'll raise;
But oh! eternity's too short
   To utter all thy praise.

*Joseph Addison*
*1672–1719*

# Two Graces for Children

What God gives, and what we take,
'Tis a gift for Christ his sake:
Be the meal of beans and peas,
God be thanked for those, and these.
Have we flesh, or have we fish,
All are fragments from his dish.
He his church save, and the king,
And our peace here, like a spring,
Make it ever flourishing.

Here a little child I stand,
Heaving up my either hand;
Cold as paddocks* though they be
Here I lift them up to thee,
For a benison* to fall
On our meat, and on us all.

*Robert Herrick*
*1591–1674*

* *paddocks:* toads; *benison:* blessing

# God Is Near

## God Made Known

Lord, grant us calm, if calm can set forth thee;
  Or tempest, if a tempest set thee forth;
Wind from the east or west or south or north,
  Or congelation of a silent sea,
With stillness of each tremulous aspen tree.

Still let fruit fall, or hang upon the tree;
  Still let the east and west, the south and north,
Curb in their winds, or plough a thundering sea;
  Still let the earth abide to set thee forth,
Or vanish like a smoke to set forth thee.

*Christina Rossetti*
*1830–94*

## The Uninvited Guest

He seems to come in like the leaves –
Blown in at the open window,
And always on a light and airy day.
Never in stormy weather.
And always, I've noticed,
At an inconvenient time –
Right in the middle of the washing.
He looks at me and shows me these holes in his hands.
And, well, I can see them in his feet.
'Not again,' I say.
'Please don't stand there bleeding
All over the kitchen floor.'

Sometimes he comes softly, sadly,
At night – close, by the side of my bed –
Sometimes I latch the door –

But he never goes away.

*Thelma Laycock*
*20th century*

# Approaches

When thou turn'st away from ill,
Christ is this side of thy hill.

When thou turnest towards good,
Christ is walking in thy wood.

When thy heart says, 'Father, pardon!'
Then the Lord is in thy garden.

When stern Duty wakes to watch,
Then his hand is on the latch.

But when Hope thy song doth rouse,
Then the Lord is in the house.

When to love is all thy wit,
Christ doth at thy table sit.

When God's will is thy heart's pole,
Then is Christ thy very soul

*George MacDonald*
*1824–1905*

# God in Everything

I am the wind which breathes upon the sea,
I am the wave of the ocean,
I am the murmur of the billows,
I am the ox of the seven combats,
I am the vulture upon the rocks,
I am a beam of the sun,
I am the fairest of plants,
I am a wild boar in valour,
I am a salmon in the water,
I am a lake in the plain,
I am a word of knowledge,
I am the point of the lance in battle,
I am the God who creates in the head the fire.
Who is it that throws light into the meeting on the
     mountain?
Who announces the ages of the moon?
Who teaches the place where couches the sun?

*Anonymous.*
*Said to be by the legendary poet Amergin, when he first set foot in Ireland.*

# News

The only news I know
Is bulletins all day
From immortality.

The only shows I see
Tomorrow and today,
Perchance eternity.

The only one I meet
Is God, the only street
Existence; this traversed,

If other news there be
Or admirabler show,
I'll tell it you.

*Emily Dickinson*
*1830–84*

# God's Aid

God to enfold me,
　God to surround me,
God in my speaking,
　God in my thinking.

God in my sleeping,
　God in my waking,
God in my watching,
　God in my hoping.

God in my life,
　God in my lips,
God in my soul,
　God in my heart.

God in my sufficing,
　God in my slumber,
God in mine ever-living soul,
　God in mine eternity.

*Traditional Celtic*
*Collected by Alexander Carmichael*
*19th century*

## 'Lo, I am with you always'

Wide fields of corn along the valleys spread;
The rain and dew mature the swelling vine;
I see the Lord in multiplying bread;
   I see him turning water into wine;
   I see him working all the works divine
He wrought when Salemward his steps were led;
   The selfsame miracles around him shine;
He feeds the famished; he revives the dead;
   He pours the flood of light on darkened eyes;
He chases tears, diseases, fiends away;
   His throne is raised upon these orient skies;
His footstool is the pave whereon we pray.
   Ah, tell me not of Christ in Paradise,
For he is all around us here today.

*John Charles Earle*
*late 19th–20th century?*

## God's Dwelling

What happy, secret fountain,
Fair shade or mountain,
Whose undiscovered virgin glory
Boasts it this day, though not in story
Was then thy dwelling? did some cloud
Fixed to a tent, descend and shroud
My distrest Lord? or did a star
Beckoned by thee, though high and far,
In sparkling smiles haste gladly down
To lodge light and increase her own?
My dear, dear God! I do not know
What lodged thee then, nor where, nor how;
But I am sure, thou dost now come
Oft to a narrow, homely room,
Where thou too hast but the least part
My God, I mean *my sinful heart.*

*Henry Vaughan*
*1621–95*

# The Divine Image

To Mercy, Pity, Peace, and Love
All pray in their distress;
And to these virtues of delight
Return their thankfulness.

For Mercy, Pity, Peace, and Love
Is God, our father dear,
And Mercy, Pity, Peace, and Love
Is Man, his child and care.

For Mercy has a human heart,
Pity a human face,
And Love, the human form divine,
And Peace, the human dress.

Then every man, of every clime,
That prays in his distress,
Prays to the human form divine,
Love, Mercy, Pity, Peace.

And all must love the human form,
In Heathen, Turk, or Jew;
Where Mercy, Love, and Pity dwell
There God is dwelling too.

*William Blake*
*1757–1827*

# After St Augustine

Sunshine let it be or frost,
Storm or calm, as thou shalt choose;
Though thine every gift were lost,
Thee thyself we could not lose.

*Mary Coleridge*
*1861–1907*

# The Guest

Yet if his Majesty, our sovereign lord,
Should of his own accord
Friendly himself invite,
And say 'I'll be your guest tomorrow night,'
How should we stir ourselves, call and command
All hands to work! 'Let no man idle stand!

'Set me fine Spanish tables in the hall;
See they be fitted all;
Let there be room to eat
And order taken that there want no meat.
See every sconce and candlestick made bright,
That without tapers they may give a light.

'Look to the presence: are the carpets spread,
The dazie* o'er the head,
The cushions in the chairs,
And all the candles lighted on the stairs?
Perfume the chambers, and in any case
Let each man give attendance in his place!'

Thus, if a king were coming, would we do;
And 'twere good reason too;
For 'tis a duteous thing
To show all honour to an earthly king,
And after all our travail and our cost,
So he be pleased, to think no labour lost.

But at the coming of the King of Heaven
All's set at six and seven;
We wallow in our sin,
Christ cannot find a chamber in the inn.
We entertain him always like a stranger,
And, as at first, still lodge him in the manger.

*Anonymous*
17th century

\* *dazie*: dais, canopy

## 'I am not worthy'

Thy God was making haste into thy roof,
Thy humble faith, and fear, keeps him aloof:
He'll be thy guest, because he may not be,
He'll come – into thy house? no, into thee.

*Richard Crashaw*
*1613–49*

## Pax

All that matters is to be at one with the living God
to be a creature in the house of the God of Life.

Like a cat asleep on a chair
at peace, in peace
and at one with the master of the house, with the mistress,
at home, at home in the house of the living,
sleeping on the hearth, and yawning before the fire.

Sleeping on the hearth of the living world,
yawning at home before the fire of life
feeling the presence of the living God
like a great reassurance
a deep calm in the heart
a presence
as of a master sitting at the board
in his own and greater being,
in the house of life.

*D.H. Lawrence*
*1885–1930*

# At Communion

Whether I kneel or stand or sit in prayer,
I am not caught in time nor held in space,
but thrust beyond this posture I am where
time and eternity come face to face;
infinity and space meet in this place
where crossbar and high upright hold the one
in agony and in all Love's embrace.
The power in helplessness that was begun
when all the brilliance of the flaming sun
contained itself in the small confines of a child
now comes to me in this strange action done
in mystery. Break me, break space, O wild
and lovely power. Break me: thus am I dead,
am resurrected now in wine and bread.

*Madeleine L'Engle*
*20th century*

# God in me

God be in my head,
And in my understanding;
God be in mine eyes,
And in my looking;
God be in my mouth
And in my speaking;
God be in my heart,
And in my thinking;
God be at my end and at my departing.

*Anonymous*
*16th century*

# Thou art God

Thou art the peace of all things calm
Thou art the place to hide from harm
Thou art the light that shines in dark
Thou art the heart's eternal spark
Thou art the door that's open wide
Thou art the guest who waits inside
Thou art the stranger at the door
Thou art the calling of the poor
Thou art my Lord and with me still
Thou art my love, keep me from ill
Thou art the light, the truth, the way
Thou art my Saviour this very day.

*David Adam*
*20th century*

# From: Christ's Victory in Heaven

What hath man done that man shall not undo,
Since God to him is grown so near akin?
Did his foe slay him? He shall slay his foe.
Hath he lost all? He all again shall win.
Is sin his master? He shall master sin.
　　Too hardy soul, with sin the field to try;
　　The only way to conquer was to fly.
But thus long death hath lived, and now death's self shall die.

He is a path, if any be misled;
He is a robe, if any naked be;
If any chance to hunger, he is bread;
If any be a bondman, he is free;
If any be but weak, how strong is he!
　　To dead men life he is, to sick men health;
　　To blind men sight, and to the needy wealth,
A pleasure without loss, a treasure without stealth.

*Giles Fletcher*
*1586–1623*

# Love and Trust

## Jesus my Knight

Jesu, I now begin
To love thee day and night.
My soul from earth to wean
I shall do all my might.
'Twas all my love to win
Jesu became my knight.

*Anonymous*
Medieval

## A Prayer to Jesus

Jesu, since thou me made and bought,
Thou be my love and all my thought,
And help that I may to thee be brought;
Withouten thee I may do nought.

Jesu, since thou must do thy will,
And nothing is that thee may let*;
With thy grace my heart fulfil,
My love and my liking in thee set.

Jesu, at thy will
I pray that I might be;
All my heart fulfil
With perfect love to thee.

That I have done ill,
Jesu, forgive thou me;
And suffer me never to spill*,
Jesu, for pity. Amen.

*Richard Rolle*
1290–1349

* *let:* forbid, stop; *spill:* perish

# Name

A name written in sand
by a child's hand;
on a San Quentin wall
by an inmate's fingernail;
in blood stains
on doorposts;
in small-print footnotes
of dissertations

a name sprinkled
on little heads;
sung over bodies
in immersion tanks

A name breathed
in wind-touched silence
of lost paradise;
carried on wings
of one-day butterflies

A name on quivering lips
of combat soldier
alone in a foxhole;
clattering between teeth
of an ageing woman;
tremored by a
protestant voice

A name remains
when writing is no more
and voices die

A name given to
what has no name

Between desire
and silence
falls a name:

Jesus, the Christ.
Paradise regained.

*Cor W. Barendrecht*
*20th century*

# True Love

All other love is like the moon
That waxeth or waneth as flower in plain
As flower that blooms and fadeth soon,
As day that showereth and ends in rain.

All other love begins with bliss,
In weeping and woe makes its endìng;
No love there is that's our whole bliss
But that which rests on heaven's king.

His love is fresh and ever green
And ever full without wanìng;
His love makes sweet and gives no pain,
His love is endless, endurìng.

All other love I flee for thee;
Tell me, tell me where thou liest.
'In Marìe, mild and free
I shall be found, but more in Christ'.

*Anonymous*
*about 1350*

# A Child my Choice

Let folly praise that fancy love, I praise and love that Child
Whose heart no thought, whose tongue no word,
　　whose hand no deed defiled.
I praise him most, I love him best, all praise and love is his;
While him I love, in him I live, and cannot live amiss.
Love's sweetest mark, laud's highest theme, man's most
　　desirèd light,
To love him life, to leave him death, to live in him delight.
He mine by gift, I his by debt, thus each to other due,
First friend he was, best friend he is, all times will try him true.

*Robert Southwell*
*1561–95*

# Discipline

Throw away thy rod,
Throw away thy wrath:
  O my God,
Take the gentle path.

For my heart's desire
Unto thine is bent:
  I aspire
To a full consent.

Not a word or look
I affect to own,
  But by book,
And thy book alone.

Though I fail, I weep;
Though I halt in pace,
  Yet I creep
To the throne of grace.

Then let wrath remove;
Love will do the deed;
  For with love
Stony hearts will bleed.

Love is swift of foot,
Love's a man of war,
  And can shoot,
And can hit from far.

Who can 'scape his bow?
That which wrought on thee,
  Brought thee low,
Needs must work on me.

Throw away thy rod:
Though man frailties hath,
  Thou art God:
Throw away thy wrath.

*George Herbert*
*1593–1633*

# Love in Action

Truth proclaims it: love the wonder healer –
No blemish left, if that herb is used.
As God wished, the world was shaped in love.
Revealed to Moses, it was the best of things,
Heaven's image, priceless, the plant of peace.
But heaven could not contain the weight of love,
Till, here on earth, it fed to the full, took
Flesh and blood. After that, no leaf there was
On tree so light as love, mobile in air, plunging
As a needle point, no steel could stop it,
Nor castle wall. So, on earth as in heaven,
Love leads God's people, like a mayor,
Agent between the commons and the king. Love
Directs all, frames law, fixes fines
For the people's crimes. Know it for sure,
Love comes surging from the power of God,
Its source, its mountain spring, the human heart.

*From Piers Plowman by William Langland*
*1330?–1400?*
*translated by Ronald Tamplin*

# 'O Lord, Seek Us'

O Lord, seek us, O Lord, find us
    In thy patient care;
By thy love before, behind us,
    Round us everywhere:
Lest the god of this world blind us,
    Lest he speak us fair,
Lest he forge a chain to bind us,
    Lest he bait a snare.
Turn not from us, call to mind us,
    Find, embrace us, bear;
Be thy love before, behind us,
    Round us, everywhere.

*Christina Rossetti*
*1830–94*

# Christ, my Beloved

Christ, my Beloved, which still doth feed
    Among the flowers, having delight
    Among his faithful lilies,
Doth take great care for me indeed,
  And I again with all my might
    Will do what so his will is.

My Love in me and I in him,
    Conjoined by love, who still abide
    Among the faithful lilies
Till day do break, and truth do dim
  All shadows dark and cause them slide,
    According as his will is.

*William Baldwin*
*about 1547*

# Love's Sacrifice

O thou who camest from above,
  The pure, celestial fire to impart,
Kindle a flame of sacred love
    On the mean altar of my heart,
There let it for thy glory burn
  With inextinguishable blaze.
And trembling to its Source return,
    In humble prayer and fervent praise.

*Jesus*, confirm my heart's desire
  To work, and speak, and think for thee,
Still let me guard the holy fire,
    And still stir up thy gift in me,
Ready for all thy perfect will
  My acts of faith and love repeat,
'Till death thy endless mercies seal,
    And make my sacrifice complete.

*Charles Wesley*
*1707–88*

# *From:* Little Gidding

IV

The dove descending breaks the air
With flame of incandescent terror
Of which the tongues declare
The one discharge from sin and error.
The only hope, or else despair
   Lies in the choice of pyre or pyre –
   To be redeemed from fire by fire.

Who then devised the torment? Love.
Love is the unfamiliar Name
Behind the hands that wove
The intolerable shirt of flame
Which human power cannot remove.
   We only live, only suspire
   consumed by either fire or fire.

*T.S. Eliot*
*1888–1965*

63

# Splendidis Longum Valedico Nugis

Leave me, O love, which reachest but to dust;
   And thou, my mind, aspire to higher things;
Grow rich in that which never taketh rust;
   Whatever fades but fading pleasure brings.
Draw in thy beams, and humble all thy might
   To that sweet yoke where lasting freedoms be;
Which breaks the clouds and opens forth the light,
   That doth both shine and give us sight to see.
O take fast hold; let that light be thy guide
In this small course which birth draws out to death,
   And think how evil becometh him to slide,
Who seeketh heaven, and comes of heavenly breath.
   Then farewell, world; thy uttermost I see;
   Eternal Love, maintain thy life in me.

*Sir Philip Sidney*
*1554–86*

# Lovest Thou Me?

Hark, my soul! It is the Lord;
'Tis thy Saviour, hear his word;
Jesus speaks, and speaks to thee:
'Say, poor sinner, lov'st thou me?

'I delivered thee when bound,
And, when wounded, healed thy wound;
Sought thee wandering, set thee right,
Turned thy darkness into light.

'Can a woman's tender care
Cease towards the child she bare?
Yes, she may forgetful be,
Yet will I remember thee.

'Mine is an unchanging love,
Higher than the heights above;
Deeper than the depths beneath,
Free and faithful, strong as death.

'Thou shalt see my glory soon,
When the work of grace is done;
Partner of my throne shalt be:
Say, poor sinner, lov'st thou me?'

Lord, it is my chief complaint
That my love is weak and faint;
Yet I love thee and adore,
O for grace to love thee more!

*William Cowper*
*1731–1800*

# 'And she washed his feet with her tears, and wiped them with the hair of her head.'

The proud Egyptian Queen, her Roman guest,
(To express her love in height of state, and pleasure)
With pearl dissolved in gold, did feast,
   Both food and treasure.

And now (dear Lord!) thy lover, on the fair
And silver tables of thy feet, behold!
Pearl in her tears, and in her hair,
   Offers thee gold.

*Sir Edward Sherburne*
*1618–1702*

# Love

Love bade me welcome; yet my soul drew back,
   Guilty of dust and sin.
But quick-eyed Love, observing me grow slack
   From my first entrance in,
Drew nearer to me, sweetly questioning
   If I lacked anything.

'A guest', I answered, 'worthy to be here.'
   Love said, 'You shall be he.'
'I, the unkind, ungrateful? Ah, my dear,
   I cannot look on thee.'
Love took my hand, and smiling did reply,
   'Who made the eyes but I?'

'Truth, Lord, but I have marred them; let my shame
   Go where it doth deserve.'
'And know you not', says Love, 'who bore the blame?'
   'My dear, then I will serve.'
'You must sit down', says Love, 'and taste my meat.'
   So I did sit and eat.

*George Herbert*
*1593–1633*

# The Measure of Love

If love be strong, hot, mighty and fervènt,
There may be trouble, grief or sorrow fall,
But that the lover would be well content
All to endure and think it eke too small,
Though it were death, so he might therewithal
The joyful presence of that person get
On whom he hath his heart and love y-set.

Thus should of God the lover be content
Any distress or sorrow to endure,
Rather than to be from God absènt,
And glad to die, so that he may be sure
By his departing hence for to procure,
After this valley dark, the heavenly light,
And of his love the glorious blessed sight.

Not only a lover content is in his heart
But coveteth eke and longeth to sustain
Some labour, incommodity, or smart,
Loss, adversity, trouble, grief or pain:
And of his sorrow, joyful is and fain,
And happy thinketh himself that he may take
Some misadventure for his lover's sake.

Thus shouldest thou, that lovest God also.
In thine heart wish, covet, and be glad
For him to suffer trouble, pain and woe:
For whom if thou be never so woe bestead,
Yet thou ne shalt sustain (be not adread)
Half the dolour, grief and adversity
That he already suffered hath for thee.

*Sir Thomas More*
*1478–1535*

# Lachrimae Amantis

What is there in my heart that you should sue
so fiercely for its love? What kind of care
brings you as though a stranger to my door
through the long night and in the icy dew

seeking the heart that will not harbour you,
that keeps itself religiously secure?
At this dark solstice filled with frost and fire
your passions's ancient wounds must bleed anew.

So many nights the angel of my house
has fed such urgent comfort through a dream,
whispered 'your lord is coming, he is close'

that I have drowsed half-faithful for a time
bathed in pure tones of promise and remorse:
'tomorrow I shall wake to welcome him.'

*Geoffrey Hill*
*20th century*

# *From:* In Memoriam

Love is and was my Lord and King,
    And in his presence I attend
    To hear the tidings of my friend,
Which every hour his couriers bring.

Love is and was my King and Lord,
    And will be, though as yet I keep
    Within his court on earth, and sleep
Encompassed by his faithful guard,

And hear at times a sentinel
    Who moves about from place to place,
    And whispers to the world of space,
In the deep night, that all is well.

*Alfred, Lord Tennyson*
*1809–92*

# Heart's Music

(FROM: CAMPIAN'S FIRST BOOK OF AIRS)

Tune thy music to thy heart
  Sing thy joy with thanks, and so thy sorrow.
  Though devotion needs not art
Sometimes of the poor the rich may borrow.

  Strive not yet for curious ways;
Concord pleaseth more the less 'tis strained.
  Zeal affects not outward praise,
Only strives to show a love unfeigned.

  Love can wondrous things effect,
Sweetest sacrifice all wrath appeasing.
  Love the Highest doth respect;
Love alone to him is ever pleasing.

*Anonymous*
*about 1600?*

# THE WORLD
# WE LIVE IN

## God's Grandeur

The world is charged with the grandeur of God.
  It will flame out, like shining from shook foil;
  It gathers to a greatness, like the ooze of oil
Crushed. Why do men then now not reck his rod?
Generations have trod, have trod, have trod;
  And all is seared with trade; bleared, smeared with toil;
  And wears man's smudge and shares man's smell: the soil
Is bare now, nor can foot feel, being shod.

And for all this, nature is never spent;
  There lives the dearest freshness deep down things;
And though the last lights off the black West went
  Oh, morning, at the brown brink eastward, springs –
Because the Holy Ghost over the bent
  World broods with warm breast and with ah! bright wings.

*Gerard Manley Hopkins*
*1844–89*

# Nature and Landscape

## Flower in the Crannied Wall

Flower in the crannied wall,
I pluck you out of the crannies; –
Hold you here, root and all, in my hand,
Little flower – but if I could understand
What you are, root and all, and all in all,
I should know what God and man is.

*Alfred, Lord Tennyson*
*1809–92*

## Six O'Clock Feeling

You ever feel
dat 6 o'clock feeling
6 o'clock shadow falling
wrappin you up
meking you stop
and tink
bout all dese tings
God doin
6 o'clock bee calling
all dem tree
tekking strange, strange shape
and stan up
sharp! sharp! gainst dat sky
you know dem 6 o'clock colour
pink an orange an blue an purple an black
dat 6 o'clock feeling
mekkin you feel like touchin
mekkin you feel so small
you could cry
or fall down pun you knee
and thank God
you could still
see he 6 o'clock sky

*Kamal Singh*
*20th century*

# Oil of Spikenard

What a spendthrift you are, sir,
a squanderseed wastrel!
Did they never teach you
the Puritan virtues?
Look at those puffball heads.
You toss your hair like a petulant schoolgirl, and there –
how untidy you are! – it's like dandruff.
Then there's sperm,
not to mention the sand and the stars and the orange pips.
It's embarrassing, all this extravagance.

And not five minutes ago you painted a skyscape
in a whole fruit salad of pastels,
a study in citrous shades.
So now what are you up to?
You've rubbed it out and started again with blue.
Stop a minute and give us viewing time,
you throwaway artist.
Even when invention funds
are unlimited, surely the waste.

Couldn't this oil of spikenard
have been sold and given to the poor?

*Anne Ashworth*
*20th century*

# Nature

The sky is low, the clouds are mean,
A travelling flake of snow
Across a barn or through a rut
Debates if it will go.

A narrow wind complains all day
How someone treated him;
Nature, like us, is sometimes caught
Without her diadem.

*Emily Dickinson*
*1830–86*

# The Very Thought

I love the very thought of Heaven:
Where angels sing
In perfect, perpetual Choir Practice.
Where Father, Son, and Spirit
Rule, unchallenged,
And are honoured in full measure.
I love the very thought of Heaven:
But I was not made
To live there.

I was not made
To walk on clouds,
And bask eternally
In immaterial splendour.
I was made for this green planet:
This tight ball
Of infinite beauty,
Alive with unending possibilities
Of his creative power.
I was made for the sunshine
That blazes through the veins of leaves,
And glints in the tiny, perfect back
Of a ladybird, crossing my arm.
I was made to be human
In this, most human place.
I was made for Earth:
The Earth is my home.
That's why I'm glad
that God, more than anyone,
Is a Friend of the Earth.
That he was prepared
To die for its restoration,
And that's why I'm glad
That the magnificent, jewelled foundations
Of the mighty Pearly Gates,
Will be anchored
Deeply and for ever
In the soil of Earth.

*Gerard Kelly*
*20th century*

# A Chant out of Doors

God of grave nights,
God of brave mornings,
God of silent noon,
Hear my salutation!
  For where the rapids rage white and scornful
  I have passed safely, filled with wonder;
  Where the sweet pools dream under willows
  I have been swimming, filled with joy.

God of round hills,
God of green valleys,
God of clear springs,
Hear my salutation!
  For where the moose feeds I have eaten berries,
  Where the moose drinks I have drunk deep;
  And under clear skies I have known love.

God of great trees,
God of wild grasses,
God of little flowers,
Hear my salutation!
  For where the deer crops and the beaver plunges
  Near the river I have pitched my tent;
  Where the pines cast aromatic needles
  On the still flowers I have known peace.

God of grave nights,
God of brave mornings,
God of silent noon,
Hear my salutation.

*Marguerite Wilkinson*
*1883–1928*

# A Pastoral Hymn

Happy choristers of air
Who by your nimble flight draw near
　　His throne, whose wondrous story
　　And unconfinèd glory
Your notes still carol, whom your sound
And whom your plumy pipes rebound.

Yet do the lazy snails no less
The greatness of our Lord confess,
　　And those whom weight hath chained
　　And to the earth restrained,
Their ruder voices do as well,
Yea and the speechless fishes tell.

Great Lord, from whom each tree receives
Then pays again as rent, his leaves;
　　Thou dost in purple set
　　The rose and violet,
And giv'st the sickly lily white,
Yet in them all, thy name doth write.

*John Hall*
*1627–56*

# Vegetation

O never harm the dreaming world,
the world of green, the world of leaves,
but let its million palms unfold
the adoration of the trees.

It is a love in darkness wrought
obedient to the unseen sun,
longer than memory, a thought
deeper than the graves of time.

The turning spindles of the cells
weave a slow forest over space,
the dance of love, creation,
out of time moves not a leaf,
and out of summer, not a shade.

*Kathleen Raine*
*20th century*

# The Storm

Rods of rain piledrive mercilessly into the tarmac
and bounce back
to the billowing, black clouds above;
the drains spew back the gurgling torrent's flow,
sweeping away bedraggled, drowning rats below.

Rrrrrumble... CRACK! The heavens tear themselves asunder;
buffeted pilots helplessly curse the thunder.
Lightning sizzles, the air's alight.
The moped driver anxiously looks for cover;
frightened children run to their frightened mother.

In agony radios hiss and spit;
a splintering tree screams as it is hit;
rain trickles from my squelching boots;
pea-pullers scatter to escape the carnage,
as God puts proud Man back into the Dark Age.

The digger's arm stretches imploringly towards the sky
but the arm of the cloud passes remorselessly by,
gradually disappearing over the hill;
the abandoned digger ruefully dips, weak and forlorn,
and thankful birds emerge to greet the second dawn.

*Trevor Hoggard*
*20th century*

# Immanence

I come in the little things
Saith the Lord:
Not borne on morning wings
Of majesty, but I have set my feet
Amidst the delicate and bladed wheat
That springs triumphant in the furrowed sod.
There so I dwell, in weakness and in power;
Not broken or divided, saith our God!
In your strait garden plot I come to flower:
About your porch my vine
Meek, fruitful, doth entwine;
Waits, at the threshold, Love's appointed hour...

*Evelyn Underhill*
*1875–1941*

# Bring me the Sunset

Bring me the sunset in a cup,
Reckon the morning's flagons up
And say how many dew,
Tell me how far the morning leaps,
Tell me what time the weaver sleeps
Who spun the breadths of blue.

Write how many notes there be
In the new robin's ecstasy
Among astonished boughs,
How many trips the tortoise makes,
How many cups the bee partakes,
The debauchee of dews.

Also, who laid the rainbow's piers,
Also, who leads the docile spheres
By withes of supple blue?
Whose fingers string the stalactite
Who counts the wampum* of the night
To see that none is due?
Who built this little alban house
And shut the windows down so close
My spirit cannot see?
Who'll let me out some gala day
With implements to fly away,
Passing pomposity?

*Emily Dickinson*
*1830–1886*

*\*wampum:* string of beads used as memory aid,
and shell beads used as currency by native Americans.

# Christ in Creation

I see his blood upon the rose
And in the stars the glory of his eyes,
His body gleams amid eternal snows,
His tears fall from the skies.

I see his face in every flower;
The thunder and the singing of the birds
Are but his voice – and carven by his power
Rocks are his written words.

All pathways by his feet are worn,
His strong heart stirs the ever-beating sea,
His crown of thorns is twined with every thorn,
His cross is every tree.

*Joseph Mary Plunkett*
*1887–1916*

# Home Pictures in May

The sunshine bathes in clouds of many hues
And morning's feet are gemmed with early dews;
Warm daffodils about the garden beds
Peep through their pale slim leaves their golden heads,
Sweet earthly suns of spring; the gosling broods,
In coats of sunny green, about the road
Waddle in ecstasy; and in rich moods
The old hen leads her flickering chicks abroad,
Oft scuttling 'neath her wings to see the kite
Hang wavering o'er them in the spring's blue light.
The sparrows round their new nests chirp with glee
And sweet the robin spring's young luxury shares,
Tootling its song in feathery gooseberry tree
While watching worms the gardener's spade unbares.

*John Clare*
*1793–1864*

# From: The Task

   One spirit – his
Who wore the plaited thorns with bleeding brows –
Rules universal nature. Not a flower
But shows some touch, in freckle, streak or stain
Of his unrivalled pencil. He inspires
Their balmy odours, and imparts their hues,
And bathes their eyes with nectar, and includes,
In grains as countless as the sea-side sands,
The forms with which he sprinkles all the earth.
Happy who walks with him! whom what he finds
Of flavour or of scent in fruit or flower,
Or what he views of beautiful or grand
In nature, from the broad majestic oak
To the green blade that twinkles in the sun,
Prompts with remembrance of a present God!
His presence, who made all so fair, perceived,
Makes all still fairer. As with him no scene
Is dreary, so with him all seasons please.
Though winter had been none, had man been true,
And earth be punished for its tenant's sake,
Yet not in vengeance; as this smiling sky,
So soon succeeding such an angry night,
And these dissolving snows, and this clear stream
Recovering fast its liquid music, prove.

*William Cowper*
*1731–1800*

# The Community

First chestnut tree, the candle master
Lights the dawn's church, birch serves the altar,
Oak in old age guides novice summer,
Elm bows to still the rooks' dark clamour,
Sycamore spreads the lessons' leaves,
Pines' song shapes the praying eaves
In needles sharp as finger tips;
Beech scurries, rustling, through the copse
And by the stream the willows tell
Litany of each circling shallow.

Gifts take a summer's life to form,
Brought to the apse with autumn's hymn,
Angel from sycamore and blood
Where holly stoops, the cornfield's bread
Where copse gives way to the wide acre,
Pasture to furrow and stooped shadow;
Pale song as spruce the crucifer
Snuffs sun and leaves the evening door
For mustard seed, the cellarer
To all the wild birds of the air.

*Martyn Halsall*
*20th century*

# Pied Beauty

Glory be to God for dappled things –
For skies of couple-colour as a brinded cow;
For rose-moles all in stipple upon trout that swim;
Fresh firecoal chestnut-falls; finches' wings;
Landscapes plotted and pieced – fold, fallow and plough;
And all trades, their gear and tackle and trim.

All things counter, original, spare, strange;
Whatever is fickle, freckled (who knows how?)
With swift, slow; sweet, sour; adazzle, dim;
He fathers-forth whose beauty is past change:
      Praise him.

*Gerard Manley Hopkins*
*1844–89*

# A Garden

(WRITTEN AFTER THE CIVIL WARS)

See how the flowers, as at parade,
Under their colours stand displayed:
Each regiment in order grows,
That of the tulip, pink, and rose.
But when the vigilant patrol
Of stars walks round about the pole,
Their leaves, that to the stalks are curled,
Seem to their staves the ensigns furled.
Then in some flower's beloved hut
Each bee, as sentinel, is shut,
And sleeps so too; but if once stirred,
She runs you through, nor asks the word.

O thou, that dear and happy isle,
The garden of the world erewhile,
Thou paradise of the four seas
Which heaven planted us to please,
But, to exclude the world, did guard
With watery,if not flaming, sword;
What luckless apple did we taste
To make us mortal and thee waste!
Unhappy! shall we never more
That sweet militia restore,
When gardens only had their towers,
And all the garrisons were flowers;
When roses only arms might bear,
And men did rosy garlands wear?

*Andrew Marvell*
*1621–78*

# Of an Orchard

Good is an orchard, the saint saith
To meditate on life and death,
With a cool well, a hive of bees,
A hermit's grot below the trees.

Good is an orchard: very good,
Though one should wear no monkish hood;
Right good when spring awakes her flute,
And good in yellowing time of fruit:

Very good in the grass to lie
And see the network 'gainst the sky,
A living lace of blue and green
And boughs that let the gold between.

The bees are types of souls that dwell
With honey in a quiet cell;
The ripe fruit figures goldenly
The soul's perfection in God's eye.

Prayer and praise in a country home
Honey and fruit: a man might come
Fed on such meats to walk abroad
And in his orchard talk with God.

*Katharine Tynan Hinkson*
*1861–1931*

# Under a Wiltshire Apple Tree

Some folks can afford,
So I've heard say,
Set up a sort of cross
Right in the garden way
To mind 'em of the Lord.

But I, when I do see
Thik apple tree
An' stoopin' limb
All spread wi' moss,
I think of him
And how he talks wi' me.

I think of God
And how he trod
That garden long ago;
He walked, I reckon, to and fro
And then sat down
Upon the groun'
Or some low limb
What suited him
Such as you see
On many a tree,
And on thik very one
Where I at set o' sun
Do sit and talk wi' he.

And, mornings too, I rise and come
An' sit down where the branch be low;
A bird do sing, a bee do hum,
The flowers in the border blow,
And all my heart's so glad and clear
As pools when mists do disappear:
As pools a-laughing in the light
When mornin' air is swep' and bright,
As pools what got all Heaven in sight
So's my heart cheer
When he be near.

He never pushed the garden door,
He left no footmark on the floor;
I never heard 'un stir nor tread
And yet his hand do bless my head,
And when 'tis time for work to start
I takes him with me in my heart.

And when I die, pray God I see
At very last thik apple tree
An' stoopin' limb,
And think of him
And all he been to me.

*Anna Bunstan*
*late 19th – 20th century?*

# Water and Seascape

## The Life-tide

Each wave that breaks upon the strand,
How swift soe'er to spurn the sand
  And seek again the sea,
Christ-like, within its lifted hand
Must bear the stigma of the land
  For all eternity.

*John Bannister Tabb*
*1845–1909*

## *From:* The Seafarer

On earth there is no man so self-assured,
so generous with his gifts or so bold in his youth,
so daring in his deeds or with such a gracious lord,
that he harbours no fears about his seafaring
as to what the Lord will ordain for him.

Wherefore my heart leaps within me,
my mind roams with the waves
over the whale's domain, it wanders far and wide
across the face of the earth, returns again to me
eager and unsatisfied; the solitary bird screams,
irresistible, urges the heart to the whale's way
over the stretch of the seas.
    So it is that the joys
of the Lord inspire me more than this dead life,
ephemeral on earth. I have no faith
that the splendours of this earth will survive for ever...

Great is the fear of God; through him the world turns.
He established the mighty plains, the face
of the earth and the sky above. Foolish is he
who fears not his Lord: death catches him unprepared.
Blessed is the humble man: mercy comes to him from heaven.
God gave man a soul because he trusts in his strength.

*Anonymous*
*about 850*

# Belize Suite

1 SEA WALL

Only a gentle swish
Where waves would touch the land
no wind no turbulence
along this wall arranged by man
dividing land from sea

No cruise-ships light this harbour end to end
only that cluster
where the army lights
ride there at anchor…
cool darkness and deluding calm

houses sit silent near the water's edge
their calm precariousness like our peace
hoisted on stilts
like mokojumbies in the carnival
listening the ocean's gentle murmur
hearing its angry wail
what seems like decades now
when death rode loud and furious
on the hissing waves

From storm and earthquake Lord
deliver us
and us
and us

*Velma Pollard*
*20th century*

# Kwikila, Waterless Place

(KWIKILA IS IN PAPUA NEW GUINEA)

Two still-green trees rub together
    as if for reassurance
    that the wind that grates
    will carry too;
    carry clouds, heavy clouds,
    full clouds and black;
    to fall and to dampen,
    to drench and to soak –
    deep into the pores of the earth.

The stream-beds are paths
  for the lizard and snake;
  the reed-beds are brown
  and blackened – (Last week
  another fire went along there)
  and the boulders which rolled along
  in the floods are quite still;
  still with the stillness of tragedy brooding,
  still with the stillness of death.

Men curse the wind
  for its transitory promises –
  dark clouds build up
  (and our hopes with them too)
  and are then blown away;
  or, worse still, come over,
  intact and enticing,
  to cynically spatter
  verandahs and faces
  before passing on…

A desk – and textbooks strewn;
  lately my eyes have been wandering
  more and more. But my window
  still frames the same picture
  of a bright, empty sky
  (called *gorgeous* in Sydney
  where water comes piped),
  and grass, grey with despair –
Dust hangs in a curl
  (thrown up by a wheel);
  it seems, almost, to have been hanging there
  for months now.

*O Lord*, I murmur, and murmur again,
  *Please send us rain.*

*Humphrey Babbage*
*20th century*

# The Shell

Upon the sandy shore an empty shell,
  Beyond the shell infinity of sea;
O Saviour, I am like that empty shell,
  Thou art the Sea to me.

A sweeping wave rides up the shore, and lo,
  Each dim recess the coiled shell within
Is searched, is filled, is filled to overflow
  By water crystalline.

Not to the shell is any glory then:
  All glory give we to the glorious sea.
And not to me is any glory when
  Thou overflowest me.

Sweep over me thy shell, as low I lie;
  I yield me to the purpose of thy will,
Sweep up, O conquering waves, and purify
  And with thy fulness fill.

*Amy Carmichael*
*1867–1951*

# The Singularity of Shells

A shell – how small an empty space,
a folding out of pink and white,
a letting in of spiral light.
How random? and how commonplace?
(A million shells along the beach
are just as fine and full of grace
as this one here within your reach.)

But lift it, hold it to your ear
and listen. Surely you can hear
the swish and sigh of all the grey
and gleaming waters, and the play
of wind with rain and sun, encased
in one small jewel box and placed,
by God and oceans, in your way.

*Luci Shaw*
*20th century*

# Town and City

## Indifference

When Jesus came to Golgotha they hanged him on a tree,
They drave great nails through hands and feet, and made a Calvary;
They crowned him with a crown of thorns, red were his wounds and deep,
For those were crude and cruel days, the human flesh was cheap.

When Jesus came to Birmingham, they simply passed him by,
They never hurt a hair of him, they only let him die;
For men had grown more tender, and they would not give him pain,
They only passed down the street, and left him in the rain.

Still Jesus cried, 'Forgive them, for they know not what they do,'
And still it rained the winter rain that drenched him through and through;
The crowds went home and left the streets without a soul to see,
And Jesus crouched against a wall and cried for Calvary.

*G.A. Studdert Kennedy*
*1883–1929*

87

## Over the Great City

Over the great city,
Where the wind rustles through the parks and gardens,
In the air, the high clouds brooding,
In the lines of street perspective, the lamps, the traffic,
The pavements and the innumerable feet upon them,
I Am: make no mistake – do not be deluded.

Think not because I do not appear at the first glance
    – because the centuries have gone by and
    there is no assured tidings of me – that therefore I am not
    there.
Think not because all goes its own way that
    therefore I do not go my own way through all.
The fixed bent of hurrying faces in the street – each
    turned towards its own light, seeing no other
    – yet I am the Light towards which they
    all look.
The toil of so many hands to such multifarious ends,
    yet my hand knows the touch and twining of them
    all.

All come to me at last.
There is no love like mine;
For all other love takes one and not another;
And other love is pain, but this is joy eternal.

*Edward Carpenter*
*1844–1929*

## Tower Block

The Council's plywood barricades
block up the frames where wired glass
was systematically smashed out.

Wet stains that pattern the bare
concrete walls, are covered up
by over-lapping spray-gun scrawls,

proclaiming loyalties and hates,
initials, names, the brute
ideograms of failing speech.

Inside the battered lifts a stench
of disinfectant still insinuates
those smells its wash has drowned.

Press on the broken button,
or climb up the glass-strewn stairs,
along the cloned, deserted landings

bolted doors conceal the warmth of homes
the pride of fitted carpets,
comforts of a frayed armchair, and

families as alive to laughter and pain
as those behind herbaceous borders,
safe along the neat suburban lanes.

*Tony Lucas*
*20th century*

# Yours, Not Ours

You are as inevitable as morning
and you are there
long before the first Woodbine croak is heard
at the bleary eyed bus stops of the city.
You watch and wonder
as the sound of waking
mumbles its chorus across roof tops
You see and hear lovers readjust their dreams
in the not quite right of day
You listen to the out of tune clatter of newspapers
drowning out the concert pitch spot-on of the trees
This is a tired morning, as street sweepers clock on
We have stolen it from you
and fashioned it in our own image
You have not yet charged us with theft
and when you do
our defence will be inadequate
the dog ends in the gutter have no apologies written on them
there are no acknowledgements in the personal columns
the milk bottles hold no thank you notes
and the morning yawns steadily onwards
the morning that is not ours
but always yours.

*Stewart Henderson*
*20th century*

# All God's Creatures

## From: To a Fish of the Brook

Enjoy thy stream, O harmless fish;
And when an angler for his dish,
  Through gluttony's vile sin,
Attempts, a wretch, to pull thee *out*
God give thee strength, O gentle trout,
  To pull the rascal *in!*

*John Wolcot (Peter Pindar)*
*1738–1839*

## The Bells of Heaven

'Twould ring the bells of Heaven
The wildest peal for years,
If Parson lost his senses
And people came to theirs,
And he and they together
Knelt down with angry prayers
For tamed and shabby tigers,
And dancing dogs and bears,
And wretched, blind pit ponies,
And little hunted hares.

*Ralph Hodgson*
*1872–1962*

# A Dream of Nature

            Birds I saw in bushes made nests.
Even a simple one no man
Could ever make. And when and where
I wondered did the magpie learn
To weave sticks one with another
To secure her nest? Carpenters
Couldn't do anything as good,
No designer make a blueprint
For it either. It astonished
Me even more that many birds
Hid their eggs, carefully concealed,
So that only the parent birds
Themselves could find them. Some I saw
Did their breeding high in the trees
And hatched their young way up above
The ground. Diving birds plumped deep down
In swamps, moorland ponds and reedbeds,
Wherever there was water. 'Dear
God,' I cried, 'What school do all these
Wild things go to, to get such sense?'
And then the peacock; I saw how
He mated, how roughly the bird
Went about it. I marvelled at
His splendour along with his crude
Screaming voice. I looked at the sea
And on further to the high stars.
The whole world was full of wonders
Too many to put down now, flowers
In the fields, their dazzling colours,
So many different shades, sprung
From the same earth and grassy fields,
Some bitter to the taste, some sweet.
It seemed all one great miracle
Ranged too wide for me to record.
But what struck me and set me back
Was that reason seemed to govern
All creatures and how they acted
Except for man, except mankind.

*From Piers Plowman by William Langland*
*1330?–1400?*
*translated by Ronald Tamplin*

# Jubilate Agno

Rejoice in God, O ye tongues; give glory to the Lord, and the Lamb.
Nations and languages, and every creature, in which is the breath of life.
Let man and beast appear before him, and magnify his name together.

Let Noah and his company approach the throne of grace,
  and do homage to the ark of their salvation.
Let Abraham present a ram, and worship the God of his redemption.
Let Isaac, the bridegroom, kneel with his camels,
  and bless the hope of his pilgrimage.
Let Jacob, and his speckled drove adore the good Shepherd of Israel.
Let Esau offer a scape goat for his seed,
  and rejoice in the blessing of God his father.
Let Nimrod, the mighty hunter, bind a leopard to the altar,
  and consecrate his spear to the Lord.
Let Ishmael dedicate a tyger, and give praise for the liberty,
  in which the Lord has let him at large.
Let Balaam appear with an ass, and bless the Lord his people
  and his creatures for a reward eternal...
Let Daniel come forth with a lion,
  and praise God with all his might through faith in Christ Jesus...
Let David bless with the bear – The beginning of victory to the Lord –
  to the Lord the perfection of excellence –
Hallelujah from the heart of God,
  and from the hand of the artist inimitable,
  and from the echo of the heavenly harp
  in sweetness magnifical and mighty.
Let Solomon praise with the ant,
  and give the glory to the Fountain of all wisdom...
Let Mephibosheth with the cricket
  praise the God of cheerfulness, hospitality, and gratitude...
Let Job bless with the worm –
  the life of the Lord is in humiliation,
  the spirit also and the truth.
Let Benjamin bless and rejoice with the redbird,
  who is soft and soothing.
Let Dan rejoice with the blackbird,
  who praises God with all his heart, and biddeth to be of good cheer.

*Christopher Smart*
*1722–71*

# The House Sparrow

Citizen Philip Sparrow, who likes
To build and breed about our habitations –
    The little birds that fly through the city smoke –

Prolific, adaptable, bold,
Untidy, cheerfully vocal –
    The little birds that quarrel in the eaves –

Grant him his right of freedom and, of your charity,
His dole of crumbs and kitchen scraps –
    The little birds that stand in the eye of God

*John Heath-Stubbs*
*20th century*

# The Unemployed

the cormorants
    a black dole queue
stand on Marsden rock
    totally unemployed

there are still the working ones
the kittiwakes mewing busily
around the rocks in the sea

but for the cormorants there is
nothing to do

    one flaps off slowly
and another returns
    with no news of work
the rest just stand around.

*Rodney Ward*
*20th century*

# The Visitor

Twice,
that sleety twilit afternoon
I glanced up sharply from the ironing
and saw, out in the dismal garden,
beyond the thickening window
our reluctant great-tit,
persuaded by winter's argument
towards the pendulous, swinging coconut; –

almost as if the Lord,
temporarily leaving aside weightier matters
had quietly entered the room
and tapped me on the shoulder,
saying

Do look, don't miss him,
isn't he wonderful?
Put down that shirt, just for a moment,
and join in my delight,
for I love you even as I love him,
and I want you to share my pleasure
in this tiny ruffled topknot
of my Creation,

pecking at life's cold shell
cupped in my wide hands; –

and tasting joy.

*Jan Godfrey*
*20th century*

# The Sparrow's Skull

MEMENTO MORI: WRITTEN AT THE FALL OF FRANCE

The kingdoms fall in sequence, like the waves on the shore.
All save divine and desperate hopes go down, they are no more.
Solitary is our place, the castle in the sea,
And I muse on those I have loved, and on those who have loved me.

I gather up my loves, and keep them all warm,
While above our heads blows the bitter storm:
The blessed natural loves, of life-supporting flame,
And those whose name is Wonder, which have no other name.

The skull is in my hand, the minute cup of bone,
And I remember her, the tame, the loving one,
Who came in at the window, and seemed to have a mind
More towards sorrowful man than to those of her own kind.

She came for a long time, but at length she grew old;
And on her death-day she came, so feeble and so bold;
And all day, as if knowing what the day would bring,
She waited by the window, with her head beneath her wing.

And I will keep the skull, for in the hollow here
Lodged the minute brain that had outgrown a fear;
Transcended an old terror, and found a new love,
And entered a strange life, a world it was not of.

Even so, dread God! even so, my Lord!
The fire is at my feet, and at my breast the sword:
And I must gather up my soul, and clap my wings, and flee
Into the heart of terror, to find myself in thee.

*Ruth Pitter*
*20th century*

95

# Saint Francis Preaches to the Computers

Saint Francis found his way (saints, in a dream,
An ecstasy, slip in and out of time)
Into the computer shop. The chipper little chaps
All chrome and plastic, stainless steel,
Gleaming and winking, chirped and buzzed and whirred
And pipped and peeped, much like the congregation
The saint had just been preaching to – of Ruddocks, Dunnocks
Citrils, Serins, Siskins, Spinks,
Orphean warblers, Ortolans, Golden Orioles.
So he began to do his stuff again –
You know the kind of thing that he would say: – he told them
To praise the Lord who had created them,
Had made them bright and new, had programmed them
Had plugged them in, and kept them serviceable.
But somehow they looked glum; hint of a minor key
Seemed to infect their electronic singing:
'Alas,' they said, 'for we were not created
By God, whoever he or she may be,
But by the shaved ape, the six-foot Siamang
The pregnant mandrake root, cumulus in pants,
Glassily-essenced Man. We are no more clever
Than he who made us, though we think faster. Nor
   were we programmed
With thoughts that take off into timelessness,
Nor trans-death longings. But we have one fear,
And it is rust, is rust, is rust,
The eternal rubbish tip and the compressor.'
'My little mechanical brothers,' rejoined the saint
'I'll tell you something that a Mullah said,
One that was in the Soldan's entourage,
That time I visited his camp. They postulate
A moderate-sized menagerie in heaven.
I'll only mention Balaam's percipient ass,
Tobias' toby dog, that other faithful fido
Who hunted in his dreams in that Ephesian den
The seven sleepers snorted in, and snarled
At Roman persecutors, and, golden-crested,
Cinnamon-breasted, with broad dappled wings
The hoopoe, which was wise King Solomon's
Special envoy to the queen of Sheba –
That sweet blue-stocking with the donkey's toes.'

'If these could pass into eternity,
It was for love and service. And Eternity,
Loving through mankind, loved them,
And lifted them into a resurrection, as shall be lifted
The whole creation, groan though it does and travail.
And if these brute beasts were loved, then so may you be,
Along with the Puffing Billies, Chitty Chitty Bang Bangs,
Barnacled Old Superbs, Ezekiel's Wheels,
Elijah's fiery space-ship. You shall be built as stones
That gleam in the High-priestly breastplate
Which is the wall of that bright golden city –
Itself the human body glorified.'

*John Heath-Stubbs*
20th century

## St Francis and the Birds

When Francis preached love to the birds
They listened, fluttered, throttled up
Into the blue like a flock of words

Released for fun from his holy lips,
Then wheeled back, whirred about his head,
Pirouetted on brothers' capes.

Danced on the wing, for sheer joy played
And sang, like images took flight.
Which was the best poem Francis made,

His argument true, his tone light.

*Seamus Heaney*
20th century

# Dear St Francis

Some creatures of our God and King
distract one at funeral moments
trundle across the floor on six legs
in their own gospel procession

Other creatures of our God and Queen
pop in and out feeding young
At the frantic nestbox when I try to join
in spirit in committal prayers.

*Diana Downing*
*20th century*

# The Prayer of the Cock

Do not forget, Lord,
it is I who make the sun rise.
I am your servant
but, with the dignity of my calling,
I need some glitter and ostentation.
Noblesse oblige...
all the same,
I am your servant,
only... do not forget, Lord,
I make the sun rise.

*Carmen de Gasztold*
*20th century*
*translated by Rumer Godden*

# The Butterfly

My hands are warm to the butterfly
I am trying to set free.
Delicate, frail creature of beauty,
what can it know of me?
I am outside its comprehension.
It knows sunshine and showers,
darkness and the feel of flowers.
We do not ask it to do the impossible
and know Man.

So we, with God,
who looks with tenderness upon our frailty,
trying to guide us.
Trust him!
He knows the way, and, if we let him,
will open windows,
and, cradling us gently in hands we cannot comprehend.
will lift us up and set us free.

*Margaret Orford*
*20th century*

# Be a Butterfly

Don't be a kyatta-pilla
Be a butterfly
old preacher screamed
to illustrate his sermon
of Jesus and the higher life

rivulets of well-earned
sweat sliding down
his muscly mahogany face
in the half-empty school church
we sat shaking with muffling
laughter
watching our mother trying to save
herself from joining the wave

only our father remaining poker face
and afterwards we always went home to
split peas Sunday soup
with dumplings, fufu and pigtail

Don't be a kyatta-pilla
Be a butterfly
Be a butterfly

That was de life preacher
and you was right

*Grace Nichols*
*20th century*

# The Fly

The Lord in his wisdom made the fly,
And then forgot to tell us why.

*Ogden Nash*
20th century

# Student Taper

When
 – At end of moon,
At end of day –
My lamp is lit,
Grant me a boon,
I pray,
And do
So order it

 – That the small creatures,
Terrified and blind;
The gold and silvern moths
Of lovely kind,
Do not whirl to my taper,
Nor, therein,
Die, painfully,
And bring my light
To sin.

My light
Is innocent!
Grant
 – That it may be
Harmless,
And helpful,
And remarked
Of thee.

*James Stephens*
1882–1950

# The Prayer of the Ant

Lord,
I am always made out to be wrong;
a fable to the whole world.
Certainly I hoard
and make provision!
I have my rights!
And surely I can take a little joy
in the fruits of all my work
without some sob singer
coming to rob my store?
There is something in your justice
that I scarcely understand,
and, if you would allow me to advise,
it might be thought over again.
I have never been a burden to anybody,
and, if I may say so,
I manage my own business very well.
Then,
to the incorrigible improvidence
of some people,
must I, for all eternity, say
Amen.

*Carmen de Gasztold*
*20th century*
*translated by Rumer Godden*

# Go To The Ant

I have always considered
the grasshopper
to be the finer fellow
He did not scrape and hoard
worldly possessions
He would not have turned away
a friend hungry
He had more fun
in one fiddle foot
than the ant in his
whole diligent body

Gladly the grasshopper
glorified God by the
sensuous enjoyment
of each irretrievable moment
while the ant
grieved his yesterdays
and grumbled each tomorrow

IS THERE A LIFE BEFORE DEATH?

wrote the grasshopper
on the lavatory wall
and added

NOT FOR ANTS

*Barbara Dickinson*
*20th century*

## Song of the Death-Watch Beetle

Here come I, the death-watch beetle
Chewing away at the great cathedral;

Gnawing the mediaeval beams
And the magnificent carved rood screen

Gorging on gospels and epistles
From the illuminated missals;

As once I ate the odes of Sappho
And the histories of Manetho,

The lost plays of Euripides
And all the thought of Parmenides.

The Sibyl's leaves which the wind scattered,
And great Aunt Delia's love letters.

Turn down the lamp in the cooling room:
There stand I with my little drum.

Death. Watch, You are watching death.
Blow out the lamp with your last breath.

*John Heath-Stubbs*
*20th century*

# CATS AND OTHER ANIMALS

## From: Jubilate Agno

For I will consider my cat Jeoffrey.
For he is the servant of the living God duly and daily serving him.
For at the first glance of the glory of God in the East he worships in his way.
For this is done by wreathing his body seven times round with elegant quickness.
For then he leaps up to catch the musk, which is the blessing of God
    upon his prayer.
For he rolls upon prank to work it in.
For having done duty and received blessing he begins to consider himself.
For this he performs in ten degrees.
For first he looks upon his fore-paws to see if they are clean.
For secondly he kicks up behind to clear away there.
For thirdly he works upon stretch with the fore-paws extended.
For fourthly he sharpens his paws by wood.
For fifthly he washes himself.
For sixthly he rolls upon wash.
For seventhly he fleas himself, that he may not be interrupted upon the beat.
For eighthly he rubs himself against a post.
For ninthly he looks up for his instruction.
For tenthly he goes in quest of food.
For when his day's work is done his business more properly begins.
For he keeps the Lord's watch in the night against the adversary.
For he counteracts the powers of darkness by his electrical skin and glaring eyes.
For he counteracts the Devil, who is death, by brisking about the life.
For in his morning orisons he loves the sun and the sun loves him.
For he is of the tribe of tiger.
For the cherub cat is a term of the angel tiger.
For he has the subtlety and hissing of a serpent, which in goodness
    he suppresses.
For he will not do destruction, if he is well-fed, neither will he spit
    without provocation.
For he purrs in thankfulness, when God tells him he's a good cat.
For he is an instrument for the children to learn benevolence upon.
For every house is incomplete without him and a blessing is lacking in the spirit...
For he knows that God is his Saviour.
For there is nothing sweeter than his peace when at rest.
For there is nothing brisker than his life when in motion...
For the divine spirit comes about his body to sustain it in complete cat.

*Christopher Smart*
1722–71

# The Tyger

Tyger! Tyger! burning bright
In the forests of the night,
What immortal hand or eye
Could frame thy fearful symmetry?

In what distant deeps or skies
Burnt the fire of thine eyes?
On what wings dare he aspire?
What the hand dare seize the fire?

And what shoulder, and what art,
Could twist the sinews of thy heart?
And when thy heart began to beat,
What dread hand? and what dread feet?

What the hammer? What the chain?
In what furnace was thy brain?
What the anvil? what dread grasp
Dare its deadly terrors clasp?

When the stars threw down their spears,
And watered heaven with their tears,
Did he smile his work to see?
Did he who made the lamb make thee?

Tyger! Tyger! burning bright
In the forests of the night,
What immortal hand or eye,
Dare frame thy fearful symmetry?

*William Blake*
*1757–1827*

# Reluctant Prophet

Both were dwellers
in deep places (one
in the dark bowels
of ships and great fish
and wounded pride.
The other
in the silvery belly
of the seas.) Both
heard God saying
'Go!'
but the whale
did as he was told.

*Luci Shaw*
*20th century*

# The Lamb

Little lamb, who made thee?
Dost thou know who made thee?
Gave thee life, and bid thee feed,
By the stream and o'er the mead;
Gave thee clothing of delight,
Softest clothing, woolly, bright;
Gave thee such a tender voice,
making all the vale rejoice?
Little lamb, who made thee?
Dost thou know who made thee?

Little lamb, I'll tell thee,
Little lamb, I'll tell thee:
He is callèd by thy name,
For he calls himself a lamb.
He is meek and he is mild;
He became a little child.
I a child, and thou a lamb,
We are callèd by his name.
Little lamb, God bless thee!
Little lamb, God bless thee!

*William Blake*
*1757–1827*

# The Late Passenger

The sky was low, the sounding rain was falling dense and dark,
And Noah's sons were standing at the window of the Ark.

The beasts were in, but Japhet said, 'I see one creature more
Belated and unmated there come knocking at the door.'

'Well let him knock,' said Ham, 'Or let him drown or learn to swim.
We're overcrowded as it is; we've got no room for him.'

'And yet it knocks, how terribly it knocks,' said Shem, 'Its feet
Are hard as horn – but oh the air that comes from it is sweet.'

'Now hush,' said Ham, 'You'll waken Dad, and once he comes to see
What's at the door, it's sure to mean more work for you and me.'

Noah's voice came roaring from the darkness down below,
'Some animal is knocking. Take it in before we go.'

Ham shouted back, and savagely he nudged the other two,
'That's only Japhet knocking down a brad-nail in his shoe.'

Said Noah, 'Boys, I hear a noise that's like a horse's hoof.'
Said Ham, 'Why, that's the dreadful rain that drums upon the roof.'

Noah tumbled up on deck and out he put his head;
His face went grey, his knees were loosed, he tore his beard and said,

'Look, look! It would not wait. It turns away. It takes its flight.
Fine work you've made of it, my sons, between you all tonight!

'Even if I could outrun it now, it would not turn again
– Not now. Our great discourtesy has earned its high disdain.

'Oh noble and unmated beast, my sons were all unkind;
In such a night what stable and what manger will you find?

Oh golden hoofs, oh cataracts of mane, oh nostrils wide
With indignation! Oh the neck wave-arched, the lovely pride!

'Oh long shall be the furrows ploughed across the hearts of men
Before it comes to stable and to manger once again,

And dark and crooked all the ways in which our race shall walk,
And shrivelled all their manhood like a flower with broken stalk,

'And all the world, oh Ham, may curse the hour when you were born;
Because of you the Ark must sail without the Unicorn...'

*C.S. Lewis*
*1898–1963*

# The Donkey

When fishes flew and forests walked
  And figs grew upon thorn,
Some moment when the moon was blood
  Then surely I was born.

With monstrous head and sickening cry
  And ears like errant wings,
The devil's walking parody
  On all four-footed things.

The tattered outlaw of the earth,
  Of ancient crooked will;
Starve, scourge, deride me: I am dumb,
  I keep my secret still.

Fools! For I also had my hour;
  One far fierce hour and sweet:
There was a shout about my ears,
  And palms about my feet.

*G.K. Chesterton*
*1874–1936*

# The Exile

The fool said to the animals:
'You are merely my chattels,
With one lesson to learn –
That what happens to you is not your concern
But mine; for a just God has set
You on earth for my profit.'

The animals answered the fool
Nothing at all,
But for a single moment
Turned on him their wild, true, innocent
Eyes, where an Angel of the Lord
Holds Eden's flaming sword.

*Frances Bellerby*
*20th century*

# In the Wilderness

Christ of his gentleness
Thirsting and hungering
Walked in the wilderness;
Soft words of grace he spoke
Unto lost desert-folk
That listened wondering.
He heard the bitterns call
From ruined palace-wall,
Answered them brotherly.
He held communion
With the she-pelican
Of lonely piety.
Basilisk, cockatrice,
Flocked to his homilies,
With mail of dread device,
With monstrous barbed stings,
With eager dragon-eyes;
Great rats on leather wings
And poor blind broken things,
Foul in their miseries.
And ever with him went,
Of all his wanderings
Comrade, with ragged coat,
Gaunt ribs – poor innocent –
Bleeding foot, burning throat,
The guileless old scape-goat;
For forty nights and days
Followed in Jesus' ways,
Sure guard behind him kept,
Tears like a lover wept.

*Robert Graves*
*1895–1985*

# Good-Nature to Animals

The man of Mercy (says the Seer)
 Shows mercy to his beast;
Learn not of churls to be severe,
 But house and feed at least.

Shall I melodious prisoners take
 From out the linnet's nest,
And not keep busy care awake,
 To cherish every guest?

What, shall I whip in cruel wrath
 The steed that bears me safe,
Or 'gainst the dog, who plights his troth,
 For faithful service chafe?...

Let thine industrious silk-worms reap
 Their wages to the full,
Nor let neglected dormice sleep
 To death within thy wool.

Know when the frosty weather comes,
 'Tis charity to deal
To wren and redbreast all thy crumbs,
 The remnant of thy meal.

Tho' these some spirits think but light,
 And deem indifferent things;
Yet they are serious in the sight
 Of CHRIST, the King of kings.

*Christopher Smart*
1722–71

# At the Last Judgment

A dog starved at his master's gate
Predicts the ruin of the state.

A horse misused upon the road
Cries to Heaven for human blood.

Each outcry of the hunted hare
A fibre from the brain does tear.

Kill not the moth nor butterfly;
For the Last Judgment draweth nigh.

*William Blake*
1757–1827

# Times and Seasons

## For Everything There is a Season
(ECCLESIASTES 3)

The time to weep is in the heart's winter.
  Grief is the grip of ice and silence,
snow and vast grey skies. Bending under
  tree-caught snow, nerves hold the sad immense.

The time to laugh is when new is sprung
  suddenly. Renewal – new love, new
light, new green, new morning, blossom-hung
  delight – makes the Spring of the heart due.

There is a time for living. Into
  a wide green under a thoughtful sun
we move and struggle. Who is the True
  must reach here, must judge what we have done.

There is also a time for dying.
  The green leaves become brown, the grass fades,
the unplucked fruit drops and rots. Sighing
  tree-sung rain makes cold decaying shades.

*Colin Duriez*
*20th century*

# SPRING AND SUMMER

## The Flower

How fresh, O Lord, how sweet and clean
Are thy returns! E'en as the flowers in Spring,
  To which, besides their own demesne,
The late-past frosts tributes of pleasure bring;
    Grief melts away
    Like snow in May,
As if there were no such cold thing.

Who would have thought my shrivelled heart
Could have recovered greenness? It was gone
  Quite under ground; as flowers depart
To see their mother-root, when they have blown,
    Where they together
    All the hard weather,
Dead to the world, keep house unknown.

These are thy wonders, Lord of power,
Killing and quickening, bringing down to Hell
  And up to Heaven in an hour;
Making a chiming of a passing-bell.
    We say amiss
    This or that is;
Thy word is all, if we could spell.

O that I once past changing were,
Fast in thy Paradise, where no flower can wither;
  Many a spring I shoot up fair,
Offering at Heaven, growing and groaning thither;
    Nor doth my flower
    Want a spring-shower,
My sins and I joining together.

But while I grow in a straight line,
Still upwards bent, as if Heaven were mine own,
  Thy anger comes, and I decline:
What frost to that? what pole is not the zone
    Where all things burn,
    When thou dost turn,
And the least frown of thine is shown?

And now in age I bud again,
After so many deaths I live and write;
  I once more smell the dew and rain,
And relish versing: O, my only Light,
    It cannot be
    That I am he
On whom thy tempests fell at night.

These are thy wonders, Lord of love,
To make us see we are but flowers that glide;
  Which when we once can find and prove,
Thou hast a garden for us where to bide;
    Who would be more,
    Swelling through store,
Forfeit their Paradise by their pride.

*George Herbert*
*1593–1633*

# Spring Flowers

Bowing adorers of the gale,
Ye cowslips delicately pale,
  Upraise your loaded stems,
Unfold your cups in splendour; speak!
Who decked you with that ruddy streak,
  And gilt your golden gems?

Violets, sweet tenants of the shade,
In purple's richest pride arrayed,
  Your errand here fulfil!
Go, bid the artist's simple stain
Your lustre imitate, in vain,
  And match your Maker's skill.

Daisies, ye flowers of lowly birth,
Embroiderers of the carpet earth,
  That stud the velvet sod;
Open to spring's refreshing air,
In sweetest smiling bloom declare
  Your Maker and my God.

*John Clare*
*1793–1864*

# fenscape

after winter rain the enormous sky
opens blue eyes in wet-lashed wonder

at its own shattered reflection
a blink a breath caught held in

cracked ice mirrors, thin light
fingering heaven's seamless hem of

broken clouds spilling colour into
painted pools of living moving water

shining turquoise puddles scooped from
pumpernickel earth's harsh richness of

clumbered furrows, black bones converging
to a narrow ribbed sharp-cut perspective

hardly peopled or housed this iron bleakness
broken tree scarecrow-man land taut to

time's horizon: mocked pecked he stands
dumb wooden guardian of all our innocences

as a man once swung between the heavens
and all the frozen darkened earth

*Jan Godfrey*
*20th century*

# Spring Sonnet

The lilac bush puts forth its purple spikes
and pink-tipped blossom decks the apple tree,
while on the ground the bright-faced primrose likes
to highlight shaded violet's modesty;
and on the cherry bough full-throated thrush
sings out in answer to the cuckoo's call,
and over all the earth the first fair flush
of Spring unfolds its beauty to enthral.
In full accord but by more wondrous means
the Holy Spirit quickens all that lives
and like Spring's sun on many-shaded greens
new Life to people's varied natures gives.
And as Spring blooms are rendered safe from frost
may God save us from sin, else we are lost.

*Cyril Lloyd*
*20th century*

# Virtue

Sweet day, so cool, so calm, so bright,
The bridal of the earth and sky,
The dew shall weep your fall tonight;
    For thou must die.

Sweet rose, whose hue angry and brave
Bids the rash gazer wipe his eye,
Thy root is ever in its grave,
    And thou must die.

Sweet spring, full of sweet days and roses,
A box where sweets compacted lie,
My music shows ye have your closes,
    And all must die.

Only a sweet and virtuous soul,
Like seasoned timber, never gives;
And though the whole world turn to coal,
    Then chiefly lives.

*George Herbert*
*1593–1633*

# Spring

Nothing is so beautiful as spring –
When weeds, in wheels, shoot long and lovely and lush;
Thrush's eggs look little low heavens, and thrush
Through the echoing timber does so rinse and wring
The ear, it strikes like lightnings to hear him sing;
The glassy peartree leaves and blooms, they brush
The descending blue; that blue is all in a rush
With richness; the racing lambs too have fair their fling.
What is all this juice and all this joy?
A strain of the earth's sweet being in the beginning
In Eden garden. – Have, get, before it cloy,
Before it cloud, Christ, lord, and sour with sinning,
Innocent mind and Mayday in girl and boy,
Most, O maid's child, thy choice and worthy the winning.

*Gerard Manley Hopkins*
*1844–89*

# Lent

Lent is a tree without blossom, without leaf,
than blackthorn in its winter sleep,
All unadorned. Unlike Christmas which decrees
The setting-up, the dressing-up of trees,
Lent is a taking down, a stripping bare,
A starkness after all has been withdrawn
Of surplus and superfluous,
Leaving no hiding-place, only an emptiness
Between black branches, a most precious space
Before the leaf, before the time of flowers;
Lest we should see only the leaf, the flower,
Lest we should miss the stars.

*Jean M. Watt*
*20th century*

## Villanelle for a Season's End

Autumn is here and summer will not stay
The season cuts a bloodline on the land
And all earth's singing green is stripped away.

Our parting drains the colour from the day.
The oak leaves' red is clotting in your hand.
Autumn is here and summer will not stay.

The sea fog settles. Even noon is grey.
The light recedes as though this dusk were planned.
The green of field and tree is stripped away.

We shiver on the beach and watch the way
The berries' blood is spilled along the sand.
The green of all our fields is stripped away.

See how the wind has scattered the salt hay
Across the dunes! Too well we understand:
Autumn is here, bright summer will not stay
And all earth's love and green are stripped away.

*Luci Shaw*
*20th century*

## Falling Leaves

Fall, leaves, fall; die, flowers, away;
Lengthen night and shorten day;
Every leaf speaks bliss to me
Fluttering from the autumn tree.
I shall smile when wreaths of snow
Blossom where the rose should grow;
I shall sing when night's decay
Ushers in a drearier day.

*Emily Brontë*
*1818–48*

# The Song of the Reapers

We know a field.
A sheltered, fertile ground,
Well-favoured by the sun.
    There the first yield
Of corn is reaped and bound
Before the harvest is begun.

    It is a sheaf
Of whitest gold, the green
Half-fainted from the stem.
    Upon the leaf
Spring's last veins are seen.
Each ear is a Jerusalem.

    Now from this first
Pure sheaf the bread is baked.
And offered, fragrant, fresh,
    To God. – Who thirst
And hunger shall be slaked
By holy wine, fed by this flesh.

    For when we eat
This bread that is new-made
We take into our blood
    His grace, our meat.
By faith, the earth is fed
And by His love we have our bread.

*James Kirkup*
*20th century*

# The Burning of the Leaves

Now is the time for the burning of the leaves.
They go to the fire; the nostril pricks with smoke
Wandering slowly into a sweeping mist.
Brittle and blotched, ragged and rotten sheaves!
A flame seizes the smouldering ruin and bites
On stubborn stalks that crackle as they resist.

The last hollyhock's falled tower is dust;
All the spices of June are a bitter reek,
All the extravagant riches spent and mean.
All burns! The reddest rose is a ghost;
Sparks whirl up, to expire in the mist: the wild
Fingers of fire are making corruption clean.

Now is the time for stripping the spirit bare,
Time for the burning of days ended and done,
Idle solace of things that have gone before:
Rootless hopes and fruitless desires are there;
Let them go to the fire, with never a look behind.
The world that was ours is a world that is ours no more.

They will come again, the leaf and the flower, to arise
From squalor of rottenness into the old splendour,
And magical scents to a wondering memory bring;
The same glory, to shine upon different eyes.
Earth cares for her own ruins, naught for ours.
Nothing is certain, only the certain spring.

*Laurence Binyon*
*1869–1943*

# The Golden Boy

In March he was buried
    And nobody cried
Buried in the dirt
    Nobody protested
Where grubs and insects
    That nobody knows
With outer-space faces
    That nobody loves
Can make him their feast
    As if nobody cared.

But the Lord's mother
  Full of her love
Found him underground
  And wrapped him with love
As if he were her baby
  Her own born love
She nursed him with miracles
  And starry love
And he began to live
  And to thrive on her love

He grew night and day
  And his murderers were glad
He grew like a fire
  And his murderers were happy
He grew lithe and tall
  And his murderers were joyful
He toiled in the fields
  And his murderers cared for him
He grew a gold beard
  And his murderers laughed.

With terrible steel
  They slew him in the furrow
With terrible steel
  They beat his bones from him
With terrible steel
  They ground him to powder
They baked him in ovens
  They sliced him on tables
They ate him they ate him
  They ate him they ate him

  Thanking the Lord
  Thanking the Wheat
  Thanking the Bread
  For bringing them Life
  Today and Tomorrow
  Out of the dirt.

*Ted Hughes*
*20th century*

# Broad Autumn

True faith matures without discarding.
All I unearthed, each sky-sign crudely mapped
On the white rasped hills of youth,
Warms me still by rowan-tapped crags,
Far up the autumnal mountain,
Incredibly remote in climate, texture, weathering
Of bare stones, from my first insights:
I leave no wreckage on those low rasped cones.

There is no snarl of tools
Where broad wisdom calls across the cordial heather,
But the hacked glints my young heart stored
Still tone the subtle comforts and the sharp
Fearful shifts of shade as the blood cools
To admit, and clarify, the expanding mental range.

No pestilence of proud ripeness,
Urbane, agnostic, cankers the wide braes
Which my spirit, eagle-keen now, calls native
In the pale sun's gloss. The spikes of raw praise,
Sparse once on the white hills,
Glow ruddier here against the thinned
Thieving of the schooled foreign crows.

I have not changed my country; I have grown and explored
In my faith's undivided world.
I discard no primal certainty, no rasped
Sky-sign of the Cross;
But now in broad autumn, feeling a new peace
And the old poise of defence,
I accept the pure trysting lochs,
The full antler in the glens.

*Jack Clemo*
*20th century*

# WINTER

## A Better Resurrection

I have no wit, no words, no tears;
  My heart within me like a stone
Is numbed too much for hopes or fears;
  Look right, look left, I dwell alone;
I lift mine eyes, but dimmed with grief
  No everlasting hills I see;
My life is in the falling leaf
  O Jesus, quicken me.

My life is like a faded leaf,
  My harvest dwindled to a husk;
Truly my life is void and brief
  And tedious in the barren dusk;
My life is like a frozen thing,
  No bud nor greenness can I see:
Yet rise it shall – the sap of Spring;
  O Jesus, rise in me.

My life is like a broken bowl,
  A broken bowl that cannot hold
One drop of water for my soul
  Or cordial in the searching cold;
Cast in the fire the perished thing,
  Melt and remould it, till it be
A royal cup for him my King:
  O Jesus, drink of me.

*Christina Rossetti*
*1830–94*

## Winter Woe

Winter wakens all my care,
Now the leaves are waxing bare;
Oft I sigh and mourn sare*
When it come in my thought
Of this world's joy, how it goes all to nought.

*Anonymous*
*about 1300*

* *sare*: sore

# November Sonnet

Spirit of place. Spirit of time. Re-form
The rugged oaks and chestnuts. Now they stand
Naked and pallid giants out of storm
And out of sorts. It is the Autumn's end

And this is Winter brought in by All Saints
Fast followed by All Souls to keep us in
Touch with chill and death. Each re-acquaints
Us with the year's end. Yet we now begin

A life of realism, watching out
For a red sunset, grateful for a dawn
Of rich light now. Tall shadows step and strut

Facing the big wind daily coming on
Faster. This is the season of right doubt
While that elected child waits to be born.

*Elizabeth Jennings*
*20th century*

# Winter Now

'Tis winter now; the fallen snow
   Has left the heavens all coldly clear;
Through leafless boughs the sharp winds blow,
   And all the earth lies dead and drear.

And yet God's love is not withdrawn;
   His life within the keen air breathes;
His beauty paints the crimson dawn,
   And clothes the boughs with glittering wreaths.

And though abroad the sharp winds blow,
   And skies are chill, and frosts are keen,
Home closer draws her circle now,
   And warmer glows her light within.

O God! who giv'st the winter's cold,
   As well as summer's joyous rays,
Us warmly in thy love enfold,
   And keep us through life's wintry days.

*Samuel Longfellow*
*1819–92*

# Flos Campi

The rooftree of the year is fallen, fallen
and fallen is the splendour of the grass.
The great trees, barebone senators, observe
gravely the crepuscular season pass.

Here in the stripped pathology of winter
time's bleak agenda lately comes to light;
Summer's fluorescence now, and the autumn idyll
matters for hindsight, else an oversight.

This iron season, cloaked in fictive beauty,
the icefield's glory and the blizzard's pride;
and which of us at length has his desire?
or which in having it, is satisfied?

New rose, effulgent, out of time and season
flower of grace on Jesse's ancient tree,
Ah, be the benison of all beginnings,
the steadfast root in our declension be.

*Kevin Nichols*
*20th century*

# Dance of the Months

January comes with his ice-crown.
February spilling thaw and snowdrops.
March, bursting loud cheeks!
Then April, with a troop of lambs and daffodils.
May, keeper of peat-hill and cuithe-stream.
June, covering the night fire in the north.
July, tall and blue as lupins.
August with the cut cornstalks.
September, dusting cobwebs from the lamp.
October, good witch, with apples and nuts.
November, host to shades and hallows.
December, with snowflake and star.

In the inn of December, a fire.
A loaf, a bottle of wine.
Travellers, rich and poor, are on the roads.

*George Mackay Brown*
*20th century*

# Shadows

And if to-night my soul may find her peace
in sleep, and sink in good oblivion,
and in the morning wake like a new-opened flower
then I have been dipped again in God, and new-created.

And if, as weeks go round, in the dark of the moon
my spirit darkens and goes out, and soft strange gloom
pervades my movements and my thoughts and words
then I shall know that I am walking still
with God, we are close together now the moon's in shadow.

And if, as autumn deepens and darkens
I feel the pain of falling leaves, and stems that break in storms
and trouble and dissolution and distress
and then the softness of deep shadows folding,
    folding around my soul and spirit, around my lips
so sweet, like a swoon, or more like the drowse of a low, sad song
singing darker than the nightingale, on, on to the solstice
and the silence of short days, the silence of the year, the shadow,
then I shall know that my life is moving still
with the dark earth, and drenched
with the deep oblivion of earth's lapse and renewal.

And if, in the changing phases of man's life
I fall in sickness and in misery
my wrists seem broken and my heart seems dead
and strength is gone, and my life
is only the leavings of a life:

and still, among it all, snatches of lovely oblivion, and snatches
    of renewal
odd, wintry flowers upon the withered stem, yet new, strange flowers
such as my life has not brought forth before, new blossoms of me:

then I must know that still
I am in the hands of the unknown God,
he is breaking me down to his own oblivion
to send me forth on a new morning, a new man.

*D.H. Lawrence*
*1885–1930*

# THE PILGRIM'S WAY

## From: The Lord of the Rings

The Road goes ever on and on
   Down from the door where it began.
Now far ahead the Road has gone,
   And I must follow, if I can,
Pursuing it with eager feet,
   Until it joins some larger way
Where many paths and errands meet.
   And whither then? I cannot say.

*J.R.R. Tolkien*
*1892–1973*

# The Journey

## The Pilgrim's Song

Who would true valour see
Let him come hither;
One here will constant be,
Come wind, come weather.
There's no discouragement
Shall make him once relent
His first avowed intent,
To be a pilgrim.

Who so beset him round
With dismal stories,
Do but themselves confound;
His strength the more is.
No lion can him fright,
He'll with a giant fight,
But he will have a right
To be a pilgrim.

Hobgoblin, nor foul fiend
Can daunt his spirit:
He knows he, at the end,
Shall life inherit.
Then fancies flee away,
He'll fear not what men say,
He'll labour night and day
To be a pilgrim.

*John Bunyan*
*1628–88*

# Vox Ultima Crucis

Tarry no longer; toward thine heritage
Haste on thy way, and be of right good cheer.
Go each day onward on thy pilgrimage;
Think how short time thou hast abiden here.
Thy place is built above the starès clear,
No earthly palace wrought in so stately wise.
Come on, my friend, my brother may enter!
For thee I offered my blood in sacrifice.

*John Lydgate*
*1370?–1450?*

# *From:* The Wanderer

Often the wanderer pleads for pity
and mercy from the Lord; but for a long time,
sad in mind, he must dip his oars
into icy waters, the lanes of the sea;
he must follow the paths of exile: fate is inflexible...
A wise man must fathom how eerie it will be
when all the riches of the world stand waste,
as now in diverse places in this middle-earth
walls stand, tugged at by winds
and hung with hoar-frost, buildings in decay.
The wine-halls crumble, lords lie dead...
'Here possessions are fleeting, here friends are fleeting,
here man is fleeting, here kinsman is fleeting,
the whole world becomes a wilderness.'
So spoke the wise man in his heart as he sat apart in thought.
Brave is the man who holds to his beliefs; nor shall he ever
show the sorrow in his heart before he knows how he
can hope to heal it. It is best for a man to seek
mercy and comfort from the Father in heaven where
security stands for us all.

*Anonymous*
*about 850*
*translated by Kevin Crossley-Holland*

# The Pilgrim's Aiding

God be with thee in every pass,
Jesus be with thee on every hill,
Spirit be with thee on every stream,
   Headland and ridge and lawn;

Each sea and land, each moor and meadow,
Each lying down, each rising up,
In the trough of the waves, on the crest of the billows,
   Each step of the journey thou goest.

*Traditional Celtic*
*Collected by Alexander Carmichael*
*19th century*

# Seek the Lord

Seek the Lord, and in his ways persever.
   O faint not, but as eagles fly;
   For his steep hill is high;
Then striving gain the top, and triumph ever.

When with glory there thy brows are crowned,
   New joys so shall abound in thee,
   Such sights thy soul shall see,
That worldly thoughts shall by their beams be drownèd.

Farewell, World, thou mass of mere confusion,
   False light, with many shadows dimmed,
   Old witch, with new foils trimmed,
Thou deadly sleep of soul, and charmed illusion.

I the King will seek, of kings adorèd;
   Spring of light, tree of grace and bliss,
   Whose fruit so sovereign is
That all who taste it are from death restorèd.

*Thomas Campion*
*1567–1620*

# Road of my Desire

O thou who dost direct my feet
  To right or left where pathways part,
Wilt thou not, faithful Paraclete
  Direct the journeying of my heart?

Into the love of God, I pray,
  Deeper and deeper let me press,
Exploring all along the way
  Its secret strength and tenderness.

Into the steadfastness of one
  Who patiently endured the cross.
Of him who, though he were a Son,
    Came to his crown through bitter loss.

This is the road of my desire –
  Learning to love as God loves me,
Ready to pass through flood or fire
  With Christ's unwearying constancy.

*Frank Houghton*
*1894–1972*

# Prayer for the Journey

Here I am and forth I must,
And in Jesus Christ is all my trust.
No wicked thing do me no dere*,
Neither here nor elleswhere.
The Father with me, the Son with me,
The Holy Ghost, and the Trinity,
Be betwixt my ghostly enemy and me.
    In the name of the Father and the Son
    And the Holy Ghost, Amen.

*Anonymous*
Medieval
* *do me no dere*: do me any harm

# A Journey Spell

I guard myself with this rod and give myself into God's protection,
Against the painful stroke, against the grievous stroke,
Against the grim dread,
Against the great terror which is hateful to each
And against all evil which may enter the land.
I chant a charm of victory, I bear a rod of victory,
Word-victory, work-victory. May they be of power for me...
I pray now to the God of victory, to the mercy of God,
For a good journey, a mild and gentle
Wind from these shores. I have heard of winds
Which rouse whirling waters. Thus ever preserved
From all fiends may I meet friends,
So that I may dwell in the Almighty's protection,
Guarded from the enemy who seeks my life,
Set amid the glory of the angels,
And in the holy hand of the mighty one of heaven,
Whilst I may live in this life. Amen.

*Anonymous*
From a selection of Charms in the Anglo-Saxon Exeter Book *about 800*
*translated by Ruth Etchell*

# The Passionate Man's Pilgrimage

THOUGHT TO BE WRITTEN WHILE RALEGH WAS UNDER SENTENCE OF DEATH
IN THE TOWER OF LONDON IN 1603 OR JUST BEFORE HIS DEATH.

Give me my scallop-shell* of quiet,
My staff of faith to walk upon,
My scrip of joy, immortal diet,
My bottle of salvation,
My gown of glory, hope's true gage,
And thus I'll take my pilgrimage.

Blood must be my body's balmer,
No other balm will there be given,
While my soul like a white palmer
Travels to the land of heaven,
Over the silver mountains,
Where spring the nectar fountains;
And there I'll kiss
The bowl of bliss,
And drink my eternal fill

*The Pilgrim's Way*

On every milken hill.
My soul will be a-dry before,
But after it will ne'er thirst more.

And by that happy blissful way
More peaceful pilgrims I shall see,
That have shook off their gowns of clay
And go apparelled fresh like me.
I'll bring them first
To slake their thirst,
And then to taste those nectar suckets*
At the clear wells
Where sweetness dwells,
Drawn up by saints in crystal buckets...

And this is my eternal plea
To him that made heaven, earth and sea:
Seeing my flesh must die so soon,
And want a head to dine next noon,
Just at the stroke when my veins start and spread,
Set on my soul an everlasting head.
Then am I ready, like a palmer fit,
To tread those blest paths which before I writ.

*Sir Walter Ralegh*
*about 1552–1618*

* *scallop shell:* a pilgrim's badge; *suckets:* sweetmeats, usually fruit candied in syrup.

## *From:* The Growth of Love

3

Eternal Father, who didst all create,
In whom we live, and to whose bosom move,
To all men be thy name known, which is love,
Till its loud praises sound at heaven's high gate.
Perfect thy kingdom in our passing state,
That here on earth thou may'st as well approve
Our service, as thou ownest theirs above,
Whose joy we echo and in pain await.

Grant body and soul each day their daily bread:
And should in spite of grace fresh woe begin,
Even as our anger soon is past and dead
Be thy remembrance mortal of our sin:
By thee in paths of peace thy sheep be led,
And in the vale of terror comforted.

*Robert Bridges*
*1844–1930*

## 'I Am the Way'

  Thou art the Way
Hadst thou been nothing but the goal
  I cannot say
If thou hadst ever met my soul.

  I cannot see –
I, child of process – if there lies
  An end for me
Full of repose, full of replies.

  I'll not reproach
The road that winds, my feet that err.
  Access, Approach
Art thou, Time, Way, and Wayfarer.

*Alice Meynell*
*1847–1922*

# From: Paradise Lost

ADAM AND EVE ARE BANISHED FROM PARADISE

They, looking back, all the eastern side beheld
Of Paradise, so late their happy seat,
Waved over by that flaming brand, the gate
With dreadful faces thronged and fiery arms.
Some natural tears they dropped, but wiped them soon;
The world was all before them, where to choose
Their place of rest, and Providence their guide:
They hand in hand, with wandering steps and slow,
Through Eden took their solitary way.

*John Milton*
*1608–74*

# Faith and Doubt

## Prayer

We doubt the Word that tells us: Ask,
And ye shall have your prayer:
We turn our thoughts as to a task,
With will constrained and rare.

And yet we have; these scanty prayers
Yield gold without alloy:
O God, but he that trusts and dares
Must have a boundless joy!

*George MacDonald*
*1824–1905*

## *From:* Samson Agonistes

All is best, though we oft doubt,
What the unsearchable dispose
Of highest wisdom brings about,
And ever best found in the close.
Oft he seems to hide his face,
But unexpectedly returns
And to his faithful Champion hath in place
Bore witness gloriously; whence Gaza mourns
And all that band them to resist
His uncontrollable intent.
His servants he with new acquist
Of true experience from this great event
With peace and consolation hath dismissed,
And calm of mind all passion spent.

*John Milton*
*1608–74*

# Agnosticism

It doesn't come easy.

In spite of it all,
I can't help pushing open
the doors of country churches;
shoving a coin or two
in the box on the wall,
paying twice over
for the leaflet I take.

It doesn't come easy.

Wandering among gravestones
is irresistible;
departure is almost
impossible. I delay
it over and over
to hear once more the song of the blackbird.

It doesn't come easy.

As I race back
into the modern
rationalistic world,
I think of cathedral towns
and country rectories
and gentle rectors' wives
arranging the flowers.

*John Tatum*
*20th century*

# Adrift

Unto my faith as to a spar, I bring
   My love – and Faith and Love adrift I cast
   On a dim sea. I know not if at last
They the eternal shore of God shall find.

I know that neither waves nor wind
   Can sunder them, the cords are tied so fast
   That faith shall never – doubts and dangers past –
Come safe to land and Love be left behind.

*By the wife of Edward Dowden*
*1843–1913*
*(Possibly his second wife, Elizabeth Dickinson)*

# Death on a Crossing

What he never thought to consider was whether
the thing was true. What bewildered him, mostly,
was the way that the rumours had of reaching him
from such improbable sources – illiterate pamphlets
pressed in his hand, the brash or the floundering stranger
who came to his door, the proclamations, among
so many others, on hoardings

      though sometimes waking
a brief dismay, that never quite prodded him
to the analyst's couch.

      But annunciations, he thought,
should come to a rational man in a rational way.
He walked between a skyful of midnight angels
and a patch on somebody's jeans, both saying
the same thing to his stopped ears

      till the day
when he stepped on a crossing with not enough conviction
to get him safe to the other side, and he lay
among strangers' feet, and the angels lowered their trumpets
and no sweet chariot swung, to carry him home.

*Evangeline Paterson*
*20th century*

# Thanksgiving

We give thanks for St Thomas
  All we who have known
  The darkness of disbelief,
The hollowness at the heart of Christmas,
The intolerable emptiness of Easter,
  The grief of separation.

With thy great mercy thou dost enfold us,
The waverers, the aliens, who stood apart, alone.
  For the impoverishments of our barren years
    Thou wilt atone.

Now with the faithful company we bring,
From depths of thankfulness
  Our adoration
    To thee,
  O, Christ our King.

*Edith Forrest*
*20th century*

# Paradox

Mild yoke of Christ, most harsh to me not bearing,
You bruise the neck that balks, the hands that break you;
Sweet bread and wine, bitter to me not sharing,
You scar and scorch the throat that will not take you;
Mount where he taught, you cripple feet not bloody
From your sharp flints of eight-fold benediction;
Bright cross, most shameful stripped of the stripped body,
You crucify me safe from crucifixion:
Yet I, who am my own dilemma, jolting
My mind with thought lest it unthink its stiffness,
Rise to revolt against my own revolting
Blind me to blindness, deafen me to deafness.
So will your gifts of sight and hearing plunder
My eyes with lightning and my ears with thunder.

*Vassar Miller*
*20th century*

# Mock on! Mock on!

Mock on, mock on, Voltaire, Rousseau;
Mock on, mock on: 'tis all in vain!
You throw the sand against the wind,
And the wind blows it back again.

And every sand becomes a gem
Reflected in the beams divine;
Blown back they blind the mocking eye,
But still in Israel's path they shine.

The atoms of Democritus
And Newton's particles of light
Are sands upon the Red Sea shore,
Where Israel's tents do shine so bright.

*William Blake*
*1757–1827*

# E Tenebris

Come down, O Christ, and help me! reach thy hand,
For I am drowning in a stormier sea
Than Simon on the lake of Galilee:
The wine of life is spilt upon the sand,
My heart is as some famine-murdered land
Whence all good things have perished utterly,
And well I know my soul in Hell must lie
If I this night before God's throne should stand.
'He sleeps perchance, or rideth to the chase,
Like Baal, when his prophets howled that name
From morn to noon on Carmel's smitten height.'
Nay, peace, I shall behold, before the night,
The feet of brass, the robe more white than flame,
The wounded hands, the weary human face.

*Oscar Wilde*
*1856–1900*

# Tidal

The waves run up the shore
and fall back. I run
up the approaches of God
and fall back. The breakers return
reaching a little further,
gnawing away at the main land.
They have done this thousands
of years, exposing little by little
the rock under the soil's face.
I must imitate them only
in my return to the assault,
not in their violence. Dashing
my prayers at him will achieve
little other than the exposure
of the rock under the surface.
My returns must be made
on my knees. Let despair be known
as my ebb-tide; but let prayer
have its springs, too, brimming,
disarming him; discovering somewhere
among his fissures deposits of mercy
where trust may take root and grow.

*R.S. Thomas*
*20th century*

# Amor Dei

Give me to be thy child, and learn for ever at thy knee.
Give me to grow weak and grey-headed, since thou willst it so.
Bid me aside
Lay all the pleasures of my youth and pride,
Gladness as well,
Sweet ardours and bright hopes – I'll not rebel.

Only, I pray, keep me beside thee all the night and day,
Only for all thou takest give thyself and past recall!
And when youth's gone
As men count going, twixt us two alone
Still let me be
Thy little child, left learning at thy knee.

*Anonymous*

## After reading the life of Mrs Catherine Stubbs,
## in Isaac Ambrose's *War with the Devils*

Devil! I tell thee without nubbs or jubbs.
Thou wert no match at all for Catherine Stubbs,
And if her God give grace to play the man,
Thou wilt come off as bad with Isaac Hann.
For all the arguments she used shall be
The arguments which he will use with thee:
And when thou canst those arguments repel
He must submit to go with thee to hell;
But while his Saviour God doth live and reign
He is secure – gang off with thy cracked brain!
God is a sun and shield to every saint,
A cordial to their souls whene'er they faint;
He will give grace and glory we are told
And no good thing will he from them withhold.

*Isaac Hann*
*1690–1778*

## No Worst

No worst, there is none. Pitched past pitch of grief,
More pangs will, schooled at forepangs, wilder wring.
Comforter, where, where is your comforting?
Mary, mother of us, where is your relief?
My cries heave, herds-long; huddle in a main, a chief-
woe, world-sorrow; on an age-old anvil wince and sing –
Then lull, then leave off. Fury had shrieked 'No linge-
ring! Let me be fell: force I must be brief'.
O the mind, mind has mountains; cliffs of fall
Frightful, sheer, no-man-fathomed. Hold them cheap
May who ne'er hung there. Nor does long our small
Durance deal with that steep or deep. Here! creep,
Wretch, under a comfort serves in a whirlwind: all
Life death does end and each day dies with sleep.

*Gerard Manley Hopkins*
*1844–89*

# Dover Beach

The sea is calm to-night,
The tide is full, the moon lies fair
Upon the Straits; – on the French coast, the light
Gleams and is gone; the cliffs of England stand,
Glimmering and vast, out in the tranquil bay.
Come to the window, sweet is the night air!
Only, from the long line of spray
Where the ebb meets the moon-blanched sand,
Listen! you hear the grating roar
Of pebbles which the waves suck back, and fling,
At their return, up the high strand,
Begin, and cease, and then again begin,
With tremulous cadence slow, and bring
The eternal note of sadness in.

Sophocles long ago
Heard it on the Aegean, and it brought
Into his mind the turbid ebb and flow
Of human misery; we
Find also in the sound a thought,
Hearing it by this distant northern sea.

The sea of faith
Was once, too, at the full, and round earth's shore
Lay like the folds of a bright girdle furled;
But now I only hear
Its melancholy, long, withdrawing roar,
Retreating to the breath
Of the night-wind down the vast edges drear
And naked shingles of the world.

Ah, love, let us be true
To one another! for the world, which seems
To lie before us like a land of dreams,
So various, so beautiful, so new,
Hath really neither joy, nor love, nor light,
Nor certitude, nor peace, nor help for pain;
And we are here as on a darkling plain
Swept with confused alarms of struggle and flight,
Where ignorant armies clash by night.

*Matthew Arnold*
*1822–88*

# *From:* The Eternal Goodness

I know not what the future hath
   Of marvel or surprise,
Assured alone that life and death
   His mercy underlies.

And if my heart and flesh are weak
   To bear an untried pain,
The bruised reed he will not break,
   But strengthen and sustain.

No offering of my own I have,
   Nor works my faith to prove;
I can but give the gifts he gave,
   And plead his love for love.

And so beside the silent sea
   I wait the muffled oar;
No harm from him can come to me
   On ocean or on shore.

I know not where his islands lift
   Their fronded palms in air;
I only know I cannot drift
   Beyond his love and care.

*John Greenleaf Whittier*
*1807–92*

# Latter Day Psalms

2

The tree waves in the wind
But does not break unless
The bough is over-burdened.
When spring disrupts the dead days
Buds, leaves, and birds praise God
In song and silent sound.

The dead dock, stiff
With last year's pride,
Leans unwillingly in the gale.

My heart, Lord, is unyielding.
My joints are stiff
The knuckles of my knees

Refuse to bend.
The knife is at my neck,
My back breaks.

I will say my matutinal prayers
From a crippled position,
Perhaps the Lord will hear?

4

On the estate, Lord, the people
Take counsel one with another
And in the public house
There is lamentation.
The cost of living soars
Like wild duck rising
After morning feed.
Man has neither means nor meaning.
The cry of the young in the street
Rouses a protest in the market place.
    What shall I do, Lord?
Though I bring my sad soul
And place it at your feet,
My mouth is bitter, for fear
Infects my hand and heart.
The pit of hell yawns wide
Before my floundering feet,
I slip, I slide, I fall,
I try to grasp a skylark
But it flies south for summer.
    My mind is melancholic,
    I cannot praise my maker.

*Cliff Ashby*
*20th century*

# From: Abt Vogler

### IX

Therefore to whom turn I but to thee, the ineffable Name?
Builder and maker, thou, of houses not made with hands!
What, have fear of change from thee who art ever the same?
Doubt that thy power can fill the heart that thy power expands?
There shall never be one lost good! What was, shall live as before;
The evil is null, is nought, is silence implying sound;
What was good shall be good, with, for evil, so much good more;
On the earth the broken arcs; in the heaven, a perfect round.

### X

All we have willed or hoped or dreamed of good shall exist;
Not its semblance, but itself; no beauty, nor good, nor power
Whose voice has gone forth, but each survives for the melodist
When eternity affirms the conception of an hour.
The high that proved too high, the heroic for earth too hard,
The passion that left the ground to lose itself in the sky,
Are music sent up to God by the lover and the bard;
Enough that he heard it once: we shall hear it by-and-by.

*Robert Browning*
*1812–89*

# Aridity

O soul, canst thou not understand
Thou art not left alone,
As a dog to howl and moan
His master's absence? Thou art as a book
Left in a room that he forsook,
But returns to by and by,
A book of his dear choice, –
That quiet waiteth for his Hand,
That quiet waiteth for his Eye,
That quiet waiteth for his Voice.

*Michael Field*
*(Katharine Bradley 1846–1914*
*and Edith Cooper 1862–1913)*

# Faith Unfaithful

Mute, with signs I speak:
Blind, by groping seek:
Heed; yet nothing hear:
Feel; find no one near.

Deaf, eclipsed, and dumb,
Through this gloom I come
On the time-path trod
Towards ungranted God.

Carnal, I can claim
Only his known name
Dying, can but be
One with him in me.

*Siegfried Sassoon*
*1886–1967*

# Auguries of Innocence

To see a World in a grain of sand,
And a Heaven in a wild flower,
Hold Infinity in the palm of your hand,
And Eternity in an hour…

The bat that flits at close of eve
Has left the brain that won't believe.
The owl that calls upon the night
Speaks the unbeliever's fright…

Joy and woe are woven fine,
A clothing for the soul divine;
Under every grief and pine
Runs a joy with silken twine…

He who doubts from what he sees
Will ne'er believe, do what you please.
If the Sun and Moon should doubt,
They'd immediately go out…

God appears and God is Light,
To those poor souls who dwell in Night;
But does a Human Form display
To those who dwell in realms of Day…

*William Blake*
*1757–1827*

# Last Lines

('THE FOLLOWING ARE THE LAST LINES MY SISTER EMILY EVER WROTE.'
CHARLOTTE BRONTË)

No coward soul is mine,
No trembler in the world's storm-troubled sphere:
I see Heaven's glories shine,
And faith shines equal, arming me from fear.

O God within my breast,
Almighty, ever-present Deity!
Life – that in me has rest,
As I – undying Life – have power in thee!

Vain are the thousand creeds
That move men's hearts: unutterably vain;
Worthless as withered weeds,
Or idlest froth amid the boundless main,

To waken doubt in one
Holding so fast by thine infinity;
So surely anchored on
The steadfast rock of immortality.

With wide-embracing love
Thy spirit animates eternal years,
Pervades and broods above,
Changes, sustains, dissolves, creates and rears.

Though earth and man were gone,
And suns and universes ceased to be,
And thou wert left alone,
Every existence would exist in thee.

There is not room for Death,
Nor atom that his might could render void:
Thou – THOU art Being and Breath,
And what THOU art may never be destroyed.

*Emily Brontë*
*1818–48*

## From: Bishop Blougram's Apology

Why first, you don't believe, you don't and can't,
(Not statedly, that is, and fixedly
And absolutely and exclusively)
In any revelation called divine.
No dogmas nail your faith; and what remains
But say so, like the honest man you are?
First, therefore, overhaul theology!
Nay, I too, not a fool, you please to think,
Must find believing every whit as hard:
And if I do not frankly say as much,
The ugly consequence is clear enough.

Now wait, my friend: well, I do not believe –
If you'll accept no faith that is not fixed,
Absolute and exclusive, as you say.
You're wrong – I mean to prove it in due time.
Meanwhile, I know where difficulties lie
I could not, cannot solve, nor ever shall,
So give up hope accordingly to solve –
(To you, and over the wine). Our dogmas then
With both of us, though in unlike degree,
Missing full credence – overboard with them!
I mean to meet you on your own premise:
Good, there go mine in company with yours!

And now what are we? unbelievers both,
Calm and complete, determinately fixed
Today, to-morrow and for ever, pray?
You'll guarantee me that? Not so, I think!
In no wise! All we've gained is, that belief,
As unbelief before, shakes us by fits,
Confounds us like its predecessor. Where's
The gain? how can we guard our unbelief,
Make it bear fruit to us – the problem here.
Just when we are safest, there's a sunset-touch,
A fancy from a flower-bell, someone's death,
A chorus-ending from Euripides, –
And that's enough for fifty hopes and fears
As old and new at once as nature's self,
To rap and knock and enter in our soul,
Take hands and dance there, a fantastic ring,
Round the ancient idol, on his base again, –

The grand Perhaps! We look on helplessly.
There the old misgivings, crooked questions are –
This good God, – what he could do if he would,
Would if he could – then must have done long since:
If so, when, where and how? some way must be, –
Once feel about, and soon or late you hit
Some sense, in which it might be, after all.
Why not, 'The Way, the Truth, the Life'?

*Robert Browning*
*1812–89*

## Adam in the Garden

Adam in the suburban garden
Among the television trees,
Tasting the fruit of the Tree of Knowledge,
Carelessly tosses the core over his shoulder.

It explodes, brilliant as a million acetylene torches,
Deafening as a million sonic booms.
It shatters the picture windows and knocks
The cross of First Church out of the sky.

The sun hides his face behind a mushroom cloud.
The clock on the Federal Building and Loan Office
No longer reports the interest rate
Or flashes the time and temperature.

The net alert station is silent,
Huntley and Brinkley fail to report the flash,
Church bells are silent. Sermons on
Unilateral disarmament have been cancelled.

God, abandoned, lonely, obscured by smoke,
Stubs his toe on a steeple
Buried in the ashes of the garden and
Calls, 'Adam, where are you?'

*Elmer F. Suderman*
*20th century*

# A Highland Testimony

We had our ritual too. Down the long glen
While startled curlews cried on ebb-tide sands,
We all would walk, our Bibles in our hands,
And winter sunshine turned to rain again.

The crisp and cutting edge of our dark suits
Served as a weekly penance. We, in turn
Would kick some chuckies into ditch or burn,
And scuff the polish on our Sunday boots.

The church bell spread its iron news abroad,
Dull through the trees or clear across the bay.
With quickened step we hastened on our way.
And so we entered in the house of God.

Thus went the ritual of that far-off day.
The creak of bell and bell-rope clanged and jarred.
The psalms were dignified. The pews were hard.
The rain was soft. The lowering skies were grey.

Grey too the tenor of our world today.
The death of humanism, sick and sad.
And I could wish that once again we had
That child's acceptance of the Christian way.

Faith of my fathers. If it came again,
I would not change a moment of my youth,
The grey kirk and the straight unflinching truth,
Clean as the stones at the burn-side in the glen.

*Alistair Halden*
20th century

# Abdication of Belief

Those – dying then,
Knew where they went –
They went to God's Right Hand
That Hand is amputated now
And God cannot be found –

The abdication of Belief
Makes the Behaviour small –
Better an ignis fatuus
Than no illume at all –

*Emily Dickinson*
*1830–86*

# The Journey

And if you go up that way, you will meet with a man
Leading a horse, whose eyes declare:
There is no God. Take no notice.
There will be other roads and other men
With the same creed, whose lips yet utter
Friendlier greeting, men who have learned
To pack a little of the sun's light
In their cold eyes, whose hands are waiting
For your hand. But do not linger.
A smile is payment; the road runs on
With many turnings towards the tall
Tree to which the believer is nailed.

*R.S. Thomas*
*20th century*

## From: In Memoriam

Strong Son of God, immortal Love,
 Whom we, that have not seen thy face,
 By faith, and faith alone, embrace,
Believing where we cannot prove;

Thine are these orbs of light and shade;
 Thou madest life in man and brute;
 Thou madest death; and lo, thy foot
Is on the skull which thou hast made.

Thou wilt not leave us in the dust:
 Thou madest man, he knows not why,
 He thinks he was not made to die;
And thou hast made him: thou art just.

Thou seemest human and divine,
 The highest, holiest manhood, thou:
 Our wills are ours, we know not how;
Our wills are ours, to make them thine.

Our little systems have their day;
 They have their day and cease to be:
 They are but broken lights of thee,
And thou, O Lord, art more than they.

We have but faith: we cannot know;
 For knowledge is of things we see;
 And yet we trust it comes from thee,
A beam in darkness: let it grow...

Forgive these wild and wandering cries,
 Confusion of a wasted youth;
 Forgive them where they fail in truth,
And in thy wisdom make me wise.

*Alfred, Lord Tennyson*
*1809–92*

# Light Shining out of Darkness

God moves in a mysterious way
   His wonders to perform;
He plants his footsteps in the sea,
   And rides upon the storm.

Deep in unfathomable mines
   Of never-failing skill
He treasures up his bright designs
   And works his sovereign will.

Ye fearful saints, fresh courage take:
   The clouds ye so much dread
Are big with mercy, and shall break
   In blessings on your head.

Judge not the Lord by feeble sense,
   But trust him for his grace;
Behind a frowning providence
   He hides a smiling face.

His purposes will ripen fast,
   Unfolding every hour;
The bud may have a bitter taste,
   But sweet will be the flower.

Blind unbelief is sure to err,
   And scan his work in vain;
God is his own interpreter,
   And he will make it plain.

*William Cowper*
*1731–1800*

## The Harrowing of Hell

Love asks to penetrate
The hot dark place,
The place of pain,
From which the sons of light
Hide their modest faces.
Love is allowed.
And oh! what gnashing of teeth
Among the demons
Who thought it was their own!

*D.M. Lewis*
*20th century*

## The Crucifixion

'String him up,' some repoman shouted,
'He's a weirdo.' 'In the bin, in the bin,'
Yelled another and grabbed some thorns,
Sharp as needles, twisting them round
A fresh-cut thorn branch. He made
A wreath and forced it down on his head,
The pain piercing his flesh. 'Morning, vicar,'
This comedian said and darted twigs
At him, aiming at his eyes. With three
Nails, he nailed him naked to a cross,
Lifted bitter drink to his lips, telling
Him drink and stop dropping off, hang
On a bit longer. 'Now if he's really something,'
He said, 'He'll get himself out of this one.
If you're Christ, and if Christ is God's
Son, come on down, off that cross.
We'll believe it then, you've got life
On a string, you're never going to be
            A goner.'
            'That's it,'
            Christ said,
            'That's it.'

His senses
Began to fade
Pale and piteous
Like a prisoner
In death, the lord
Of life and light
Closed his eyes, day
Shrank back, appalled,
And the sun darkened.
The Temple wall
Shattered and split,
The solid rocks
Of earth ruptured.
It was dark
As thickest night,
Earth convulsed,
Quaked like a live thing. The noise brought
Dead men clambering up
From the coffined depths
Who told why the tempest
Raged so long.
One corpse said,
'There is in darkness
Here a bitter fight.
Life and Death
Destroy each other.
None can know
For sure who wins
Till Sunday
As the sun rises,'
And with these words
Sank back in earth.

*From Piers Plowman, by William Langland*
*1330?–1400?*
*translated by Ronald Tamplin*

# Retreat

The enclosed garden, sensuous and chaste;
darkly, through bars, perceive angelic bees
dusting with gilded fur the flowers' lips.
The calf and the young lion lying down
beneath the laden, scented shade of trees
and guards with flaming swords at the east gates.

Outside, never enough to storm them,
never one enough. Heroic sacrifice
brings babel siege-towers down about our ears;
scapegoats and saboteurs are freighted out
on dwindling rails that meet the wilderness;
gardens of wire and huts with floors of blood.

The blood for milk and tears for honeydew
and smoke which never palls, always disperses
under heaven like perjurious prayers;
strong fingers dip into torn carcasses
and tongues lap sweetness hid in hives of bone.

There is a way, retreat. A swathe runs back
through thistles to skull-hill; one bare tree's shade
cast in the rocks' arena of defeat.
Deserted now, through-route when stone rolls back,
the tomb, unstoppered, spills the garden's light.

*Paul Hyland*
*20th century*

# Hope in the Darkness

Say not the struggle naught availeth,
　　The labour and the wounds are vain,
The enemy faints not, nor faileth,
　　And as things have been they remain.

If hopes were dupes, fears may be liars;
　　It may be, in yon smoke concealed,
Your comrades chase e'en now the fliers,
　　And, but for you, possess the field.

For while the tired waves, vainly breaking,
　　Seem here no painful inch to gain,
Far back, through creeks and inlets making,
　　Comes silent, flooding in, the main.

And not by eastern windows only,
　　When daylight comes, comes in the light;
In front the sun climbs slow, how slowly!
　　But westward, look, the land is bright!

*Arthur Hugh Clough*
*1819–61*

# *From:* To Keep the Cold Wind Away

There blows a cold wind today, today,
   The wind blows cold today;
Christ suffered his passion for man's salvation,
   To keep the cold wind away.

This wind by reason is called temptation
   It rages both night and day.
Remember, man, how the Saviour was slain
   To keep the cold wind away.

Pride and presumption and false extortion,
   That many man doth betray –
Man, come to contrition and ask confession
   To keep the cold wind away.

O Mary mild, for love of the child
   That died on Good Friday,
Be our salvation from mortal damnation
   To keep the cold wind away.

He was nailed, his blood was haled*,
   Our remission for to buy;
And for our sins all he drank both eisel* and gall
   To keep the cold wind away

Sloth, envy, covetousness and lechery
   Blow the cold wind, as I dare say;
Against such poison he suffered his passion
   To keep the cold wind away.

*Anonymous*
*about 1500*

* *haled:* drawn; *eisel:* vinegar

# St Patrick's Hymn before Tara

Christ, as a light,
Illumine and guide me!
Christ, as a shield, o'ershadow and cover me!
Christ be under me! Christ be over me!
Christ be beside me
On left hand and right!
Christ be before me, behind me, about me!
Christ this day be within and without me!

Christ, the lowly and meek,
Christ, the All-powerful, be
In the heart of each to whom I speak,
In the mouth of each who speaks to me!
In all who draw near me,
Or see me or hear me!

At Tara to-day, in this awful hour,
I call on the Holy Trinity!
Glory to him who reigneth in power,
The God of the elements, Father, and Son,
And Paraclete Spirit, which Three are in One,
The ever-existing Divinity!

Salvation dwells with the Lord,
With Christ, the Omnipotent Word.
From generation to generation
Grant us, O Lord, thy grace and salvation!

*St Patrick*
*about 372–466*
*translated from the Irish by James Mangan*

# Be Thou my Vision

Be thou my vision, O Lord of my heart,
Naught be all else to me save that thou art;
Be thou my best thoughts in the day and night,
Waking and sleeping thy presence my light.

Be thou my wisdom, be thou my true word,
I ever with thee and thou with me, Lord;
Thou my great Father, and I thy true son;
Thou in me dwelling, and I with thee one.

Be thou my breast-plate, my sword for the fight,
Be thou my armour, and be thou my might,
Thou my soul's shelter, and thou my high tower,
Raise thou me heavenward, O Power of my power.

Riches I heed not, nor man's empty praise,
Thou mine inheritance through all my days;
Thou, and thou only, the first in my heart,
High King of heaven, my treasure thou art!

High King of heaven, when battle is done,
Grant heaven's joy to me O bright heaven's sun,
Christ of my own heart, whatever befall,
Still be my vision, O Ruler of all.

*Gaelic*
*8th century*
*translated by Eleanor Hull*

# Battle Hymn of the Republic

Mine eyes have seen the glory of the coming of the Lord:
He is trampling out the vintage where the grapes of wrath are stored:
He has loosed the fateful lightning of his terrible swift sword:
    His truth is marching on.

I have seen him in the watch-fires of a hundred circling camps;
They have builded him an altar in the evening dews and damps;
I can read his righteous sentence by the dim and flaring lamps:
    His day is marching on.

I have read a fiery gospel, writ in burnished rows of steel:
'As ye deal with my contemners, so with you my grace shall deal;
Let the Hero, born of woman, crush the serpent with his heel!
    Since God is marching on.'

He has sounded forth the trumpet that shall never call retreat;
He is sifting out the hearts of men before his Judgement Seat;
O, be swift, my soul, to answer him, be jubilant my feet!
    Our God is marching on.

In the beauty of the lilies Christ was born, across the sea,
With a glory in his bosom that transfigures you and me:
As he died to make men holy, let us die to make men free,
    While God is marching on.

*Julia Ward Howe*
*1819–1910*

# The Harrowing of Hell

'Hold still,'
Truth said: 'I hear some spirit
Speaking to the guards of hell,
And see him too, telling them
Unbar the gates. "Lift your heads
    You gates."'
  And from the heart
    of light
A loud voice spoke.
    'Open
These gates, Lucifer,
Prince of this land: the king of glory
  A crown upon his head
    Comes,'

Satan groaned and said to his hell's angels,
'It's that sort of light sprung Lazarus.
Unstoppable. This'll be big, big
Trouble, I mean all sorts of bother
For the lot of us...

    Again
  The light said, 'Unlock.'
    Said Lucifer, 'Who
      Goes there?'

A huge voice replied, 'The lord
Of power, of strength, that made
All things. Dukes of this dark place
Undo these gates so Christ come
In, the son of heaven's King.'
With that word, hell split apart,
Burst its devil's bars; no man
Nor guard could stop the gates swing
Wide. The old religious men,
Prophets, people who had walked
In darkness, 'Behold the Lamb
Of God,' with Saint John sang now.
But Lucifer could not look
At it, the light blinding him.
And along that light all those
Our Lord loved came streaming out.

'Body and soul,' Christ said,
'I am here. Look on me.
I come for all sinners,
To give both the devil
His due and claiming mine...

'So, Lucifer, don't let yourself think
I'm bringing any of these sinners
Out illegally, by power alone.
I ransom my people in justice
And in law. I come not to destroy
The law but to fulfil it. And so
    What a trick
      Took
      Grace
    Has regained.

     As Adam
And all his people
  Died
Through a tree
  So
Through a tree
  Adam
And all his people
  Shall
Rise again.

Your tricks begin to turn upon you.
My grace, everywhere, spreads wider,
Wider. The bitter drink you have brewed,
Taste it yourself. Doctor of Death, drink
The prescription you have made. I am
Lord of life and so love is my drink.'

*From Piers Plowman, by William Langland*
*1330?–1400?*
*translated by Ronald Tamplin*

## Healing

Sick wards. The sailed beds
becalmed. The nurses tack
hither and fro. The chloroform
breeze rises and falls.
Hospitals are their own
weather. The temperatures
have no relation
to the world outside. The surgeons,
those cunning masters
of navigation, follow
their scalpels' compass through
hurricanes of pain to a calm
harbour. Somewhere far down
in the patient's darkness,
where faith died, like a graft
or a transplant prayer
gets to work, repairing
the soul's tissue, leading
the astonished self between
twin pillars, where life's angels
stand wielding their bright swords of flame.

R.S. *Thomas*
20th century

# From: Litany to the Holy Spirit

In the hour of my distress,
When temptations me oppress,
And when I my sins confess,
    Sweet Spirit comfort me!

When I lie within my bed,
Sick in heart, and sick in head,
And with doubts discomforted,
    Sweet Spirit comfort me!

When the house doth sigh and weep,
And the house is drowned in sleep,
Yet mine eyes the watch do keep;
    Sweet Spirit comfort me!

When the artless doctor sees
Not one hope, but of his fees,
And his skill runs on the lees;
    Sweet Spirit comfort me!

When his potion and his pill,
Has, or none, or little skill,
Meet for nothing, but to kill;
    Sweet Spirit comfort me!

When the passing-bell doth toll,
And the furies in a shoal
Come to fright a parting soul;
    Sweet Spirit comfort me!...

When the flames and hellish cries
Fright mine ears, and fright mine eyes,
And all terrors me surprise;
    Sweet Spirit comfort me!

When the judgement is revealed,
And that opened which was sealed,
When to thee I have appealed;
    Sweet Spirit comfort me!

*Robert Herrick*
*1591–1674*

# Hymn to God, my God, in my Sickness

Since I am coming to that holy room,
   Where, with thy choir of saints for evermore,
I shall be made thy music; as I come
      I tune the instrument here at the door,
      And what I must do then, think here before.

Whilst my physicians by their love are grown
   Cosmographers, and I their map, who lie
Flat on this bed, that by them may be shown
      That this is my south-west discovery
      *Per fretum febris*, by these straits to die,

I joy, that in these straits, I see my west;
   For, though their currents yield return to none,
What shall my west hurt me? As west and east
      In all flat maps (and I am one) are one,
      So death doth touch the resurrection.

Is the pacific sea my home? Or are
   The eastern riches? Is Jerusalem?
Anyan, and Magellan, and Gibraltar,
      All straits, and none but straits, are ways to them,
      Whether where Japhet dwelt, or Cham, or Sem.

We think that Paradise and Calvary,
   Christ's Cross, and Adam's tree, stood in one place;
Look Lord, and find both Adams met in me;
      As the first Adam's sweat surrounds my face,
      May the last Adam's blood my soul embrace.

So, in his purple wrapped receive me, Lord,
   By these his thorns give me his other crown;
And as to others' souls I preached thy word,
      Be this my text, my sermon to mine own,
      Therefore that he may raise the Lord throws down.

*John Donne*
*1572–1631*

# Before the Anaesthetic

OR
A REAL FRIGHT

Intolerably sad, profound
St. Giles's bells are ringing round,
They bring the slanting summer rain
To tap the chestnut boughs again
Whose shadowy cave of rainy leaves
The gusty belfry-song receives.
Intolerably sad and true,
Victorian red and jewel blue,
The mellow bells are ringing round
And charge the evening light with sound,
And I look motionless from bed
On heavy trees and purple red
And hear the midland bricks and tiles
Throw back the bells of stone St. Giles,
Bells, ancient now as castle walls,
Now hard and new as pitchpine stalls,
Now full with help from ages past,
Now dull with death and hell at last.
Swing up! and give me hope of life,
Swing down! and plunge the surgeon's knife.
I, breathing for a moment, see
Death wing himself away from me
And think, as on this bed I lie,
Is it extinction when I die?
I move my limbs and use my sight;
Not yet, thank God, not yet the Night.
Oh better far those echoing hells
Half-threaten'd in the pealing bells
Than that this 'I' should cease to be –
Come quickly, Lord, come quick to me.
St. Giles's bells are asking now
'And hast thou known the Lord, hast thou?'
St. Giles' bells, they richly ring
'And was that Lord our Christ the King?'
St. Giles's bells they hear me call
*I never knew the Lord at all.*
Oh not in me your Saviour dwells
You ancient, rich St.Giles's bells.
Illuminated missals – spires –
Wide screens and decorated quires –

All these I loved, and on my knees
I thanked myself for knowing these
And watched the morning sunlight pass
Through richly stained Victorian glass
And in the colour-shafted air
I, kneeling, thought the Lord was there.
Now, lying in the gathering mist
I know that Lord did not exist;
Now, lest this 'I' should cease to be,
Come, real Lord, come quick to me.
With every gust the chestnut sighs,
With every breath, a mortal dies;
The man who smiled alone, alone,
And went his journey on his own
With 'Will you give my wife this letter,
In case, of course, I don't get better?'
Waits for his coffin lid to close
On waxen head and yellow toes.
Almighty Saviour, had I Faith
There'd be no fight with kindly Death.
Intolerably long and deep
St. Giles's bells swing on in sleep:
'But still you go from here alone'
Say all the bells about the Throne.

*John Betjeman*
*20th century*

## Prayer

God stir the soil,
Run the ploughshare deep,
Cut the furrows round and round,
Overturn the hard, dry ground,
Spare no strength nor toil,
Even though I weep.
In the loose, fresh mangled earth
Sow new seed.
Free of withered vine and weed
Bring fair flowers to birth.

*Anonymous*

# Intercession Against the Plague

Set free thy people, set free thy servants,
Lighten thine anger, Ruler most holy;
Look on their anguish, bitter their weeping,
    Christ, in thy mercy.

Thou art our Father, Master exalted,
We are thy servants, thou the Good Shepherd,
Bearing thy token of blood and of crimson
    Marked on our foreheads.

Deep in thy hell who then shall confess thee?
Yea, shall the dead give praise to thy name?
Judge of our dread, thy rod is of iron,
    Spare us, we pray thee.

Bring not so near to thy people, thy servants,
The cup of thine anger, thy merited wrath:
Lighten upon us thine ancient compassion.
    We cry. Do thou hear!

Loosen, we pray thee, our load of transgression.
Vouchsafe to keep us, Prince ever blessed.
Vanquish the shadow that darkens our spirits,
    Light of the world.

Saint of all saints and king of all kingships,
Visit thy people with thy right hand.
Lift up the light of thy countenance upon us,
    Lord, or we perish.

*Sedulius Scottus*
*about 848–74*
*translated by Helen Waddell*

# OUT OF THE DEPTHS:
# PSALMS OF SUFFERING

## Psalm 6

Lord, in thine anger do not reprehend me,
  Nor in thy hot displeasure me correct;
Pity me, Lord, for I am much deject,
  Am very weak and faint; heal and amend me,
For all my bones, that even with anguish ache,
  Are troubled, yea, my soul is troubled sore.
And thou, O Lord, how long? turn, Lord, restore
  My soul, O save me for thy goodness sake,
For in death no remembrance is of thee;
  Who in the grave can celebrate thy praise?
Wearied I am with sighing out my days,
  Nightly my couch I make a kind of sea;
My bed I water with my tears; mine eye
  Through grief consumes, is waxen old and dark
I' the midst of all mine enemies that mark.
  Depart, all ye that work iniquity,
Depart from me, for the voice of my weeping
  The Lord hath heard; the Lord hath heard my prayer;
My supplication with acceptance fair
  The Lord will own, and have me in his keeping.
Mine enemies shall all be blank and dashed
  With much confusion; then grow red with shame;
They shall return in haste the way they came
  And in a moment shall be quite abashed.

*John Milton*
*1608–74*

# Psalm 13

How long, O Lord, shall I forgotten be?
   What? Ever?
How long wilt thou thy hidden face from me
   Dissever?

How long shall I consult with careful sprite*
   In anguish?
How long shall I with foes triumphant might
   Thus languish?

Behold me, Lord; let to thy hearing creep
   My crying;
Nay, give me eyes and light, lest that I sleep
   In dying:

Lest my foe brag, that in my ruin he
   Prevailed;
And at my fall they joy that, troublous, me
   Assailed.

No! no! I trust on thee, and joy in thy
   Great pity:
Still, therefore, of thy graces shall be my
   Song's ditty.

*Mary Herbert, Countess of Pembroke*
*1561–1621*

* sprite: spirit

## The Fell of Dark

I wake and feel the fell of dark, not day.
What hours, O what black hours we have spent
This night! What sights you, heart, saw; ways you went!
And more must, in yet longer light's delay.

With witness I speak this. But where I say
Hours I mean years, mean life. And my lament
Is cries countless, cries like dead letters sent
To dearest him that lives alas! away.

I am gall, I am heartburn. God's most deep decree
Bitter would have me taste: my taste was me;
Bones built in me, flesh filled, blood brimmed the curse.

Selfyeast of spirit a dull dough sours. I see
The lost are like this, and their scourge to be
As I am mine, their sweating selves; but worse.

*Gerard Manley Hopkins*
*1844–89*

## Remorse

Remorse is memory awake,
Her parties all astir,
A presence of departed acts
At window and at door.

It's past set down before the soul
And lighted with a match,
Perusal to facilitate
And help belief to stretch.

Remorse is cureless – the disease
Not even God can heal,
For 'tis his institution and
The adequate of Hell.

*Emily Dickinson*
*1830–86*

# I Am

I am – yet what I am none cares or knows,
My friends forsake me like a memory lost;
I am the self-consumer of my woes,
They rise and vanish in oblivions host,
Like shadows in love – frenzied stifled throes
And yet I am, and live like vapours tossed.

Into the nothingness of scorn and noise,
Into the living sea of waking dreams,
Where there is neither sense of life or joys,
But the vast shipwreck of my life's esteems;
And e'en the dearest – that I love the best –
Are strange – nay, rather stranger than the rest.

I long for scenes where man has never trod,
A place where woman never smiled or wept;
There to abide with my Creator, God,
And sleep as I in childhood sweetly slept:
Untroubling and untroubled where I lie,
The grass below – above the vaulted sky.

*John Clare*
*1793–1864*

# Lines Written During a Period of Insanity

Hatred and vengeance, my eternal portion
Scarce can endure delay of execution,
Wait, with impatient readiness, to seize my
    Soul in a moment.

Damned below Judas: more abhorred than he was
Who for a few pence sold his holy Master.
Twice betrayed Jesus me, the last delinquent,
    Deems the profanest.

Man disavows, and Deity disowns me:
Hell might afford my miseries a shelter;
Therefore hell keeps her ever hungry mouths all
    Bolted against me.

Hard lot! encompassed with a thousand dangers;
Weary, faint, trembling with a thousand terrors;
I'm called, if vanquished, to receive a sentence
    Worse than Abiram's.

*Him* the vindictive rod of angry justice
Sent quick and howling to the centre headlong;
I, fed with judgement, in a fleshly tomb, am
    Buried above ground.

*William Cowper*
*1731–1800*

## Anguish

I shall know why, when time is over,
And I have ceased to wonder why;
Christ will explain each separate anguish
In the fair schoolroom of the sky.

He will tell me what Peter promised,
And I, for wonder at his woe,
I shall forget the drop of anguish
That scalds me now, that scalds me now.

*Emily Dickinson*
*1830–86*

## Casting all your Care upon God, for he careth for you

Come, heavy souls, oppressed that are
With doubts, and fears, and carking care.
Lay all your burdens down, and see
There's one that carried once a tree
Upon his back, and, which is more,
A heavier weight, your sins, he bore.
Think then how easily he can
Your sorrows bear that's God and man;
Think too how willing he's to take
Your care on him, who for your sake
Sweat bloody drops, prayed, fasted, cried,
Was bound, scourged, mocked and crucified.
He that so much for you did do,
Will do yet more, and care for you.

*Thomas Washbourne*
*1606–87*

# God our Help

With floods and storms thus we be tossed,
Awake, good Lord, to thee we cry.
Our ship is almost sunk and lost.
Thy mercy help our misery.

Man's strength is weak: man's wit is dull:
Man's reason's blind. These things to amend,
Thy hand, O Lord, of might is full;
Awake betime, and help us send.

In thee we trust, and in no wight:
Save us as chickens under the hen.
Our crookedness thou canst make right
Glory to thee for aye. Amen.

*Anonymous*
*17th century*

# PEACE AND ACCEPTANCE

# *From:* The Brewing of Soma

Drop thy still dews of quietness,
    Till all our strivings cease;
Take from our souls the strain and stress,
And let our ordered lives confess
    The beauty of thy peace.

*John Greenleaf Whittier*
*1807–92*

# Quiet Peace

O Lord, my heart is all a prayer,
 But it is silent unto thee;
I am too tired to look for words,
 I rest upon thy sympathy
To understand when I am dumb;
 And well I know thou hearest me.

I know thou hearest me because
 A quiet peace comes down to me,
And fills the places where before
 Weak thoughts were wandering wearily;
And deep within me it is calm,
 Though waves are tossing outwardly.

*Amy Carmichael*
*1867–1951*

# God, the Port of Peace

Now come all you who have been brought
In bondage full of busy bitterness,
Earthly desire abiding in your thought!
Here is the rest from all your busyness,
Here is the port of peace and restfulness
To those who stand in storms and in dis-ease,
Open refuge to wretches in distress,
And all comfort from trouble and mis-ease.

*Adapted from John Walton*
*about 1410*

# *From:* The Thoughts of God

They say there is a hollow, safe and still,
A point of coolness and repose
Within the centre of a flame, where life might dwell
Unharmed and unconsumed, as in a luminous shell,
Which the bright walls of fire enclose
In breachless splendour, barrier that no foes
    Could pass at will.

    There is a point of rest
At the great centre of the cyclone's force
  A silence at its secret source; –
A little child might slumber undistressed,
Without the ruffle of one fairy curl,
In that strange central calm amid the mighty whirl.

So in the centre of these thoughts of God,
Cyclones of power, consuming glory-fire,
  As we fall o'erawed
Upon our faces, and are lifted higher
By his great gentleness, and carried nigher
Than unredeemèd angels, till we stand
  Even in the hollow of his hand, –
  Nay more! we lean upon his breast –
*There*, there we find a point of perfect rest
  And glorious safety. There we see
  His thoughts to us-ward, thoughts of peace
That stoop to tenderest love; that still increase
With increase of our need; that never change,
That never fail, or falter, or forget.
    O pity infinite!
    O royal mercy free!
    O gentle climax of the depth and height
Of God's most precious thoughts, most wonderful, most strange!
    'For I am poor and needy, yet
The Lord himself, Jehovah, *thinketh upon me!*'

*Frances Ridley Havergal*
*1836–79*

# The Good Shepherd

Christ who knows all his sheep
Will all in safety keep;
He will not lose his blood,
    Nor intercession:
Nor we the purchased good
    Of his dear passion.

I know my God is just,
To him I wholly trust
All that I have and am,
    All that I hope for.
All's sure and seen to him,
    Which I here grope for.

Lord Jesus, take my spirit:
I trust thy love and merit:
Take home this wandering sheep,
    For thou hast sought it:
This soul in safety keep,
    For thou hast bought it.

*Richard Baxter*
*1615–91*

# Intimations

Henry Vaughan saw eternity
and far beyond star countries;
Blake met angels in the garden
pleasantly building green Jerusalem.

I border bred, London extended,
little matchstick man
for whom the sparrows do not care two farthings,
remain untutored by exceptions

Lord keep us in our proper stations.

If the communion of saints
is not only the shining ones
but the incompetent and ineffective,
let grace sidle down the repeated street
and a wing flash in ambiguous sunlight

*Raymond Chapman*
*20th century*

# City of God

Glorious things of thee are spoken,
  Zion, city of our God;
He, whose word cannot be broken,
  Formed thee for his own abode:
On the Rock of Ages founded,
  What can shake thy sure repose?
With salvation's walls surrounded,
  Thou mayst smile at all thy foes.

See, the streams of living waters,
  Springing from eternal love,
Well supply thy sons and daughters,
  And all fear of want remove:
Who can faint, while such a river
  Ever flows their thirst to assuage –
Grace, which like the Lord the giver,
  Never fails from age to age.

Blest inhabitants of Zion,
  Washed in the Redeemer's blood;
Jesus, whom their souls rely on,
  Makes them kings and priests to God.
'Tis his love his people raises
  Over self to reign as kings;
And as priests, his solemn praises
  Each for a thankoffering brings.

Saviour, if of Zion's city
  I, through grace, a member am,
Let the world deride or pity,
  I will glory in thy name:
Fading is the worldling's pleasure,
  All his boasted pomp and show;
Solid joys and lasting treasure
  None but Zion's children know.

*John Newton*
*1725–1807*

# The Hands of God

It is a fearful thing to fall into the hands of the living God.
But it is a much more fearful thing to fall out of them.

Did Lucifer fall through knowledge?
oh then, pity him, pity him that plunge!

Save me, O God, from falling into the ungodly knowledge
of myself as I am without God.

Let me never know, O God
let me never know what I am or should be
when I have fallen out of your hands, the hands of the living
God.

That awful and sickening endless sinking, sinking
through the slow corruptive levels of disintegrative knowledge
when the self has fallen from the hands of God
and sinks, seething and sinking, corrupt
and sinking still, in depth after depth of disintegrative
consciousness
sinking in the endless undoing, the awful katabolism into the
abyss!
even of the soul, fallen from the hands of God!

Save me from that, O God!
Let me never know myself apart from the living God!

*D.H. Lawrence*
*1885–1930*

# Dum vivimus, vivamus

Live while you live, the Epicure would say,
And seize the pleasures of the present day.
Live while you live, the sacred Preacher cries,
And give to God each moment as it flies.
Lord, in my view, let both united be,
I live in pleasure if I live to thee.

*Philip Doddridge*
*1702–51*

# On His Blindness

When I consider how my light is spent,
    Ere half my days, in this dark world and wide,
    And that one talent which is death to hide
    Lodged with me useless, though my soul more bent
To serve therewith my Maker, and present
    My true account, lest he returning chide,
    'Doth God exact day-labour, light denied?'
    I fondly ask. But Patience, to prevent
That murmur, soon replies: 'God does not need
    Either man's work or his own gifts; who best
    Bear his mild yoke, they serve him best. His state
    Is kingly: thousands at his bidding speed,
And post o'er land and ocean without rest;
They also serve who only stand and wait.'

*John Milton*
*1608–74*

# The Holy Man

A trapped bird
A wrecked ship
An empty cup
A withered tree
Is he
Who scorns the will of the King above.

Pure gold
Bright sun
Filled wine-cup
Happy beautiful holy
Is he
Who does the will of the King of love.

*Brendan Kennelly*
*20th century*

# True Felicity

Contentment is a sleepy thing!
If it in death alone must die;
A quiet mind is worse than poverty!
   Unless it from enjoyment spring!
That's blessedness alone that makes a king!
Wherein the joys and treasures are so great,
They all the powers of the soul employ,
     And fill it with a work complete,
       While it doth all enjoy.
True joys alone contentment do inspire,
Enrich content, and make our courage higher.
    Content alone's a dead and silent stone:
      The real life of bliss
    Is glory reigning in a throne,
      Where all enjoyment is
The soul of man is so inclined to see,
Without his treasures no man's soul can be,
    Nor rest uncrowned!
     Desire and love
Must in the height of all their rapture move,
     Where there is true felicity.

*Thomas Traherne*
*1636?–74*

# The Shepherd's Song

He that is down needs fear no fall,
   He that is low no pride;
He that is humble ever shall
   Have God to be his guide.

I am content with what I have,
   Little be it or much:
And, Lord, contentment still I crave,
   Because thou savest such.

Fulness to such a burden is
   That go on pilgrimage:
Here little, and hereafter bliss,
   Is best from age to age.

*John Bunyan*
*1622–88*

# The Pulley

When God at first made man,
Having a glass of blessings standing by,
'Let us,' said he, 'pour on him all we can;
Let the world's riches, which dispersèd lie,
    Contract into a span.'

So strength first made a way;
Then beauty flowed, then wisdom, honour, pleasure;
When almost all was out, God made a stay,
Perceiving that, alone of all his treasure,
    Rest in the bottom lay.

'For if I should,' said he,
'Bestow this jewel also on my creature,
He would adore my gifts instead of me,
And rest in Nature, not the God of Nature:
    So both should losers be.

'Yet let him keep the rest,
But keep them with repining restlessness;
Let him be rich and weary, that at least,
If goodness lead him not, yet weariness
    May toss him to my breast.'

*George Herbert*
*1593–1633*

# Faith's Review and Expectation

Amazing grace! how sweet the sound
    That saved a wretch like me!
I once was lost, but now am found,
    Was blind, but now I see.

'Twas grace that taught my heart to fear,
    And grace my fears relieved;
How precious did that grace appear
    The hour I first believed.

Through many dangers, toils, and snares
    I have already come;
'Tis grace has brought me safe thus far
    And grace will lead me home.

The Lord has promised good to me,
    His word my hope secures;
He will my shield and portion be
    As long as life endures.

*John Newton*
*1725–1807*

## Shadow and Coolness

Shadow and coolness, Lord, art thou to me;
Cloud of my soul, lead on, I follow thee.
What though the hot winds blow,
Fierce heat beat up below,
Fountains of water flow –
    Praise, praise to thee.

Clearness and glory, Lord, art thou to me;
Light of my soul, lead on, I follow thee.
All through the moonless night,
Making its darkness bright,
Thou art my heavenly light –
    Praise, praise to thee.

Shadow and shine art thou, dear Lord, to me;
Pillar of cloud and fire, I follow thee.
What though the way be long,
In thee my heart is strong,
Thou art my joy, my song –
    Praise, praise to thee.

*Amy Carmichael*
*1867–1951*

# Character of a Happy Life

How happy is he born and taught
That serveth not another's will;
Whose armour is his honest thought
And simple truth his utmost skill!

Whose passions not his masters are,
Whose soul is still prepared for death,
Not tied unto the world with care
Of public fame, or private breath;

Who envies none that chance doth raise,
Or vice; who never understood
How deepest wounds are given by praise;
Nor rules of state, but rules of good:

Who hath his life from rumours freed,
Whose conscience is his strong retreat;
Whose state can neither flatterers feed,
Nor ruin make oppressors great;

Who God doth late and early pray
More of his gifts than grace to lend;
And entertains the harmless day
With a well-chosen book or friend;

– This man is freed from servile bands
Of hope to rise, or fear to fall;
Lord of himself, though not of lands;
And having nothing, yet hath all.

*Henry Wotton*
*1568–1639*

# Ballade of Good Counsel

Flee from the crowd and dwell with truthfulness:
   Suffice thee with thy goods, tho' they be small:
To hoard brings hate, to climb brings giddiness;
   The crowd has envy, and success blinds all;
   Desire no more than to thy lot may fall;
Work well thyself to counsel others clear,
And Truth shall make thee free, there is no fear!

Torment thee not all crooked to redress,
   Nor put thy trust in fortune's turning ball;
Great peace is found in little busy-ness;
   And war but kicks against a sharpened awl;
   Strive not, thou earthen pot, to break the wall;
Subdue thyself, and others thee shall hear;
And Truth shall make thee free, there is no fear!

What God doth send, receive in gladsomeness;
   To wrestle for this world foretells a fall.
Here is no home, here is but wilderness:
   Forth, pilgrim, forth; up, beast, and leave thy stall!
   Know thy country, look up, thank God for all:
Hold the high way, thy soul the pioneer,
And Truth shall make thee free, there is no fear!

ENVOY

Therefore, poor beast, forsake thy wretchedness;
   No longer let the vain world be thy stall.
His mercy seek who in his mightiness
   Made thee of naught but not to be a thrall.
   Pray freely for thyself and pray for all
Who long for larger life and heavenly cheer;
And Truth shall make thee free, there is no fear!

*Geoffrey Chaucer*
*1343?–1400*
*translated by Henry Van Dyke*

# With Christ

Lord, it belongs not to my care,
  Whether I die or live;
To love and serve thee is my share,
  And this thy grace must give.

If life be long I will be glad,
  That I may long obey;
If short – yet why should I be sad
  To soar to endless day?

Christ leads me through no darker rooms
  Than he went through before;
He that unto God's kingdom comes,
  Must enter by this door.

Come, Lord, when grace has made me meet
  Thy blessed face to see;
For if thy work on earth be sweet,
  What will thy glory be!

Then I shall end my sad complaints,
  And weary, sinful days,
And join with the triumphant saints,
  To sing Jehovah's praise.

My knowledge of that life is small,
  The eye of faith is dim,
But 'tis enough that Christ knows all,
  And I shall be with him.

*Richard Baxter*
*1615–91*

# JESUS THE CHRIST

## Wit Wonders

A God and yet a man,
A maid and yet a mother:
Wit wonders what wit can
Conceive this or the other.

A God and can he die?
A dead man, can he live?
What wit can well reply?
What reason reason give?

God, Truth itself, doth teach it.
Man's wit sinks too far under
By reason's power to reach it:
Believe and leave to wonder.

*Anonymous*
*15th century*

# Christ the Child: Christmas Nativity

## THE ANNUNCIATION

### The annunciation

The angel and the girl are met.
Earth was the only meeting place.
For the embodied never yet
Travelled beyond the shore of space.
The eternal spirits in freedom go.

See, they have come together, see,
While the destroying minutes flow,
Each reflects the other's face
Till heaven in hers and earth in his
Shine steady there. He's come to her
From far beyond the farthest star,
Feathered through time. Immediacy
Of strangest strangeness is the bliss
That from their limbs all movement takes.
Yet the increasing rapture brings
So great a wonder that it makes
Each feather tremble on his wings.

Outside the window footsteps fall
Into the ordinary day
And with the sun along the wall
Pursue their unreturning way.
Sounds perpetual roundabout
Rolls its numbered octaves out
And hoarsely grinds its battered tune.

But through the endless afternoon
These neither speak nor movement make,
But stare into their deepening trance
As if their gaze would never break.

*Edwin Muir*
*1887–1959*

# 'I Sing of a Maiden'

I sing of a maiden
   That is matchless:
King of all kings
   For her son she ches*.

He came all so stillè
   Where his mother was,
As dew in Aprillè
   That falls on the grass.

He came all so stillè
   To his mother's bower,
As dew in Aprillè
   That falls on the flower.

He came all so stillè
   Where his mother lay,
As dew in Aprillè
   That falls on the spray.

Mother and maiden
   Was never none but she
Well may such a lady
   God's mother be.

*Anonymous*
*15th century*

\* *ches:* chose

# THE SAVIOUR COMES

## *From:* Messiah

The Saviour comes! by ancient bards foretold:
Hear him, ye deaf, and all ye blind, behold!
He from thick films shall purge the visual ray,
And on the sightless eyeball pour the day:
'Tis he the obstructed paths of sound shall clear,
And bid new music charm the unfolding ear:
The dumb shall sing, the lame his crutch forego,
And leap exulting like the bounding roe.
No sigh, no murmur the wide world shall hear,
From every face he wipes off every tear.
In adamantine chains shall Death be bound,
And hell's grim tyrant feel the eternal wound.
As the good shepherd tends his fleecy care,
Seeks freshest pasture and the purest air,
Explores the lost, the wandering sheep directs,
By day o'ersees them, and by night protects,
The tender lambs he raises in his arms,
Feeds from his hand, and in his bosom warms;
Thus shall mankind his guardian care engage,
The promised father of the future age.

*Alexander Pope*
*1688–1744*

## Salus Mundi

I saw a stable, low and very bare,
   A little child in a manger.
The oxen knew him, had him in their care,
   To men he was a stranger.
The safety of the world was lying there,
   And the world's danger.

*Mary Coleridge*
*1861–1907*

# Joy to the World

Joy to the world! the Lord is come;
Let earth receive her King.
Let every heart prepare him room
And heaven and nature sing.

Joy to the earth! the Saviour reigns;
Let men their songs employ,
While fields and floods, rocks, hills, and plains
Repeat the sounding joy.

No more let sins and sorrows grow,
Nor thorns infest the ground;
He comes to make his blessings flow
Far as the curse is found.

He rules the world with truth and grace
And makes the nations prove
The glories of his righteousness
And wonders of his love.

*Isaac Watts*
*1674–1748*

# The Oxen

Christmas Eve, and twelve of the clock,
  'Now they are all on their knees,'
An elder said as we sat in a flock
  By the embers in hearthside ease.

We pictured the meek mild creatures where
  They dwelt in their strawy pen
Nor did it occur to one of us there
  To doubt they were kneeling then.

So fair a fancy few would weave
  In these years! Yet, I feel,
If someone said on Christmas Eve,
  'Come, see the oxen kneel

In the lonely barton by yonder coomb
  Our childhood used to know,'
I should go with him in the gloom,
  Hoping it might be so.

*Thomas Hardy*
*1840–1928*

# Noel: Christmas Eve, 1913

PAX HOMINIBUS BONAE VOLUNTATIS

A frosty Christmas Eve
  when the stars were shining
Fared I forth alone
  where westward falls the hill,
And from many a village
  in the water'd valley
Distant music reach'd me
  peals of bells aringing:
The constellated sounds
  ran sprinkling on earth's floor
As the dark vault above
  with stars was spangled o'er.
Then sped my thoughts to keep
  that first Christmas of all
When the shepherds watching
  by their folds ere the dawn
Heard music in the fields
  and marvelling could not tell
Whether it were angels
  or the bright stars singing.
Now blessed be the tow'rs
  that crown England so fair
That stand up strong in prayer
  unto God for our souls:
Blessed be their founders
  (said I) an' our country folk
Who are ringing for Christ
  in the belfries tonight
With arms lifted to clutch
  the rattling ropes that race
Into the dark above
  and the mad romping din.

But to me heard afar
  it was starry music
Angels' song, comforting
  as the comfort of Christ
When he spake tenderly
  to his sorrowful flock:

The old words came to me
　by the riches of time
Mellow'd and transfigured
　as I stood on the hill
Heark'ning in the aspect
　of th'eternal silence.

*Robert Bridges*
*1844–1930*

## Chanticleer

All this night shrill chanticleer,
Day's proclaiming trumpeter,
　Claps his wings and loudly cries,
　Mortals, mortals, wake and rise!
　　See a wonder
　　Heaven is under;
From the earth is risen a Sun
Shines all night, though day be done.

Wake, O earth, wake everything!
Wake and hear the joy I bring;
　Wake and joy; for all this night
　Heaven and every twinkling light,
　　All amazing,
　　Still stand gazing.
Angels, powers, and all that be,
Wake, and joy this Sun to see.

Hail, O Sun, O blessed light,
Sent into the world by night!
　Let thy rays and heavenly powers
　Shine in these dark souls of ours;
　　For most duly
　　Thou art truly
God and man, we do confess:
Hail, O Sun of righteousness!

*William Austin*
*1587–1634*

# All in Tune

All in tune to William's flute
Now is Robin's tabor,
Dance tonight and sing high praise
As they did in other days,
Every kindly neighbour.
All in tune, all in tune,
Are the flute and tambourine,
All in tune, all in tune,
Heaven and earth tonight are seen.

God and man are in accord,
More than flute or tabor,
Dance for joy and sing with awe,
For the child upon the straw
Is our God and neighbour.
God and man, God and man,
Are like flute and tambourine,
God and man, God and man,
As true neighbours here are seen.

*Anonymous*

# CHRISTMAS DAY:
## THE INCARNATION

## *From:* Ode on the Morning of Christ's Nativity

COMPOSED 1629

This is the month, and this the happy morn,
Wherein the Son of heaven's eternal King,
Of wedded maid and virgin mother born,
Our great redemption from above did bring;
For so the holy sages once did sing,
  That he our deadly forfeit should release,
And with his Father work us a perpetual peace.

That glorious form, that light insufferable,
And that far-beaming blaze of majesty,
Wherewith he wont at heaven's high council-table
To sit the midst of trinal unity,
He laid aside; and here with us to be,
  Forsook the courts of everlasting day,
And chose with us a darksome house of mortal clay.

Say, heavenly muse, shall not thy sacred vein
Afford a present to the infant God?
Hast thou no verse, no hymn, or solemn strain,
To welcome him to this his new abode,
Now while the heaven, by the sun's team untrod,
  Hath took no print of the approaching light,
And all the spangled host keep watch in squadrons bright?

See how from far upon the eastern road
The star-led wizards haste with odours sweet!
O run, prevent them with thy humble ode,
And lay it lowly at his blessed feet;
Have thou the honour first thy Lord to greet,
  And join thy voice unto the angel quire,
From out his secret altar touched with hallowed fire.

*John Milton*
*1608–74*

# Psalm for Christmas Day

Fairest of morning lights appear,
  Thou blest and gaudy day*,
On which was born our Saviour dear;
  Arise and come away!

This day prevents his day of doom;
  His mercy now is nigh;
The mighty God of love is come,
  The dayspring from on high!

Behold the great Creator makes
  Himself a house of clay,
A robe of virgin-flesh he takes
  Which he will wear for aye.

Hark, hark, the wise eternal Word
  Like a weak infant cries:
In form of servant is the Lord,
  And God in cradle lies.

This wonder struck the world amazed,
  It shook the starry frame;
Squadrons of spirits stood and gazed,
  Then down in troops they came.

Glad shepherds ran to view this sight;
  A quire of angels sings;
And eastern sages with delight
  Adore this King of kings.

Join them all hearts that are not stone,
  And all our voices prove,
To celebrate this holy one,
  The God of peace and love.

*Thomas Pestel*
*1584?–1659?*

* *gaudy day*: festival

# Mangers

Who knows the name and country now
    Of that rich man who lived of old;
Whose horses fed at silver mangers,
    And drank of wine from troughs of gold?

He who was in a manger born,
    By gold and silver undefiled –
Is known as Christ to every man
    And Jesus to a little child.

*W.H. Davies*
*1871–1940*

# Song for a Winter Birth

Under the watchful lights
    A child was born
From a mortal house of flesh
    Painfully torn.

And we, who later assembled
    To praise or peer,
Saw merely an infant boy
    Soft sleeping there;

Till he awoke and stretched
    Small arms wide
And, for food or comfort,
    Quavering cried.

A cry and attitude
    Rehearsing, in small,
The deathless death still haunting
    The Place of the Skull.

Outside, in the festive air,
    We lit cigars;
The night was nailed to the sky
    With hard bright stars.

*Vernon Scannell*
*20th century*

# A Christmas Carol

In the bleak mid-winter
    Frosty wind made moan,
Earth stood hard as iron,
    Water like a stone;
Snow had fallen, snow on snow,
    Snow on snow,
In the bleak mid-winter
    Long ago.

Our God, heaven cannot hold him,
    Nor earth sustain;
Heaven and earth shall flee away
    When he comes to reign:
In the bleak mid-winter
    A stable-place sufficed
The Lord God Almighty
    Jesus Christ.

Enough for him whom cherubim
    Worship night and day,
A breastful of milk
    And a mangerful of hay;
Enough for him whom angels
    Fall down before,
The ox and ass and camel
    Which adore.

Angels and archangels
    May have gathered there,
Cherubim and seraphim
    Thronged the air,
But only his mother
    In her maiden bliss
Worshipped the Beloved
    With a kiss.

What can I give him,
    Poor as I am?
If I were a shepherd
    I would bring a lamb,
If I were a wise man
    I would do my part, –
Yet what I can I give him,
    Give my heart.

*Christina Rossetti*
*1830–94*

# Christmas Bells

I heard the bells on Christmas day
Their old familiar carols play,
   And wild and sweet
   The words repeat,
Of 'Peace on earth, good will to men!'

And thought how, as the day had come,
The belfries of all Christendom
   Had rolled along
   The unbroken song,
Of 'Peace on earth, good will to men!'

Till ringing, singing on its way,
The world revolved from night to day –
   A voice, a chime,
   A chant sublime,
Of 'Peace on earth, good will to men!'

And in despair I bowed my head;
'There is no peace on earth,' I said,
   'For hate is strong
   And mocks the song
Of peace on earth, good will to men!'

Then pealed the bells more loud and deep:
'God is not dead; nor doth he sleep!
   The wrong shall fail,
   The right prevail,
With peace on earth, good will to men!'

*Henry Wadsworth Longfellow*
*1807–82*

# At the Manger Mary Sings

O shut your bright eyes that mine must endanger
With their watchfulness; protected by its shade
Escape from my care: what can you discover
From my tender look but how to be afraid?
Love can but confirm the more it would deny.
   Close your bright eye.

Sleep. What have you learned from the womb that bore you
But an anxiety your Father cannot feel?
Sleep. What will the flesh that I gave do for you,
Or my mother love, but tempt you from his will?
Why was I chosen to teach his Son to weep?
   Little One, sleep.

Dream. In human dreams earth ascends to Heaven
Where no one need pray nor ever feel alone.
In your first few hours of life here, O have you
Chosen already what death must be your own?
How soon will you start on the Sorrowful Way?
   Dream while you may.

*W.H. Auden*
*20th century*

# Balulalow

O my dear heart, young Jesus sweet,
Prepare thy cradle in my spirit,
And I shall rock thee in my heart
And never more from thee depart.

But I shall praise thee evermore
With songs sweet to thy glory;
The knees of my heart shall I bow,
And sing that right *Balulalow*!

*James, John and Robert Wedderburn*
*about 1567*

# Joseph's Lullaby

Sleep now, little one.
I will watch while you and your mother sleep.
I wish I could do more.
This straw is not good enough for you.
Back in Nazareth I'll make a proper bed for you
Of seasoned wood, smooth, strong, well-pegged.
A bed fit for a carpenter's son.

Just wait till we get back to Nazareth.
I'll teach you everything I know.
You'll learn to use the cedarwood, eucalyptus and fir.
You'll learn to use the drawshave, axe, and saw.
Your arms will grow strong, your hands rough – like these.
You will bear the pungent smell of new wood
and wear shavings and sawdust in your hair.

You'll be a man whose life centres
on hammer and nails and wood.
But for now,
sleep, little Jesus, sleep.

*Ron Klug*
*20th century*

# The Burning Babe

As I in hoary winter's night stood shivering in the snow,
Surprised I was with sudden heat which made my heart to glow;
And lifting up a fearful eye to view what fire was near,
A pretty Babe all burning bright did in the air appear;
Who scorchèd with excessive heat, such floods of tears did shed,
As though his floods should quench his flames which with his tears were fed.
'Alas!' quoth he, 'but newly born in fiery heats I fry,
Yet none approach to warm their hearts or feel my fire but I.
My faultless breast the furnace is, the fuel wounding thorns;
Love is the fire, and sighs the smoke, the ashes shame and scorns;
The fuel justice layeth on, and mercy blows the coals;
The metal in this furnace wrought are men's defilèd souls:
For which, as now on fire I am to work them to their good,
So will I melt into a bath to wash them in my blood.'
With this he vanished out of sight and swiftly shrunk away,
And straight I callèd unto mind that it was Christmas day.

*Robert Southwell*
*1561–95*

# A Christmas Carol

The other night
I saw a light!
  A star as bright as day!
And ever among
A maiden sung:
  'By-by, baby, lullay.'

This virgin clear
Who had no peer
  Unto her son did say,
'I pray thee, son,
Grant me a boon
  To sing by-by, lullay.

'Let child or man,
Whoever can
  Be merry on this day,
And blessings bring –
So I shall sing
  "By-by, baby, lullay."'

*Anonymous*
*about 1500*

# The Wonder of the Incarnation

To spread the azure canopy of heaven,
And make it twinkle with those spangs of gold,
To stay the ponderous globe of earth so even,
That it should all, and nought should it uphold;
To give strange motions to the planets seven,
Or Jove to make so meek, or Mars so bold,
To temper what is moist, dry, hot, and cold,
Of all their jars that sweet accords are given:
Lord, to thy wisdom's nought; nought to thy might.
But that thou shouldst (thy glory laid aside)
Come meanly in mortality to bide,
And die for those deserved eternal plight,
A wonder is so far above our wit,
That angels stand amazed to muse on it.

*William Drummond*
*1585–1649*

# At Christmas

Always
in the dark centre
of this season
the birth occurs
noiseless and marvellous
the seers
move on their journeys
there are gestures
of wonder, and at midnight
a resting star.
Always
it is amazing
that the mountains
do not relinquish
their momentary grandeur,
bend to the stable,
let the ermine tremble
there
where the oxen
and the angels are.

*Jean Kenward*
*20th century*

# It is as if Infancy were the Whole of Incarnation

One time of the year
the new-born child
is everywhere,
planted in madonnas' arms
hay mows, stables,
in palaces or farms,
or quaintly, under snowed gables,
gothic angular or baroque plump,
naked or elaborately swathed,
encircled by Della Robbia wreaths,
garnished with whimsical
partridges and pears,
drummers and drums,
lit by oversize stars,

partnered with lambs,
peace doves, sugar plums,
bells, plastic camels in sets of three
as if these were what we need
for eternity.

But Jesus the Man is not to be seen.
We are too wary, these days,
of beards and sandalled feet.

Yet if we celebrate, let it be
that he
has invaded our lives with purpose,
striding over our picturesque traditions,
our shallow sentiment,
overturning our cash registers,
wielding his peace like a sword,
rescuing us into reality,
demanding much more
than the milk and the softness
and the mother warmth
of the baby in the storefront creche,
(only the Man would ask
all, of each of us)
reaching out
always, urgently, with strong
effective love
(only the Man would give
his life and live
again for love of us).

Oh come, let us adore him –
Christ – *the Lord*.

*Luci Shaw*
*20th century*

# Unto Us a Son is Given

Given, not lent,
And not withdrawn – once sent,
This Infant of mankind, this One,
Is still the little welcome Son.

New every year,
New born and newly dear,
He comes with tidings and a song,
The ages long, the ages long;

Even as the cold
Keen winter grows not old,
As childhood is so fresh, foreseen,
And spring in the familiar green.

Sudden as sweet
Come the expected feet.
All joy is young, and new all art,
And he, too, whom we have by heart.

*Alice Meynell*
*1847–1922*

# Judah's Lion

Where does the lion, Judah's lion walk?
Stealthy under star by winter night his soft paws stalk.
Out on lonely hills a cold wind howls and darkness scowls;
Shepherds shiver – danger in the dark! – some wild beast prowls.
Suddenly up springs a light; a voice rings like a bell;
'Joy, O men of Judah! Come and see! Noel! Noel!'
Where lies Judah's longed-for lion? 'Come and see the sight!
Fear not – your golden one is couched among the lambs
     tonight.'

*Keith Patman*
*20th century*

# Kid Stuff

The wise guys
tell me
that Christmas
is Kid Stuff...
Maybe they've got
something there –
Two thousand years ago
three wise guys
chased a star
across a continent
to bring
frankincense and myrrh
to a Kid
born in a manger
with an idea in his head...
And as the bombs
crash
all over the world today
the real wise guys know
that we've all got to go
chasing stars
again
in the hope
that we can get back
some of that
Kid Stuff
born two thousand years ago.

*Frank Horne*
*20th century*

# THE SHEPHERDS

## From: A Christmas Sequence

IV THE SHEPHERDS

He is so small the stars bow down
  The fierce winds ease their breath,
And careful shepherds look upon
  The one unsullied birth.
They kneel and stare while time seems gone
  And goodness rules the earth.

The blight on man is all undone
  And there will be no death,
For though this child will be nailed on
  A cross, he'll be so since
He is the jewel of untold worth,
  For him all stars have shone.

*Elizabeth Jennings*
*20th century*

## The Angels for the Nativity of our Lord

Run, shepherds, run, where Bethlem blest appears,
We bring the best of news, be not dismayed,
A Saviour there is born more old than years,
Amidst heaven's rolling heights this earth who stayed.
In a poor cottage inned, a virgin maid
A weakling did him bear, who all upbears;
There is he, poorly swaddled, in manger laid,
To whom too narrow swaddlings are our spheres:
Run, shepherds run, and solemnize his birth,
This is that night – no, day, grown great with bliss,
In which the power of Satan broken is;
In heaven be glory, peace unto the earth!
  Thus singing, through the air the angels swam,
  And cope of stars re-echoèd the same.

*William Drummond of Hawthornden*
*1585–1649*

# The Shepherd's Carol

We stood on the hills, Lady,
Our day's work done,
Watching the frosted meadows
That winter had won.

The evening was calm, Lady,
The air so still,
Silence more lovely than music
Folded the hill.

There was a star, Lady,
Shone in the night,
Larger than Venus it was
And bright, so bright.

Oh, a voice from the sky, Lady,
It seemed to us then
Telling of God being born
In the world of men.

And so we have come, Lady,
Our day's work done,
Our love, our hopes, ourselves
We give to your son.

*Anonymous*

# NEW YEAR: THE MAGI

## The Blade of Grass

'A SWORD SHALL GO THROUGH THINE OWN HEART.'
PROPHECY OF SIMEON

Oh! little blade of grass,
  A little sword thou art,
That in thy haste to pass
  Hast pierced thy mother's heart!

Oh! little blade of grass,
  A little tongue thou art
Of cleaving flame, – alas!
  Thou hast cleft thy mother's heart.

Oh! little blade, upcurled
  Leaf, sword, or fiery dart,
To win thy Father's world
  Thou must break thy mother's heart!

*Dora Greenwell*
*1821–82*

## The New-Year's Gift

Let others look for pearl and gold,
Tissues or tabbies* manifold;
One only look of that sweet hay
Whereon the blessed Baby lay,
Or one poor swaddling-clout, shall be
The richest New-Year's gift to me.

*Robert Herrick*
*1591–1674*

* *tabbies:* silks

# *From:* Three Kings Came Riding

The Three Kings rode through the gate and the guard,
 Through the silent street, till their horses turned
And neighed as they entered the great inn-yard;
But the windows were closed, and the doors were barred,
 And only a light in the stable burned.

And cradled there in the scented hay,
 In the air made sweet by the breath of kine,
The little child in the manger lay,
The child that would be King one day
 Of a kingdom not human but divine.

His mother, Mary of Nazareth,
 Sat watching beside his place of rest,
Watching the even flow of his breath,
For the joy of life and the terror of death
 Were mingled together in her breast.

They laid their offerings at his feet:
 The gold was their tribute to a King,
The frankincense, with its odour sweet,
Was for the Priest, the Paraclete,
 The myrrh for the body's burying.

And the mother wondered and bowed her head,
 And sat as still as a statue of stone;
Her heart was troubled yet comforted,
Remembering what the angel had said,
 Of an endless reign and of David's throne.

*Henry Wadsworth Longfellow*
*1807–82*

# Royal Presents

The off'rings of the Eastern kings of old
Unto our lord were incense, myrrh and gold;
Incense because a God; gold as a king;
And myrrh as to a dying man they bring.
Instead of incense (blessed Lord) if we
Can send a sigh or fervent prayer to thee,
Instead of myrrh if we can but provide
Tears that from penitential eyes do slide,
And though we have no gold; if for our part
We can present thee with a broken heart
Thou wilt accept: and say those Eastern kings
Did not present thee with more precious things.

*Nathaniel Wanley*
*1634–80*

# The Offering

They gave to thee
Myrrh, frankincense and gold
But, Lord, with what shall we
Present ourselves before thy majesty,
Whom thou redeemedst when we were sold?
We've nothing but ourselves, and scarce that neither;
Vile dirt and clay;
Yet it is soft and may
Impression take.
Accept it, Lord, and say, this thou hadst rather;
Stamp it, and on this sordid metal make
Thy holy image, and it shall outshine
The beauty of the golden mine.

*Jeremy Taylor*
*1613–67*

# Twelfth Night

No night could be darker than this night,
no cold so cold,
as the blood snaps like a wire,
and the heart's sap stills,
and the year seems defeated.

O never again, it seems, can green things run,
or sky birds fly,
or the grass exhale its humming breath
powdered with pimpernels,
from this dark lung of winter.

Yet here are lessons for the final mile
of pilgrim kings;
the mile still left when all have reached
their tether's end: that mile
where the Child lies hid.

For see, beneath the hand, the earth already
warms and glows;
for men with shepherd's eyes there are
signs in the dark, the turning stars,
the lamb's returning time.

Out of this utter death he's born again,
his birth our saviour;
from terror's equinox he climbs and grows,
drawing his finger's light across our blood
the son of heaven, and the son of God.

*Laurie Lee*
*20th century*

# The Star of the Heart

The star has risen in the heart,
The sweet light flushes every part.
The shepherds of the body know,
The rumour reached them long ago,
Abiding in the field were they
When deity informed the clay.
The wise kings of the mind bow down,
They yield the wiser king his crown;
Before a cradle they unfold
The myrrh and frankincense and gold.

*Susan Mitchell*
*1866–1926*

# Epiphany

(…ANGELS BENDING NEAR THE EARTH
TO TOUCH THEIR HARPS OF GOLD.'
*Edmund Hamilton Sears 1810–76*)

Thank you
Edmund Hamilton Sears
for your carol about the angels,
Thank you, Fra Angelico
for the feather detail of their wings.

Were your pipes frozen
Christina Georgina Rossetti
that you wrote of bleak mid-winter,
earth like iron, snow on snow
and water like a stone. Gas-fired
my central heating keeps the ice out.

Who's that knocking?
A king with a gift of aromatic herbs.
The stick insects, for whom parthenogenesis
is a fact of daily life, sway hopefully
on the drying privet in their tank.
We offer wine. His camel chews the roses.

He insists there is a miracle
In this untidy house.

*Jeffery Wheatley*
*20th century*

# Words for the Magi

'Shall I bring you wisdom, shall I bring you power?'
The first great stranger said to the child.
Then he noticed something he'd never felt before –
A wish in himself to be innocent and mild.

'Shall I bring you glory, shall I bring you peace?'
The second great stranger said when he saw
The star shine down on entire helplessness.
The gift that he offered was his sense of awe.

'Shall I show you riches' the third one began
Then stopped in terror because he had seen
A God grown-up and a tired tempted man.
'Suffering's my gift' he said
'That is what I mean.'

*Elizabeth Jennings*
*20th century*

# Rich Man

Rich man, rich man, who are you?
Do you seek the Christ Child, too?
In your palace and your court,
Life is busy, life is short.
Have you time to go away
To find a baby in the hay?
Can you get your camel through
The needle's eye, as you must do?

Rich man, rich man, you've come far.
Where did you learn to trust a star
Instead of turning to a king
To guide you in your wandering?
Rich man, how did you grow wise
In spite of all your kingly guise?
Who taught you to play your part,
To bring an educated heart
To the stable in the west
So you could kneel there and be blessed?

*Elizabeth Rooney*
*20th century*

# The Journey of the Magi

'A cold coming we had of it,
Just the worst time of the year
For a journey, and such a long journey:
The ways deep and the weather sharp,
The very dead of winter.'
And the camels galled, sore-footed, refractory,
Lying down in the melting snow.
There were times we regretted
The summer palaces on slopes, the terraces,
And the silken girls bringing sherbet.
Then the camel men cursing and grumbling
And running away, and wanting their liquor and women,
And the night-fires going out, and the lack of shelters,
And the cities hostile and the towns unfriendly
And the villages dirty and charging high prices:
A hard time we had of it.
At the end we preferred to travel all night,
Sleeping in snatches,
With the voices singing in our ears, saying
That this was all folly.
Then at dawn we came down to a temperate valley,
Wet, below the snow line, smelling of vegetation,
With a running stream and a water-mill beating the darkness,
And three trees on the low sky.
And an old white horse galloped away in the meadow.
Then we came to a tavern with vine-leaves over the lintel,
Six hands at an open door dicing for pieces of silver,
And feet kicking the empty wine-skins.
But there was no information, and so we continued
And arrived at evening, not a moment too soon
Finding the place; it was (you may say) satisfactory.

All this was a long time ago, I remember,
And I would do it again, but set down
This set down
This; were we led all that way for
Birth or Death? There was a Birth, certainly,
We had evidence and no doubt. I had seen birth and death,
But had thought they were different; this Birth was
Hard and bitter agony for us, like Death, our death.

We returned to our places, these Kingdoms,
But no longer at ease here, in the old dispensation,
With an alien people clutching their gods.
I should be glad of another death.

*T.S. Eliot*
*1888–1965*

Christ the Child: Christmas Nativity

## The Southern Cross

Three ancient men in Bethlehem's cave,
  With awful wonder stand:
A voice had called them from their grave,
  In some far Eastern land.

They lived: they trod the former earth,
  When the old waters swelled,
The ark, that womb of second birth,
  Their house and lineage held.

Pale Japhet bows the knee with gold,
  Bright Sem sweet incense brings,
And Cham the myrrh his fingers hold:
  Lo! the three Orient kings.

Types of the total earth, they hailed
  The signal's starry frame;
Shuddering with second life, they quailed
  At the Child Jesu's Name.

Then slow the Patriarchs turned and trod,
  And this their parting sigh:
'Our eyes have seen the living God,
  And now – once more to die.'

*Robert Stephen Hawker*
*1804–75*

# HEROD'S SLAUGHTER
# OF THE CHILDREN

## Innocent's Song

Who's that knocking on the window,
Who's that standing at the door,
What are all those presents
Lying on the kitchen floor?

Who is the smiling stranger
With hair as white as gin,
What is he doing with the children
And who could have let him in?

Why has he rubies on his fingers,
A cold, cold crown on his head,
Why, when he caws his carol,
Does the salty snow run red?

Why does he ferry my fireside
As a spider on a thread,
His fingers made of fuses
And his tongue of gingerbread?

Why does the world before him
Melt in a million suns,
Why do his yellow, yearning eyes
Burn like saffron buns?

Watch where he comes walking
Out of the Christmas flame,
Dancing, double-talking:

Herod is his name.

*Charles Causley*
*20th century*

# Christk the Man:
## Easter Death and Resurrection

## The Call

My blood so red
For thee was shed,
Come home again, come home again:
My own sweet heart, come home again!
You've gone astray
Out of your way,
Come home again, come home again!

*Anonymous*
*17th century*

## HOLY WEEK

## Palm Sunday

Astride the colt and claimed as King
that Sunday morning in the spring,
He passed a thornbush flowering red
that one would plait to crown his head.

He passed a vineyard where the wine
was grown for men of royal line
and where the dregs were also brewed
into a gall for Calvary's rood.

A purple robe was cast his way,
then caught and kept until that day
when, with its use, a trial would be
profaned into a mockery.

His entourage was forced to wait
to let a timber through the gate,
a shaft that all there might have known
would be an altar and a throne.

*Marie J. Post*
*20th century*

# Ride on!

Ride on! Ride on in majesty!
Hark, all the tribes hosanna cry;
Thy humble beast pursues his road
With palms and scattered garments strowed.

Ride on! Ride on in majesty!
In lowly pomp ride on to die;
O Christ, thy triumphs now begin
O'er captive death and conquered sin.

Ride on! Ride on in majesty!
The wingèd squadrons of the sky
Look down with sad and wondering eyes
To see the approaching sacrifice.

Ride on! Ride on in majesty!
Thy last and fiercest strife is nigh;
The Father on his sapphire throne
Expects his own anointed Son.

Ride on! Ride on in majesty!
In lowly pomp ride on to die;
Bow thy meek head to mortal pain,
Then take, O God, thy power, and reign.

*Henry Hart Milman*
*1791–1868*

# A Psalm for Maundy Thursday

Tonight
Lord Jesus Christ
You sat at supper
with your friends.
It was a simple meal
that final one
of lamb
unleavened bread
and wine.
Afterward
You went out to die.
How many other meals you shared
beside the lake
fried fish and toasted bread
at Simon's banquet hall a feast
at Lazarus' home in Bethany
the meal that Martha cooked
on mountain slope
where you fed the hungry crowd
at close of tiring day.
Please sit with us tonight
at our small meal
of soup and rolls and tea.
Then go with us
to feast of bread and wine
that you provide
because afterward
you went out to die.

*Joseph Bayley*
*20th century*

# A Ballad of Trees and the Master

Into the woods my Master went,
Clean forspent, forspent.
Into the woods my Master came,
Forspent with love and shame.
But the olives they were not blind to him,
The little grey leaves were kind to him:
The thorn-trees had a mind to him
   When into the woods he came.

Out of the woods my Master went,
And he was well content.
Out of the woods my Master came,
Content with death and shame.
When death and shame would woo him last,
From under the trees they drew him last:
'Twas on a tree they slew him – last
   When out of the woods he came.

*Sidney Lanier*
*1842–81*

## Good Friday

O heart, be lifted up; O heart be gay,
Because the Light was lifted up today –
Was lifted on the Rood, but did not die,
To shine eternally for such as I.

O heart, rejoice with all your humble might
That God did kindle in the world this Light,
Which stretching on the Cross could not prevent
From shining with continuous intent.

Why weep, O heart, this day? Why grieve you so?
If all the glory of the Light had lost its glow
Would the sun shine or earth put on her best –
Her flower-entangled and embroidered vest?

Look up, O heart; and then, O heart, kneel down
In humble adoration: give no crown
Nor golden diadem to your fair Lord,
But offer love and beauty by your word...

The everlasting fire of love, O heart,
Has blazed in you and it will not depart.
Wherefore, O heart, exult and praises sing:
Lift up your voice and make the echoes ring...

O heart, rise up: O heart be lifted high.
Rejoice; for Light was slain today, yet did not die.

*Anonymous*

# The Saviour Speaks

Thou who createdst everything,
Sweet Father, heavenly King,
Hear me – I, thy son, implore:
For Man this flesh and bone I bore.

Clear and bright my breast and side,
Blood over whiteness spilling wide,
Holes in my body crucified.

Stiff and stark my long arms rise,
Dimness and darkness cloud my eyes;
Like sculpted marble hang my thighs.

Red my feet with the flowing blood,
Holes in them washed through with that flood.
Mercy on Man's sins, Father on high!
Through all my wounds to thee I cry!

*Anonymous*
*13th century*

# Good Friday: the Third Nocturn

Alone to sacrifice thou goest, Lord,
Giving thyself to death whom thou hast slain.
For us thy wretched folk is any word,
Who know that for our sins this is thy pain?

For they are ours, O Lord, our deeds, our deeds,
Why must thou suffer torture for our sin?
Let our hearts suffer for thy passion, Lord,
That sheer compassion may thy mercy win.

This is that night of tears, the three days' space,
    Sorrow abiding of the eventide,
Until the day break with the risen Christ,
    And hearts that sorrowed shall be satisfied.

So may our hearts have pity on thee, Lord,
    That they may sharers of thy glory be:
Heavy with weeping may the three days pass,
    To win the laughter of thine Easter Day.

*Peter Abelard*
*1079–1142*
translated from Latin by Helen Waddell

# Crucifixion to the World
# by the Cross of Christ

When I survey the wondrous Cross
   Where the young Prince of Glory died,
My richest gain I count but loss,
   And pour contempt on all my pride.

Forbid it, Lord, that I should boast
   Save in the death of Christ my God;
All the vain things that charm me most,
   I sacrifice them to his blood.

See from his head, his hands, his feet,
   Sorrow and love flow mingled down;
Did e'er such love and sorrow meet,
   Or thorns compose so rich a crown?

His dying crimson, like a robe,
   Spreads o'er his body on the tree;
Then am I dead to all the globe,
   And all the globe is dead to me.

Were the whole realm of nature mine
   That were a present far too small;
Love so amazing, so divine,
   Demands my soul, my life, my all.

*Isaac Watts*
*1674–1748*

# *From:* The Dream of the Rood

Listen! I will describe the best of dreams
which I dreamed in the middle of the night
when, far and wide, all men slept.
It seemed that I saw a wondrous tree
soaring into the air, surrounded by light,
the brightest of crosses; that emblem was entirely
cased in gold; beautiful jewels
were strewn around its foot, just as five
studded the cross-beam. All the angels of God
fair creations, guarded it. That was no cross
of a criminal, but holy spirits and men on earth
watched over it there – the whole glorious universe…

      Now I look day by day
for that time when the cross of the Lord,
which once I saw in a dream here on earth,
will fetch me away from this fleeting life
and lift me to the home of joy and happiness
where the people of God are seated at the feast
in eternal bliss, and set me down
where I may live in glory unending and share
the joy of the saints. May the Lord be a friend to me,
he who suffered once for the sins of men
here on earth on the gallows-tree.
He has redeemed us; he has given life to us,
and a home in heaven.

*Anonymous*
*translated from Anglo-Saxon*
*by Kevin Crossley-Holland*

# Good Friday, 1613. Riding Westward

Let man's soul be a sphere, and then, in this,
The intelligence that moves, devotion is,
And as the other Spheres, by being grown
Subject to foreign motions, lose their own,
And being by others hurried every day,
Scarce in a year their natural form obey:
Pleasure or business, so, our souls admit
For their first mover, and are whirl'd by it.
Hence is't, that I am carried towards the west
This day, when my soul's form bends toward the east.

There I should see a sun, by rising set,
And by that setting endless day beget;
But that Christ on this cross, did rise and fall,
Sin had eternally benighted all.
Yet dare I almost be glad, I do not see
That spectacle of too much weight for me.
Who sees God's face, that is self life, must die;
What a death were it then to see God die?
It made his own lieutenant, Nature, shrink,
It made his footstool crack, and the sun wink.
Could I behold those hands which span the poles,
And turn all spheres at once, pierced with those holes?
Could I behold that endless height which is
Zenith to us, and our Antipodes,
Humbled below us? or that blood which is
The seat of all our souls, if not of his,
Made dirt of dust, or that flesh which was worn
By God, for his apparel, ragg'd and torn?
If on these things I durst not look, durst I
Upon his miserable mother cast mine eye,
Who was God's partner here, and furnished thus
Half of that sacrifice, which ransomed us?
Though these things, as I ride, be from mine eye,
They are present yet to my memory,
For that looks towards them; and thou look'st towards me,
O Saviour, as thou hang'st upon the tree;
I turn my back to thee, but to receive
Corrections, till thy mercies bid thee leave.
O think me worth thine anger, punish me,
Burn off my rusts, and my deformity,
Restore thine image, so much, by thy grace,
That thou may'st know me, and I'll turn my face.

*John Donne*
*1572–1631*

## Dead and Buried

And so we took him down
(Or thought we did),
Wiped off the sweat and spittle
From his face,
Washed the dried blood,
Threw out the crown of thorns,
And wrapped him once again
In swaddling clothes.

A tomb can be a cramped,
Confining place,
Far smaller than a stable.
We laid him there
(Or thought we did).
We were not able
To comprehend
The infinite contained.
For us it was the end.
Only the harsh realities
Of death and stone
Remained.

*Elizabeth Rooney*
*20th century*

# Before Easter

Spring;
yet frost still builds
dead palaces.

We hear the crack from
icicles of bone,
snow crowns
have snapped the throats
of daffodils,
the ice-queen walks in
her brittle dress.

No rose-blood in the stem,
no cumulus
perfume in trees,
each day
is a coffin of glass.

The sun is turned
to crystal,
it is our alchemy of winter;
inner cold.

Christ sleeps
behind the quickening stone.

*Isobel Thrilling*
20th century

# Poem for Easter

Wrapped in his shroud of wax, his swoon of wounds,
still as a winter's star he lies with death.

Still as a winter's lake his stark limbs lock
the pains that run in stabbing frosts about him.

Star in the lake, grey spark beneath the ice,
candle of love snuffed in its whitened flesh,

I, too, lie bound within your dawn of cold
while on my breath the serpent mortal moans.

O serpent in the egg, become a rod,
crack the stone shell that holds his light in coil.

O grief within the serpent sink your root
and bear the flower for which our forked tongues wail.

Cold in this hope our mortal eyes forgather
wandering like moths about the tomb's shut mouth;

Waiting the word the riven rock shall utter,
waiting the dawn to fly its bird of god.

*Laurie Lee*
*20th century*

# Easter Saturday

A curiously empty day,
As if the world's life
Had gone underground.
The April sun
Warming dry grass
Makes pale spring promises
But nothing comes to pass.

Anger
Relaxes into despair
As we remember our helplessness,
Remember him hanging there.
We have purchased the spices
But they must wait for tomorrow.
We shall keep today
For emptiness and sorrow.

*Elizabeth Rooney*
*20th century*

# Easter Midnight Service

A pagan fire to conjure in the spring –
But this fire we have lit to conjure out
The winter chill of all the pagan rout,
And conjure in the summer of the king.
Soon will the brazen bells of triumph ring,
And midnight dark be shaken by a shout
That death's cold chain that gripped the world about
Is broken link from link: and the links sing.

And fire from fire our candles take the light,
As we take fire from the eternal flame,
And flame from flame we walk down the dark aisle,
Each flame a glory gold against the night,
That trembles at the whisper of the name
That burns through all the empty halls of hell.

*Marion Pitman*
*20th century*

## Easter Night

All night had shout of men and cry
  Of woeful women filled his way;
Until that noon of sombre sky
  On Friday, clamour and display
Smote him; no solitude had he,
  No silence, since Gethsemane.

Public was Death; but Power, but Might,
  But Life again, but Victory,
Were hushed within the dead of night,
  The shuttered dark, the secrecy.
And all alone, alone, alone,
  He rose again behind the stone.

*Alice Meynell*
*1847–1922*

234

## Easter Hymn

Death and darkness get you packing,
Nothing now to man is lacking,
All your triumphs now are ended,
And what Adam marred is mended;
Graves are beds now for the weary,
Death a nap, to wake more merry;
Youth now, full of pious duty,
Seeks in thee for perfect beauty,
The weak, and agèd tired, with length
Of days, from thee look for new strength,
And infants with thy pangs contest
As pleasant, as if with the breast;
Then, unto him, who thus hath thrown
Even to contempt thy kingdom down,
And by his blood did us advance
Unto his own inheritance,
To him be glory, power, praise,
From this, unto the last of days.

*Henry Vaughan*
*1622–95*

# Lord of Life

Most glorious Lord of life, that on this day
    Didst make thy triumph over death and sin;
    And having harrowed hell didst bring away
    Captivity thence captive, us to win:
This joyous day, dear Lord, with joy begin,
    And grant that we for whom thou didest die
    Being with thy dear blood clean washed from sin,
    May live for ever in felicity.
And that thy love we weighing worthily,
    May likewise love thee for the same again;
    And for thy sake that all like dear didst buy,
    With love may one another entertain.
So let us love, dear love, like as we ought.
Love is the lesson which the Lord us taught.

*Edmund Spenser*
*1552–99*

# Love is Come Again

Now the green blade riseth from the buried grain,
Wheat that in dark earth many days has lain;
Love lives again, that with the dead has been:

> *Love is come again,*
> *Like wheat that springeth green.*

In the grave they laid him, Love whom men had slain,
Thinking that never he would wake again,
Laid in the earth like grain that sleeps unseen:

Forth he came at Easter, like the risen grain,
He that for three days in the grave had lain,
Quick from the dead my risen Lord is seen:

When our hearts are wintry, grieving, or in pain,
Thy touch may call us back to life again,
Fields of our hearts that dead and bare have been.

*J.M.C. Crum*
*1872–1958*

# Resurrection

Everything panicked. Trees shrieked
And withered in the moon's heat.
Birds rose like helium balloons.
Telephone poles popped like corks.
The night was brighter than
A hamburg stand.
The night was hotter than
A hamburg stand.

At last
There came a popping sound
And nails were popping off
The crazy iron armadillo
Like buttons. All the nails.
Fizzing high into the air
Like Roman candles,
Until the spread-eagled body
Once again lay white,
Rising like bread.
And the world and all the nations
Peeled away.

*Randall Vander Mey*
*20th century*

# Hymn Written at the Holy Sepulchre in Jerusalem

Saviour of mankind, Man, Emmanuel!
Who sinless died for sin, who vanquished hell;
The first-fruits of the grave; whose life did give
Light to our darkness; in whose death we live: –
Oh! strengthen thou my faith; convert my will,
That mine may thine obey; protect me still,
So that the latter death may not devour
My soul, sealed with thy seal. – So, in the hour
When thou (whose body sanctified this tomb,
Unjustly judged), a glorious judge shall come
To judge the world with justice; by that sign
I may be known, and entertained for thine.

*George Sandys*
*1577–1644*

# When Mary Thro' the Garden Went

When Mary thro' the garden went
  There was no sound of any bird,
And yet, because the night was spent,
  The little grasses lightly stirred,
  The flowers awoke, the lilies heard.

When Mary thro' the garden went,
  The dew lay still on flower and grass,
The waving palms about her sent
  Their fragrance out as she did pass,
  No light upon the branches was.

When Mary thro' the garden went,
  Her eyes, for weeping long, were dim,
The grass beneath her footsteps bent,
  The solemn lilies, white and slim,
  These also stood and wept for him.

When Mary thro' the garden went,
  She sought, within the garden ground,
One for whom her heart was rent,
  One who for her sake was bound,
  One who sought and she was found.

*Mary Coleridge*
*1861–1907*

# Seven Stanzas at Easter

Make no mistake
if he rose at all
it was as his body;
if the cells' dissolution did not reverse, the
  molecules reknit, the amino acids rekindle,
    the church will fall.

It was not as the flowers,
each soft Spring recurrent;
it was not as his Spirit in the mouths and
  fuddled eyes of the eleven apostles;
it was as his flesh: ours.

The same hinged thumbs and toes,
the same valved heart
that – pierced – died, withered, decayed, and then
  regathered out of his Father's might
new strength to enclose.

Let us not mock God with metaphor,
analogy, sidestepping transcendence;
making of the event a parable, a sign painted in the
  faded credulity of earlier ages;
let us walk through the door.

The stone is rolled back, not papier-mâché,
not a stone in a story,
but the vast rock of materiality that in the slow
  grinding of time will eclipse each of us
the wide light of day.

And if we will have an angel at the tomb,
make it a real angel,
weighty with Max Planck's quanta, vivid with hair,
  opaque in the dawn light, robed in real linen
spun on a definite loom.

Let us not seek to make it less monstrous,
for our own convenience, our own sense of beauty,
lest, awakened in one unthinkable hour, we are
  embarrassed by the miracle,
and crushed by remonstrance.

*John Updike*
*20th century*

# THE HOLY SPIRIT AND THE CHURCH

## From: The Rock

There shall always be the Church and the World
And the Heart of Man
Shivering and fluttering between them, choosing and chosen,
Valiant, ignoble, dark, and full of light
Swinging between Hell Gate and Heaven Gate.
And the Gates of Hell shall not prevail.
Darkness now, then
  Light.

*T.S. Eliot*
*1888–1965*

# The Holy Spirit: Pentecost

## Come Holy Ghost

Come, Holy Ghost, our souls inspire
And lighten with celestial fire;
Thou the anointing Spirit art,
Who dost thy sevenfold gifts impart.

Thy blessed unction from above
Is comfort, life, and fire of love;
Enable with perpetual light
The dulness of our blinded sight;

Anoint and cheer our soiled face
With the abundance of thy grace;
Keep far our foes; give peace at home:
Where thou art guide no ill can come.

Teach us to know the Father, Son,
And thee of both, to be but One,
That through the ages all along
This may be our endless song,
   Praise to thine eternal merit,
   Father, Son, and Holy Spirit.

*Anonymous*
*9th century*
*translated by John Cosin*

# Be the Power of All Things Within Us

O God the Holy Ghost who art Light unto thine elect,
 Evermore enlighten us.
Thou who art Fire of love,
 Evermore enkindle us.
Thou who art Lord and Giver of life,
 Evermore live in us.
Thou who bestowest sevenfold grace,
 Evermore replenish us.
As the wind is thy symbol,
 So forward our goings.
As the dove,
 So launch us heavenwards.
As water,
 So purify our spirits.
As a cloud,
 So abate our temptations.
As dew,
 So revive our languor.
As fire,
 So purge out our dross.

*Christina Rossetti*
*1830–94*

# The Holy Spirit

Come with birds' voices when the light grows dim
Yet lovelier in departure and more dear:
While the warm flush hangs yet at heavens' rim,
And the one star shines clear.

Though the swift night haste to approaching day
Stay thou and stir not, brooding on the deep:
Thy secret love, thy silent word let say
Within the senses' sleep.

Softer than dew. But where the morning wind
Blows down the world, O Spirit! show thy power:
Quicken the dreams within the languid mind
And bring thy seed to flower!

*Evelyn Underhill*
*1875–1941*

# Pentecost is Every Day

I share and share and share again
sometimes with a new language
which, if you are so open
will take you behind the sky
and award you cartwheels across the sun
I give and give and give again
not restricted by the church calendar vor concocted ritual
I have no need of anniversaries
for I have always been
I speak and speak and speak again
with the sting of purity
that can only be Me
causing joyous earthquakes in the mourning soul of man
I am and am and am again

*Stewart Henderson*
*20th century*

# Breath of God

   Breathe on me, breath of God
   Fill me with life anew,
That I may love what thou dost love,
   And do what thou wouldst do.

   Breathe on me, breath of God,
   Until my heart is pure:
Until with thee I have one will
   To do and to endure.

   Breathe on me, breath of God,
   Till I am wholly thine,
Until this earthly part of me
   Glows with thy fire divine.

   Breathe on me, breath of God,
   So shall I never die,
But live with thee the perfect life
   Of thine eternity.

*Edwin Hatch*
*1835–89*

# Pentecost

So free, so bright, so beautiful and fair,
the Holy Dove descends the earthly air:
in startling joyance come
from its immortal home,
it bears the Glory that all men may share.

Through ancient space and newest time, it brings
transcendent reason to a world of things:
it shows each mind and heart
how to assume its part
in dances born of God's imaginings.

On wings of subtlest flame, the Holy Dove
flies through the human world and offers love:
it teaches Heart and Mind
how to transcend their kind
and praise the God who lets all being move.

So free, so bright, so beautiful and fair,
the Holy Dove flies through the mortal air:
always there descending,
always there ascending,
it brings the Glory that all men may share.

*John Bennett*
20th century

## The Church the Garden of Christ

We are a Garden walled around,
Chosen and made peculiar Ground;
A little Spot enclosed by Grace
Out of the World's wide Wilderness.

Like Trees of Myrrh and Spice we stand,
Planted by God the Father's hand;
And all the Springs in Sion flow,
To make the young Plantation grow.

Awake, O heavenly Wind, and come,
Blow on this Garden of Perfume;
Spirit Divine, descend and breathe
A gracious Gale on Plants beneath.

Make our best Spices flow abroad
To entertain our Saviour-God:
And Faith, and Love, and Joy appear,
And every Grace be active here.

Let my Beloved come, and taste
His pleasant Fruits at his own Feast.
I come, my Spouse, I come, he cries,
With Love and Pleasure in his eyes.

Our Lord into his Garden comes,
Well pleased to smell our poor Perfumes,
And calls us to a Feast Divine,
Sweeter than Honey, Milk, or Wine.

Eat of the tree of Life, my Friends,
The Blessings that my Father sends;
Your taste shall all my Dainties prove,
And drink abundance of my Love.

Jesus, we will frequent thy Board,
And sing the Bounties of our Lord:
But the rich Food on which we live
Demands more Praise than Tongues can give.

*Isaac Watts*
*1674–1748*

# The Winds

There is a tree grows upside down,
   Its roots are in the sky;
Its lower branches reach the earth
   When amorous winds are nigh.

On one lone bough there starkly hangs
   A Man just crucified,
And all the other branches bear
   The choice fruits of the Bride.

When Pleasure's wind goes frisking past,
   Unhallowed by a prayer,
It swirls dead leaves from earth-born trees,
   Old growths of pride and care.

The gracious fruits are hidden by
   These leaves of human stain;
The Crucified, beneath his load
   Shudders, as if in pain.

But swift springs down a credal wind,
   It thrills through all the boughs;
The dead leaves scatter and are lost;
   The Christ renews his vows.

His hands direct the Spirit's wind
   Branch after branch to shake;
The Bride's fruit drops, and at the touch
   Elected hearts awake.

*Jack Clemo*
*20th century*

# The City of God

O thou not made with hands,
Not throned above the skies,
Nor walled with shining walls,
Nor framed with stones of price,
  More bright than gold or gem,
  God's own Jerusalem!

Where'er the gentle heart
Finds courage from above;
Where'er the heart forsook
Warms with the breath of love;
  Where faith bids fear depart,
  City of God! thou art.

Thou art where'er the proud
In humbleness melts down;
Where self itself yields up;
Where martyrs win their crown;
  Where faithful souls possess
  Themselves in perfect peace.

Where in life's common ways
With cheerful feet we go;
When in his steps we tread
Who trod the way of woe;
  Where he is in the heart,
  City of God! thou art.

Not throned above the skies,
Nor golden-walled afar,
But where Christ's two or three
In his name gathered are,
  Be in the midst of them,
  God's own Jerusalem!

*Francis Palgrave*
*1825–97*

# The Kingdom of God

'IN NO STRANGE LAND'

O world invisible, we view thee,
O world intangible, we touch thee,
O world unknowable, we know thee,
Inapprehensible, we clutch thee!

Does the fish soar to find the ocean,
The eagle plunge to find the air –
That we ask of the stars in motion
If they have rumours of thee there?

Not where the wheeling systems darken,
And our benumbed conceiving soars! –
The drift of pinions, would we hearken,
Beats at our own clay-shuttered doors.

The angels keep their ancient places; –
Turn but a stone, and start a wing!
'Tis ye, 'tis your estranged faces,
That miss the many-splendoured thing.

But (when so sad thou canst not sadder)
Cry; – and upon thy so sore loss
Shall shine the traffic of Jacob's ladder
Pitched betwixt Heaven and Charing Cross.

Yea, in the night, my Soul, my daughter,
Cry; – clinging Heaven by the hems;
And lo, Christ walking on the water
Not of Gennesareth, but Thames!

*Francis Thompson*
*1859–1907*

# The Windows

Lord, how can man preach thy eternal word?
   He is a brittle, crazy glass;
Yet in thy temple thou dost him afford
   This glorious and transcendent place,
   To be a window, through thy grace.

But when thou dost anneal in glass thy story,
   Making thy life to shine within
The holy Preacher's, then the light and glory
   More rev'rend grows, and more doth win;
   Which else shows waterish, bleak, and thin.

Doctrine and life, colours and light, in one
   When they combine and mingle, bring
A strong regard and awe; but speech alone
   Doth vanish like a flaring thing,
   And in the ear, not conscience, ring.

*George Herbert*
*1593–1633*

# Divina Commedia

Oft have I seen at some cathedral door
   A labourer pausing in the dust and heat,
   Lay down his burden, and with reverent feet
Enter, and cross himself, and on the floor
Kneel to repeat his paternoster o'er;
   Far off the noises of the world retreat;
   The loud vociferations of the street
   Become an indistinguishable roar.
So, as I enter here from day to day,
   And leave my burden at this minster gate,
   Kneeling in prayer, and not ashamed to pray,
The tumult of the time disconsolate
   To inarticulate murmurs dies away,
   While the eternal ages watch and wait.

*Henry Wadsworth Longfellow*
*1807–82*

# Thy Kingdom Come

The Lord's Prayer
   flows from facile worshippers
   like TV voices
   recounting the worries of the world
   and the wonders of anti-perspirants.

Lacking a congregation,
since all are
praying to themselves
or to impress the rest,
God seldom has a thing to do
or anyone to listen to.

Quietly he waits
to catch a man
who wants to find
but has not found
the meaning of
'Thy will be done.'
One such is worth
a thousand dissembling
'Thine be the glories'
to an idol god.

Patiently God listens
for a troubled saint
with nothing
but a sense of sin
to lean heavily
on his pew
praying 'Lord, have mercy!'
and yearning
for the Kingdom
that is yet to come.

*Elmer F. Suderman*
*20th century*

## Compound Metaphors for Sunday Morning

No war of earth or heaven darkens
the stillness of this timely church.

Earth is ours:
It blusters against the windows
and shakes the panes
we eye the sky through.

And heaven too:
Falling, it intersects the wind,
cuts through all panes
and fills with light the eyes
we close to see.

The long division of the saints
is set aside.
In the mathematics of the cross
all products, sums, and quotients
equal one.

*John Leax*
*20th century*

## Lavinia at Church

Lavinia is polite, but not profane;
To church as constant as to Drury Lane.
She decently, in form, pays heaven its due;
And makes a civil visit to her pew.
Her lifted fan, to give a solemn air,
Conceals her face, which passes for a prayer:
Curtsies to curtsies, then, with grace, succeed;
Not one the fair omits, but at the creed.
Or if she joins the service, 'tis to speak;
Through dreadful silence the pent heart might break;
Untaught to bear it, women talk away
To God himself, and fondly think they pray.
But sweet their accent, and the air refined;
For they're before their Maker – and mankind:
When ladies once are proud of praying well,
Satan himself will toll the parish bell.

*Edward Young*
*1683–1765*

# The Evangelist

'My brethren…' And a bland, elastic smile
Basks on the mobile features of Dissent.
No hypocrite, you understand. The style
Befits a church that's based on sentiment.

Solicitations of a swirling gown,
The sudden vox humana, and the pause,
The expert orchestration of a frown
Deserve, no doubt, a murmur of applause.

The tides of feeling round me rise and sink;
Bunyan, however, found a place for wit.
Yes, I am more persuaded than I think;
Which is, perhaps, why I disparage it.

You round upon me, generously keen:
The man, you say, is patently sincere.
Because he is so eloquent, you mean?
That test was never patented, my dear.

If, when he plays upon our sympathies,
I'm pleased to be fastidious, and you
To be inspired, the vice in it is this:
Each does us credit, and we know it too.

*Donald Davie*
*20th century*

# Frescoes in an Old Church

(STOWELL PARK, GLOUCESTERSHIRE)

Six centuries have gone
Since, one by one,
These stones were laid,
And in air's vacancy
This beauty made.

They who thus reared them
Their long rest have won;
Ours now this heritage –
To guard, preserve, delight in, brood upon;
And in these transitory fragments scan
The immortal longings in the soul of Man.

*Walter de la Mare*
*1873–1956*

# Celtic Chapel

A rusted grating in the ancient wall
in whose cold squares the child would frame his face;
the roofless gables held their light and space
where monks came singing to the vesper call.

This, they said, used to be the home of God,
this fading whisper of an ancient tale.
A silent chantry without altar rail,
bare ruin reaching for the sailing cloud.

*William Neill*
*20th century*

# In Canterbury Cathedral

On a day sweet with April showers
the safe tyres of our tour bus
had sung us south from London,

Sightseer pilgrims, cameras slung,
no need or time on patient plodding
horses for long diverting tales.

We stood at last at Beckett's shrine
lost in architecture and dates,
confused by Norman and Gothic.

Our ancient tiny guide seemed shrunk
into his suit, dwarfed by his clothes
as we were all dwarfed by time.

His small precise English voice went on:
pronounced 'Our Lord,' and the words
fell on us like a benediction.

'Our' – incredible assumption of union
offered in passing to American strangers,
mortar for diverse motley stones.

Time and blood and history redeemed
from meaninglessness: two words
turned sightseers into pilgrims.

*E.W. Oldenburg*
*20th century*

# In Church

Often I try
To analyse the quality
Of its silences. Is this where God hides
From my searching? I have stopped to listen,
After the few people have gone,
To the air recomposing itself
For vigil. It has waited like this
Since the stones grouped themselves about it.
These are the hard ribs
Of a body that our prayers have failed
To animate. Shadows advance
From their corners to take possession
Of places that light held
For an hour. The bats resume
Their business. The uneasiness of the pews
Ceases. There is no other sound
In the darkness but the sound of a man
Breathing, testing his faith
On emptiness, nailing his questions
One by one to an untenanted cross.

R.S. Thomas
20th century

# Te Deum Laudamus

High in the steepled church the shining bells
swing tongues unmuted to delight the air
with calls to praise, that anyone awake
might now begin this dawning hour with prayer.

Deep in the wood the hermit thrush,
in spiralled ecstasies to greet the dawn,
loops silver sounds for God's own sake alone,
flings his Te Deum now the night is gone.

If we, bell beckoned, should refuse to sing
Te Deum Laudamus to begin our days,
the very stars would ring, the rocks would shout
as now thrush, lark, and linnet spill his praise.

Marie J. Post
20th century

# DAILY LIFE

## At Dressing in the Morning

Now I arise, empowered by thee,
　The glorious sun to face;
O clothe me with humility,
　Adorn me with thy grace.

All evil of the day forefend,
　Prevent the Tempter's snare;
Thine angel on my steps attend,
　And give me fruit to prayer.

O make me useful as I go
　My pilgrimage along;
And sweetly soothe this vale of woe
　By charity and song.

Let me from Christ obedience learn,
　To Christ obedience pay;
Each parent duteous love return,
　And consecrate this day.

*Christopher Smart*
*1722–71*

# _Work_

## Market Women

(CARIBBEAN)

Down from the hills, they come
With swinging hips and steady stride
To feed the hungry Town
They stirred the steep dark land
To place within the growing seed.
And in the rain and sunshine
Tended the young green plants,
They bred, and dug and reaped.
And now, as Heaven has blessed their toil,
They come, bearing the fruits,
These hand-maids of the Soil,
Who bring full baskets down,
To feed the hungry Town.

_Daisy Myrie_
_20th century_

## Milking Croon

Bless, O God, my little cow,
Bless, O God, my desire;
Bless thou my partnership
And the milking of my hands, O God.

Bless, O God, each teat,
Bless, O God, each finger;
Bless thou each drop
That goes into my pitcher, O God!

_Traditional Celtic_

# Daily Labour

Forth in thy name, O Lord, I go,
  My daily labour to pursue;
Thee, only thee, resolved to know,
  In all I think or speak or do.

The task thy wisdom hath assigned
  O let me cheerfully fulfil,
In all my works thy presence find
  And prove thy acceptable will.

Preserve me from my calling's snare,
  And hide my simple heart above,
Above the thorns of choking care,
  The gilded baits of worldly love.

Thee may I set at my right hand,
  Whose eyes my inmost substance see,
And labour on at thy command,
  And offer all my works to thee.

Give me to bear thy easy yoke,
  And every moment watch and pray,
And still to things eternal look,
  And hasten to thy glorious day;

For thee delightfully employ
  Whate'er thy bounteous grace hath given,
And run my course with even joy
  And closely walk with thee to heaven.

*Charles Wesley*
*1707–88*

257

# Glory

Oh, you gotta get a glory
In the work you do;
A Hallelujah chorus
In the heart of you.

Paint, or tell a story,
Sing, or shovel coal,
But you gotta get a glory,
Or the job lacks soul.

*Anonymous*

# Knitting Woman

In her chosen corner she sits. Rivers of knitting
cascade plaining and purling over her lap
winter and summer together. She has her reasons,
knows that sudden contrary August weather
is worse than blizzards in winter, trusts no seasons.

Her young have escaped. She sees them
at large in the world's cold winds. Her anxious care
follows them all by post, in cumbersome parcels,
cabled and striped and ribbed. She knows no ill
that can't be cured in an Aran jacket, or better
endured in a mohair sweater. God
may temper the wind or not, but never
a lamb of hers will ever be caught shorn.

She sits defying hap and circumstance,
weak chests, ill luck, chaos and old night.

She would like to knit the whole world a pullover.

*Evangeline Paterson*
*20th century*

# Barnyard Miracle

Paulina the heifer would not stand still
while I milked her.
Five times she had kicked
so viciously
that the steel hobbles had sprung
from her legs.
Despite the tender welts where the hobble clamps
had been attached,
she was angry enough to do it again.
The fifth kick had lost me the milk
so I was angry too.
In adolescent temper I took the gutter shovel
and beat the heifer five, eight, eleven strokes
until I heard your voice, Mother.
You were in the barn for some heifer milk
for oyster stew.
Milk from other cows would do,
but heifer milk is better.
'Sietze, Sietze,
God's blessing can never rest on such temper.'
You went to the heifer's head,
served her an extra portion of cornmeal,
and talked to her woman-to-woman:
'You've go to be quiet inside, Paulina,
in order to be quiet outside.'

Paulina stood perfectly still
while I finished milking her.
I wondered guiltily
what manner of woman you were
that even the raging Paulina
obeyed you.
And what's more,
in addition to the pailful spilled,
she still gave enough milk
for oyster stew.

*Sietze Buning*
*20th century*

# *From:* The Woman's Labour

When bright Orion glitters in the skies
In winter nights, then early we must rise;
In weather ne'er so bad, wind, rain or snow,
Our work appointed, we must rise and go,
While you on easy beds may lie and sleep,
Till light does through your chamber windows peep.

When to the house we come where we should go,
How to get in, alas! we do not know:
The maid quite tired with work the day before,
O'ercome with sleep; we standing at the door,
Oppressed with cold, and often call in vain,
Ere to our work we can admittance gain.
But when from wind and weather we get in,
Briskly with courage we our work begin;
Heaps of fine linen we before us view,
Where on to lay our strength and patience too;
Cambrics and muslins, which our ladies wear,
Laces and edgings, costly, fine and rare,
Which must be washed with utmost skill and care;
With holland shirts, ruffles and fringes too,
Fashions which our forefathers never knew.
For several hours here we work and slave,
Before we can one glimpse of daylight have;
We labour hard before the morning's past,
Because we fear the time runs on too fast.

At length bright Sol illuminates the skies,
And summons drowsy mortals to arise;
Then comes our mistress to us without fail,
And in her hand, perhaps, a mug of ale
To cheer our hearts, and also to inform
Herself what work is done that very morn;
Lays her commands upon us, that we mind
Her linen well, nor leave the dirt behind.
Not this alone, but also to take care
We don't her cambrics nor her ruffles tear;
And these most strictly does of us require,
To save her soap and sparing be of fire;
Tells us her charge is great, nay furthermore,
Her clothes are fewer than the time before.

Now we drive on, resolved our strength to try,
And what we can, we do most willingly;
Until with heat and work, 'tis often known,
Not only sweat but blood runs trickling down
Our wrists and fingers: still our work demands
The constant action of our labouring hands.

*Mary Collier*
*1690?–1762*

## The List

Flawlessly typed, and spaced
At the proper intervals,
Serene and lordly, they pace
Along tomorrow's list
Like giftbearers on a frieze.

In tranquil order, arrayed
With the basic human equipment –
A name, a time, a number –
They advance on the future.

Not more harmonious who pace
Holding a hawk, a fish, a jar v(The customary offerings)
Along the valley of the kings.

Tomorrow these names will turn nasty,
Senile, pregnant, late,
Handicapped, handcuffed, unhandy,
Muddled, moribund, mute,

Be stained by living. But here,
Orderly, equal, right,
On the edge of tomorrow, they pause
Like giftbearers on a frieze

With the proper offering,
A time, a number, a home.
I am the artist, the typist;
I did my best for them.

*U.A. Fanthorpe*
*20th century*

# Loom Blessing

Thrums nor odds of thread
My hand never kept, nor shall keep,

Every colour in the bow of the shower
Has gone through my fingers beneath the cross,

White and black, red and madder,
Green, dark grey, and scarlet,

Blue and roan, and colour of the sheep,
And never a particle of cloth was wanting.

I beseech calm Bride the generous,
I beseech mild Mary the loving,
I beseech Christ Jesu the humane,
That I may not die without them,
   That I may not die without them.

*Traditional Celtic*

# Reflections

An old woman, sitting among petunias
Shelling broad beans.
Delivers one pale green baby after another:
Lumpy forehead, tucked-up legs.
Green placenta below.
She thinks of rice grains, pouring from the jar.
And blow-flies' eggs on meat:
She thinks of water at the plug-hole,
The swirling hearts of daisies,
And far imagined nebulae:
And of herself, a tiny creator
Delighting in all she makes.
An old woman, sitting in the sunshine,
Ponders on the economy of God.

*Stephanie Gifford*
*20th century*

# Washing Day

Socks and stockings
are strung like crotchets on the line.
White shirts trill a little
beside the trumpeting of
underwear let loose.
Sheets clap, trousers flap,
dishcloths drip in time.
They have come to expect
this ritual of song and dance;
fabric from my world inside.

*Rosemary A. Hector*
*20th century*

# I Sit and Sew

I sit and sew – a useless task it seems,
My hands grown tired, my head weighed down with dreams –
The panoply of war, the material tread of men,
Grim-faced, stern-eyed, gazing beyond the ken
Of lesser souls, whose eyes have not seen Death,
Nor learned to hold their lives but as a breath –
But – I must sit and sew.

I sit and sew – my heart aches with desire –
That pageant terrible, that fiercely pawing fire
On wasted fields, and writhing grotesque things
Once men. My soul in pity flings
Appealing cries, yearning only to go
There in that holocaust of hell, those fields of woe –
But – I must sit and sew.

The little useless seam, the idle patch;
Why dream I here beneath my homely thatch,
When there they lie in sodden mud and rain,
Pitifully calling me, the quick ones and the slain!
You need me, Christ! It is no roseate dream
That beckons me – this pretty futile seam,
It stifles me – God, must I sit and sew?

*Alice Dunbar Nelson*
*1875–1935*

# Housekeeper

This is my little town,
My Bethlehem,
And here, if anywhere,
My Christ Child
Will be born.

I must begin
To go about my day –
Sweep out the inn,
Get fresh hay for the manger
And be sure
To leave my heart ajar
In case there may be travellers
From afar.

*Elizabeth Rooney*
*20th century*

# Huswifery

Make me, O Lord, thy spinning wheel complete.
  Thy holy word my distaff make for me.
Make mine affections thy swift flyers neat
  And make my soul thy holy spool to be.
  My conversation make to be thy reel
  And reel the yarn thereon spun of thy wheel.

Make me thy loom then; knit therein this twine;
  And make thy Holy Spirit, Lord, wind quills;
Then weave the web thyself. The yarn is fine.
  Thine ordinances make my fulling mills.
  Then dye the same in heavenly colours choice,
  All pinked with varnished flowers of Paradise.

Then clothe therewith mine understanding, will,
  Affections, judgement, conscience, memory,
My words and actions, that their shine may fill
  My ways with glory and thee glorify.
  Then my apparel shall display before ye
  That I am clothed in holy robes for glory.

*Edward Taylor*
*1645–1729*

# The Elixir

Teach me, my God and King,
In all things thee to see,
And what I do in any thing,
To do it as for thee:

Not rudely, as a beast,
To run into an action;
But still to make thee prepossessed,
And give it his perfection.

A man that looks on glass,
On it may stay his eye;
Or if he pleaseth, through it pass,
And then the heavens espy.

All may of thee partake:
Nothing can be so mean,
Which with this tincture, 'for thy sake',
Will not grow bright and clean.

A servant with this clause
Makes drudgery divine:
Who sweeps a room, as for thy laws,
Makes that and th'action fine.

This is the famous stone
That turneth all to gold:
For that which God doth touch and own
Cannot for less be told.

*George Herbert*
*1593–1632*

# Domestic Threat

House-proud housewives, listen to the rumble –
the desert drifting daily closer to your door.
Sand is softly silting the surface like a sea-floor.
You'll snatch a broom like King Canute?
or plant some trees, house-humble?

*Grace Westerduin*
*20th century*


# Blessing

The sacred Three be over me
With my working hands this day
With the people on my way
With the labour and the toil
With the land and with the soil
With the tools that I take
With the things that I make
With the thoughts of my mind
With the sharing with mankind
With the love of my heart
With each one who plays a part
The sacred Three be over me
The blessing of the Trinity

*David Adam*
*20th century*

# By All Means Bless

By all means
bless the cloth
that wiped
the face
of Jesus

By all means
bless the towel
that unfolds
an infant
like miraculous bread

By all means
bless the towel
the boxer returns to
– a brief harbour
after a harassing round

By all means
bless the sacred silk
that garbs
the sumo's
amplitude of loin

But I say this also
bless the towel
that unwraps
your buttocks
(fresh out of the shower)
with such casual ease

we overlook
life's small epiphanies

*John Agard*
*20th century*

## Work

Close by the careless worker's side,
  Still patient stands
The Carpenter of Nazareth
  With pierced hands
Outstretched to plead unceasingly,
  His love's demands.

Longing to pick the hammer up
  And strike a blow,
Longing to feel his plane swing out,
  Steady and slow,
The fragrant shavings falling down,
  Silent as snow.

Because this is my work, O Lord,
  It must be thine,
Because it is a human task
  It is divine.
Take me, and brand me with thy cross,
  Thy slave's proud sign.

*G.A. Studdert Kennedy*
*1883–1929*

# Woodworkers' Ballad

All that is moulded of iron
Has lent to destruction and blood;
But the things that are honoured in Zion
Are most of them made from wood.

Stone can be chiselled to Beauty,
And iron shines bright for Defence;
But when Mother Earth pondered her duty
She brought forth the forest, from whence

Come tables, and chairs, and crosses,
Little things that a hot fire warps,
Old ships that the blue wave tosses,
And fiddles for music, and harps;

Oak boards where the carved ferns mingle,
Monks' shrines in the wilderness,
Snug little huts in the dingle,
All things that the sad poets bless.

King Arthur had a wood table;
And our Lord blessed wood; for you see,
He was born in a wooden stable,
And he died on a wooden tree;

And he sailed in a wooden vessel
On the waters of Galilee,
And he worked at a wooden trestle
At his wonderful carpentry.

Oh, all that is moulded of iron
Has lent to destruction and blood;
But the things that are honoured of Zion
Are most of them made from wood.

*Herbert Edward Palmer*
*born 1880*

269

# Home

## A Thanksgiving to God for his House

Lord, thou hast given me a cell
　　Wherein to dwell;
A little house, whose humble roof
　　Is weather-proof;
Under the spars of which I lie
　　Both soft and dry;
Where thou my chamber for to ward
　　Hast set a guard
Of harmless thoughts, to watch and keep
　　Me while I sleep.
Low is my porch, as is my fate,
　　Both void of state;
And yet the threshold of my door
　　Is worn by the poor,
Who thither come and freely get
　　Good words, or meat:
Like as my parlour, so my hall
　　And kitchen's small:
A little buttery, and therein
　　A little bin,
Which keeps my little loaf of bread
　　Unchipped, unflead:
Some brittle sticks of thorn or briar
　　Make me a fire,
Close by whose living coal I sit,
　　And glow like it.
Lord, I confess too, when I dine,
　　The pulse is thine,
And all those other bits, that be
　　There placed by thee;
The worts, the purslain, and the mess
　　Of water-cress,
Which of thy kindness thou hast sent;
　　And my content
Makes these and my beloved beet
　　To be more sweet.

'Tis thou that crown'st my glittering hearth
  With guiltless mirth,
And giv'st me wassail bowls to drink,
  Spiced to the brink.
Lord, 'tis thy plenty-dropping hand,
  That soils my land;
And gives me, for my bushel sown,
  Twice ten for one:
Thou mak'st my teeming hen to lay
  Her egg each day:
Besides my healthful ewes to bear
  Me twins each year:
The while the conduits of my kine
  Run cream (for wine).
All these, and better thou dost send
  Me, to this end,
That I should render, for my part,
  A thankful heart;
Which, fired with incense, I resign
  As wholly thine;
But the acceptance, that must be,
  My Christ, by thee.

*Robert Herrick*
*1591–1674*

271

# The Guardians

May a strong guardian
Stand at the door
With sword and olive branch.

May the keeper of the windows
Be eager-eyed
For dawn and first star,
   snow-light and corn-light.

May the keeper of the fire
See a loaf on the table
And faces of travellers lit with welcome
   and shadow-of-flame, in winter.

May the keeper of the beds be resolute
Against the terror that walks by night,
And herd with gentleness the flocks of sleep.

In a blue-and-silver morning
On the first winter step
Those guardians, and others who hold
   a finger to the lip, smiling
Came about her who holds now the key of the house.

*George Mackay Brown*
*20th century*

# The Kitchen

I love the sunshine in the kitchen,
The glory of the light awakens
All the familiar textures of pot and china.
This is the home of the house,
The centre of its warmth,
The articulation of its love,
In the rise of bread, the crust of pie,
And the richness of gravy.
It is the place of your caring,
Fleshed out in the daily details,
Too small to be noted one by one,
But each constructing the heart of the house.

Your delight in us is incarnated here,
And this is the place of our true receiving.
Here we come hungry, thirsty and in our need,
To meet the kindness of your hands.
And your friends came,
Finding a warmth they sought and a love they craved.
Not a pretentious place,
A good cause or a moral crusade.
If you will, another Nazareth,
Hidden in the wilderness of the world,
Where kindness feeds a poor Christ and his friends,
And bids them come in from the dark.

*Tim Marks*
*20th century*

## From: Breakfast

A dinner-party, coffee, tea,
Sandwich, or supper, all may be
In their way pleasant. But to me
Not one of these deserves the praise
That welcomer of new-born days,
A breakfast, merits; ever giving
Cheerful notice we are living
Another day refreshed by sleep,
When its festival we keep.
Now, although I would not slight
Those kindly words we use, 'Good-night',
Yet parting words are words of sorrow,
And may not vie with sweet 'Good-morrow',
With which again our friends we greet,
When in the breakfast-room we meet,
At the social table round,
Listening to the lively sound
Of those notes which never tire,
Of urn, or kettle on the fire.

*Mary Lamb*
*1765–1847*

## House Communion

Here on this accustomed table
    dull stained by family meals
    and spilled milk of past infancy,
    elbowed in friends' fellowship,

as my own house-guest I break bread,
    hosted by heart's depth,
    charged with mimetic obedience
    offer what is not my own.

May the presence hold on hasty mornings
    and through evenings of weariness
    justifying the repetitions
    of all failures that venture on worthiness.

*Raymond Chapman*
*20th century*

# Supper Being Ended

In the quiet place
at close of day
he washes the feet of my mind from the dust of its fret.

His infinite eyes
see the staining and wounds of the road, his hands
bring smarting
and cleansing
and balm.

The grace of his health
restores my soul
her place in the circling stars of perpetual praise.

Then, taking again the seamless robe, the Alpha-Omega,
Master and Lord,
we talk together,
friend with friend.

*Joan A. Bidwell*
*20th century*

# Morning and Night

## AT MORNING LIGHT

### Morning Hymn

Christ, whose glory fills the skies,
   Christ the true, the only light,
Sun of righteousness, arise,
   Triumph o'er the shades of night!
Day-spring from on high, be near!
Day-star, in my heart appear!

Dark and cheerless is the morn
   Unaccompanied by thee;
Joyless is the day's return,
   Till thy mercy's beams I see;
Till they inward light impart,
Glad my eyes, and warm my heart.

Visit then this soul of mine,
   Pierce the gloom of sin and grief!
Fill me, radiancy divine,
   Scatter all my unbelief!
More and more thyself display,
Shining to the perfect day.

*Charles Wesley*
*1707–88*

## *From:* Morning Sacrifice

Awake, my soul, and with the sun,
Thy daily stage of duty run;
Shake off dull sloth, and joyful rise,
To pay thy morning sacrifice.

Thy precious time misspent, redeem;
Each present day thy last esteem;
Improve thy talent with due care,
For the great day thyself prepare...

Wake, and lift up thyself, my heart,
And with the angels bear thy part,
Who all night long unwearied sing
High praise to the eternal King...

Glory to thee, who safe hast kept,
And hast refreshed me while I slept: –
Grant, Lord, when I from death shall wake,
I may of endless light partake.

*Thomas Ken*
*1637–1711*

277

## GOD, THE SOURCE OF LIGHT

## To Christ our Lord

Hail, heavenly beam, brightest of angels thou,
sent unto men upon this middle-earth!
Thou art the true refulgence of the sun,
radiant above the stars, and from thyself
illuminest for ever all the tides of time.
And as thou, God indeed begotten of God,
thou Son of the true Father, wast from aye,
without beginning, in the heaven's glory,
so now thy handiwork in its sore need
prayeth thee boldly that thou send to us
the radiant sun, and that thou comest thyself
to enlighten those who for so long a time
were wrapt around with darkness, and here in gloom
have sat the livelong night, shrouded in sin.

*Cynewulf*
*about 820*

## Night-time Prayer

May the Light of lights come
  To my dark heart from thy place;
May the Spirit's wisdom come
  To my heart's tablet from my Saviour.

*Celtic traditional*

## Steadfast Taper

(JOB 28:3)

His candle shines upon my head.
He trims the wick and guards the flame
and though the darkness creeps in close
the steadfast taper shines the same.

The flower of flame sways in the air.
Wind fingers snatch and try to snuff
the stalk his careful hands protect.
The light shines through. It is enough.

His candle shines on me in love,
(protective circle in the gloom)
and through the dreadful night I know
that he is with me in the room.

Throughout the weary waiting-time
the liquid flame shines thin and pure.
When tiredness dims my faith, I look
and see his light, and I am sure.

*Luci Shaw*
*20th century*

# At Undressing in the Evening

These clothes, of which I now divest
  Myself, All-seeing Eye,
Must be one day (that day be blest)
  Relinquished and laid by.

Thou cordial sleep, to death akin,
  I court thee on my knee;
O let my exit, free from sin,
  Be little more than thee.

But if much agonizing pain
  My dying hour await,
The Lord be with me to sustain,
  To help and to abate.

O let me meet thee undeterred,
  By no foul stains defiled!
According to thy holy word,
  Receive me as a child.

*Christopher Smart*
1722–71

# Evening

She sweeps with many-coloured brooms,
And leaves the shreds behind;
Oh, housewife in the evening west,
Come back, and dust the pond!

You dropped a purple ravelling in,
You dropped an amber thread;
And now you've littered all the East
With duds of emerald!

And still she plies her spotted brooms,
And still the aprons fly,
Till brooms fade softly into stars –
And then I come away.

*Emily Dickinson*
1830–86

# The Presence of God

The night is come like to the day,
Depart not thou, great God, away;
Let not my sins, black as the night
Eclipse the lustre of thy light.
Keep still in my horizon, for to me
The sun makes not the day, but thee.
Thou whose nature cannot sleep,
On my temples sentry keep;
Guard me 'gainst those watchful foes,
Whose eyes are open while mine close.
Let no dreams my head infest,
But such as Jacob's temples blest.
While I do rest, my soul advance,
Make my sleep a holy trance:
That I may, my rest being wrought,
Awake into some holy thought.
And with an active vigour run
My course, as doth the nimble sun.
Sleep is a death, O make me try
By sleeping what it is to die.
And as gently lay my head
On my grave, as now my bed.
Now ere I rest, great God, let me
Awake again at last with thee.
And thus assured, behold I lie
Securely, or to wake or die.
These are my drowsy days, in vain
I do now wake to sleep again.
O come that hour, when I shall never
Sleep again, but wake for ever!

*Sir Thomas Browne*
*1605–82*

# Night Blessing

Glory to thee, my God, this night
For all the blessings of the light;
Keep me, O keep me, King of kings,
Beneath thy own almighty wings.

Forgive me, Lord, for thy dear Son,
The ills that I this day have done,
That with the world, myself, and thee
I, ere I sleep, at peace may be.

Teach me to live, that I may dread
The grave as little as my bed;
Teach me to die, that so I may
Rise glorious at the awful day.

O may my soul on thee repose,
And with sweet sleep mine eyelids close,
Sleep that may me more vigorous make
To serve my God when I awake.

When in the night I sleepless lie,
My soul with heavenly thoughts supply;
Let no ill dreams disturb my rest,
No powers of darkness me molest.

Praise God, from whom all blessings flow,
Praise him, all creatures here below,
Praise him above, ye heavenly host,
Praise Father, Son, and Holy Ghost.

*Thomas Ken*
*1637–1711*

# Evening Praise

Ere I sleep, for every favour
   This day showed
   By my God
I will bless my Saviour.

O my Lord, what shall I render
   To thy name,
   Still the same,
Merciful and tender?

Thou hast ordered all my goings
   In thy way,
   Heard me pray,
Sanctified my doings.

Leave me not, but ever love me:
   Let thy peace
   Be my bliss,
Till thou hence remove me.

Thou my rock, my guard, my tower,
   Safely keep,
   While I sleep,
Me, with all thy power.

So, whene'er in death I slumber,
   Let me rise
   With the wise,
Counted in their number.

*John Cennick*
*1718–55*

# Before Sleep

The toil of day is ebbing,
The quiet comes again,
In slumber deep relaxing
The limbs of tired men.

And minds with anguish shaken,
And spirits racked with grief,
The cup of all forgetting
Have drunk and found relief.

The still Lethean waters
Now steal through every vein,
And men no more remember
The meaning of their pain...

Let, let the weary body
Lie sunk in slumber deep.
The heart shall still remember
Christ in its very sleep.

*Prudentius*
348–about 405
*translated from Latin by Helen Waddell*

# Who Cares?
## The Voice of Protest

## On Another's Sorrow

Can I see another's woe
And not be in sorrow too.
Can I see another's grief
And not seek for kind relief.

Can I see a falling tear,
And not feel my sorrows share,
Can a father see his child,
Weep, nor be with sorrow filled.

Can a mother sit and hear,
An infant groan an infant fear –
No no never can it be.
Never never can it be.

And can he who smiles on all
Hear the wren with sorrows small,
Hear the small birds grief & care
Hear the woes that infants bear –

And not sit beside the nest
Pouring pity on their breast,
And not sit the cradle near
Weeping tear on infant's tear...

He doth give his joy to all.
He becomes an infant small.
He becomes a man of woe
He doth feel the sorrow too.

Think not, thou canst sigh a sigh,
And thy maker is not by.
Think not, thou canst weep a tear,
And thy maker is not near.

O! he gives to us his joy,
That our grief he may destroy
Till our grief is fled & gone
He doth sit by us and moan.

*William Blake*
*1757–1827*

# The Poor of London

Almighty God, whose justice like a sun
Shall coruscate along the floors of Heaven,
Raising what's low, perfecting what's undone,
Breaking the proud and making odd things even,
The poor of Jesus Christ along the street
In your rain sodden, in your snows unshod,
They have nor hearth, nor sword, nor human meat,
Nor even the bread of men: Almighty God.

The poor of Jesus Christ whom no man hears
Have waited on your vengeance much too long.
Wipe out not tears but blood: our eyes bleed tears.
Come smite our damnèd sophistries so strong
That thy rude hammer battering this rude wrong
Ring down the abyss of twice ten thousand years.

*Hilaire Belloc*
*1870–1953*

# Feeding the Poor at Christmas

Every Christmas we feed the poor.
We arrive an hour late. Poor dears,
Like children waiting for a treat.
Bring your plates. Don't move.
Don't try turning up for more.
No. Even if you don't drink
you can't take your share
for your husband. Say thank you
and a rosary for us every evening.
No. Not a towel and a shirt,
even if they're old.
What's that you said?
You're a good man, Robert, yes,
beggars can't be, exactly.

*Eunice de Souza*
*20th century*

# Ain't I a Woman?

That man over there say
  a woman needs to be helped into carriages
and lifted over ditches
  and to have the best place everywhere.
Nobody ever helped me into carriages
  or over mud puddles
    or gives me a best place...

And ain't I a woman?
  Look at me
Look at my arm!
  I have ploughed and planted
and gathered into barns
  and no man could head me...
And ain't I a woman?
  I could work as much
and eat as much as a man –
  when I could get to it –
and bear the lash as well
  and ain't I a woman?
I have borne thirteen children
  and seen most all sold into slavery
and when I cried out a mother's grief
  none but Jesus heard me...
and ain't I a woman?
  that little man in black there say
a woman can't have as much rights as a man
  cause Christ wasn't a woman
Where did your Christ come from?
  From God and a woman!
Man had nothing to do with him!
  If the first woman God ever made
was strong enough to turn the world
  upside down, all alone
together women ought to be able to turn it
  rightside up again.

*Erlene Stetson from a speech by Isabella,*
*a slave freed in 1827 and known as Sojourner Truth*
*1797–1883*

# They Had It Coming

The South East Asians,
they were made to cry,
Look at their eyes all
narrowed up and ready to bawl.
Black Africans:
Obesity wouldn't suit them.
There's a grace about their
slenderness.
Their children would be naked
without a covering of flies.
Indians are perfect for begging
in ragged clothes
and falling dead on the streets
without too much sensation.
There are so many of them
that death is no longer a problem.
Middle Easterners, South Americans,
they were made to look anguished,
the mother crying to God,
the children just crying.
Earthquakes provide opportunity
for this.
While Westerners were made to laugh
in fast cars with beautiful friends.
They were made to drink and spend money.
Do not disturb the balance of nature.

*Steve Turner*
*20th century*

# Alcoholic

O all the problems other people face
we have intensified & could not face
until at last we feel completely alone
thick in a quart of company a day.

I knew I had a problem with that stuff
& problems with my wife & child & work;
But all what help I found left me intact
safe with a quart of feral help a day.

DT's, convulsions, hospitals galore.
Projectile vomiting hours, intravenous,
back in the nearest bar the seventh day.
God made a suggestion. I went home

and I am in the 4th week of the third treatment
& I am *hurting*, daily, and when I jerk
a few scales seem to fall away from my eyes
until with perfect clarity enough

seems to be visible to keep me sane
& sober toward the bed where I will die.
I pray that you may grant me a yielding will.

          I pray that my will may be attuned to
                your will for & with me.

*John Berryman*
20th century

# Somewhere in Suburbia

she'd have had her mother's eyes
but she never had her heart
she'd have had her father's smile
but he couldn't spare the time

she could have been a radical
a twice-born evangelical
she could have had her photo
on her grandmother's wall

but the doctors get their money
and the nurses change the bedclothes
and somewhere in suburbia
there'll be one less mouth to feed

King Herod sits in Harley Street
the land of milk and honey
while his bankers in the counting house
are counting out the money

a doctor puts his raincoat on
the nurses hurry home
the Maker gets his image back
a girl drives home alone

now the doctors get their money
and the nurses change the bedclothes
and somewhere in suburbia
there'll be one less mouth to feed

*Mike Starkey*
*20th century*

# We Were Going to be Twins

What attracted us to one another initially
was we shared the same womb
albeit the unconsidered products of flippant passion
Anyway, we were pre-natal room mates
checking each other's progress
transfixed by the budding of tiny fingernails
and the rhythm of miniscule chests
rising and falling like pale pink bellows
My brother, for that's what he was now becoming,
had a curious almost whimsical shape
his head leaning to one side
as if he were always about to ask a question
He used to poke gentle fun
at my by now rapidly expanding feet
I only had two
but on occasions because of the space they took up
they seemed to number far more
I can't remember exactly when we were terminated
My brother went first
in plunged a knife
ended his life
with a slish and a slash and a silent scream
I proved to be a more unwilling participant
like an irritating piece of dust
in the very corner of a skirting board
a long thin nozzle entered my sanctuary/death cell
and I was sucked into oblivion
along with bits of my brother
all courtesy of the National Health Service
In California some beloved dogs
when they expire
are buried in oak coffins with gold handles
Respectful mourners attend and weep accordingly
We were poured into a black plastic sack
not a hymn nor a prayer was heard
We were going to be twins
my brother and I

*Stewart Henderson*
*20th century*

# Epitaph

ON A CHILD KILLED
BY PROCURED ABORTION

O thou, whose eyes were closed in death's pale night
Ere fate revealed thee to my aching sight;
Ambiguous something, by no standard fixed,
Frail span, of naught and of existence mixed;
Embryo, imperfect as my torturing thought,
Sad outcast of existence and of naught;
Thou, who to guilty love first ow'st thy frame,
Whom guilty honour kills to hide its shame;
Dire offspring! formed by love's too pleasing power!
Honour's dire victim in a luckless hour!
Soften the pangs that still revenge thy doom:
Nor, from the dark abyss of nature's womb,
Where back I cast thee, let revolving time
Call up past scenes to aggravate my crime.

    Two adverse tyrants ruled thy wayward fate
Thyself a helpless victim to their hate;
Love, spite of honour's dictates, gave thee breath;
Honour, in spite of love, pronounced thy death.

*Anonymous*
*18th century*

## An Old Andorran Custom
## Questions the Dead

I spoke to the dead, oiled sea-bird,
questioned the poisoned fish,
saw the finger-sized foetus
asked 'Dead one, who killed you?'
And the dead gave me no answer
but the wind whispered
'You, you, you.'

I looked at the battered baby,
the man blown apart by a bomb,
the suicide pulled from the water
asked: 'Dead one, who killed you?'
And the dead gave me no answer
but the wind whispered
'You, you, you.'

I gazed at a sterile planet
– our erstwhile orbiting earth –
lifeless and pitted with craters
cried: 'Dead one, who killed you?'
And the dead gave me no answer
and there was no wind to whisper
'You, you, you.'

*Peggy Poole*
*20th century*

# Green

Green.
Green for our fear of what we have spoilt, from the turning
Wave to the grass that rots as we look, the roots
Which break in the ground. What green-sickness there is
In the world we walk on; look up, too, from the edge
  Of a field to the centre of cities where pollution
Stands in the air, blows to the suburbs, then
  Runs through corn and fruit-trees, renders barren
The bushes of blackberries, fields of strawberries, all
  That we ate with relish, bottled once and set
On a high and treasured shelf. We have set ourselves
  Too high too often, thought we ruled the sky,
Owned the arable farmlands, had a say
  In sunlight, starlight, all that atmosphere
Was rich in once. Not any longer. We have
  Watched the foxes run and die, have seen
Pigeon and pheasant fall from sky to our feet,
  And felt exultant. Almost too late we learn
Our lesson. We need a purity, a cleansing
  Ritual for the actual. We must unlearn now,
But all too slowly or else too hectically fast,
  That we must honour the earth and the flying birds,
Not spray chemicals on the delicate buds
  And poison the later fruit. We have been greedy
With land and air but also lecherous;
  We sow our seed too widely and in wrong places
So that we hinder a baby's growth, produce
  A handicapped race. We must be sorry and make
A fertile penitence, look about us, let
  Nature teach us once again. O can
We walk the difficult steps back to Eden garden
  And place the apple back on the poisoned tree?
Is it too late? Not if we deepen our sorrow,
  Give where we used to take, feed orphans, snatch
A million Christ-children back from the three-fold world
  Where the Holy Trinity broods with a lucky number.
So in a green dream of sweet fertility let us
  Kneel in sorrow, carefully plant our seeds
And exhale good air and leave it to others too,
  May the green, unpolluted waves turn over and over
Till green is the colour of safety and survival,
  And may green be our freshness for the last redemption.

*Elizabeth Jennings*
*20th century*

# Reaction to a Retard

Disgusting, really, the way it disfigures
the face – a lack of intelligence. The retard
on the ferry has nothing going for him
except his mother, who gives him a regard

I struggle to comprehend. I hear a quick
voice cry, Better to kill him before birth!
I look at him and shudder at my own depravity.
How easy it is to deny a person worth –

to limit the human, which is the image
of God, to the beautiful and clever,
and to forget that there is in every person
a spark, a spirit, that abides for ever.

There is a worse disorder than the damaged
brain that disfigures the blameless face.
It is the derangement of the cogent mind
that deforms the heart by a denial of grace.

*Andrew Lansdown*
*20th century*

# Still Falls the Rain

(THE RAIDS, 1940. NIGHT AND DAWN)

Still falls the Rain –
Dark as the world of man, black as our loss –
Blind as the nineteen hundred and forty nails
Upon the Cross.

Still falls the Rain
With a sound like the pulse of the heart that is changed to the
    hammer-beat
In the Potter's Field, and the sound of the impious feet

On the Tomb:
                                  Still falls the Rain
In the Field of Blood where the small hopes breed and the human brain
Nurtures its greed, that worm with the brow of Cain.

Still falls the Rain
At the feet of the Starved Man hung upon the Cross.
Christ that each day, each night, nails there,
                                  have mercy on us –

On Dives and on Lazarus:
Under the Rain the sore and the gold are as one.

Still falls the Rain –
Still falls the Blood from the Starved Man's wounded Side:
He bears in his Heart all wounds, – those of the light
                        that died,
The last faint spark
In the self-murdered heart, the wounds of the sad
                        uncomprehending dark,
The wounds of the baited bear, –
The blind and weeping bear whom the keepers beat
On his helpless flesh… the tears of the hunted hare.

Still falls the Rain –
Then – O Ile leape up to my God: who pulles me doune –
See, see where Christ's blood streames in the firmament:
It flows from the Brow we nailed upon the tree
Deep to the dying, to the thirsting heart
That holds the fires of the world, – dark-smirched with pain
As Caesar's laurel crown.

Then sounds the voice of One who like the heart of man
Was once a child who among beasts has lain –
'Still do I love, still shed my innocent light, my Blood, for thee.'

*Edith Sitwell*
*1887–1964*

# There Have Been Bombs Before

FOR HIROSHIMA DAY

There have been bombs before
As when:

> The serpent slid among the leaves,
> Green and glinting, to the ear,
> Twining gold, as fingers in the hair,
> Sinuous as fingers pressured on the fruit:
> The bite, the bite, so small,
> Puncturing the flesh, bursting juices,
> And crying, crying let there be
> Dark and dark there was, scales
> Dulled, leaves dried up, flesh
> Scragging, the scene cleft only
> By the fiery light arrowing west.

There have been bombs before.

There have been bombs before
As when:

> Abraham pleaded
> In sight
> Of the cities of the Plain
> For the one just man
> In desperate countdown
> For the peace of Zoar
> Should there be fifty
> Forty-five
> Will the judge
> Of the whole earth
> Not administer
> Justice?
> Forty
> Thirty
> As smoke
> From a furnace
> Twenty
> Ten

There have been bombs before.

There have been bombs before
As when:

Jonah dropped like an anchor
To the sea, to the whale's teeth,
White bolts locking him in,
Into the maw, the gulf, weeds
About his head and the bones
Of ocean, then, leagues on,
Three days, three nights, the whale
Breeches, upwards to the sun,
And the engulfed repenting prophet,
Ears murmuring with the depths,
Thrusts from his gut, bursting to the air,
Spewed up, on land, headed to Nineveh.
There have been bombs before.

There have been bombs before
As when:

In 1348, at Weymouth,
Along ship's cables, the rats
Nosed ashore, dying and spreading death.
It was the plague. Buboes, like split fruit,
Burst in a million bodies, cousins
Upon cousins, in carts, in pits.
The rotting web of kin, *magna mortalitas,*
Half the kingdom dead. Who knows
Ten thousand faces? Whose is their salvation?
They died of plague, deaths not worked in the cloths
Of war. In the villages, the hand and ink give out,
No one left to write the record, all systems gone.
There have been bombs before.

There have been bombs before
As when:

Gabriel appeared, wings promising
As rainbows, spoke the uncanny words
Of birth, virgin and angel, the twinned
Inclining heads. That time, the lilies
Flowered, and only yes the handmaid
Said and lit the fuse that burned, slow
And gathering, to whips and thorns
And nails, the sunk flesh, the lungs
Sucked in, the caked and stiffening hair.
There have been bombs before.

There have been bombs before
As at:

     The resurrection, the rock rolled
     Back, the body, perfect in its wounds,
     Bursts from the tomb, armour,
     Swords spreadeagled, breath misting
     The mirror. Life breathes, seed of the fruit,
     Not stone but bread, not east, not west,
     A great people in white raiment.
       By a river-side coming to the Lord,
     Pure water raining on pure water.
     To God all things come home.

     Come those
   Who make safe the waters;
Heal sick; make bloods once more
   Corpuscular; give back
   Eyes to the eyeless fish.

     Come those
   Who piece the bodies back
    Draw faces newly to
   The windows of raised-up
Streets; who unpile the stocks.

     Come, come those
Shoulders, arms, the hands,
    That roll back the rock;
    All other bombs annul.

*Ronald Tamplin*
*20th century*

# Epitaph

They hanged him on a clement morning, swung
between the falling sunlight and women's
breathing, like a black apostrophe to pain.
All morning while the children hushed
their hopscotch joy and the cane kept growing
he hung there sweet and low.
                              At least that's how
they tell it. It was long ago
and what can we recall of a dead slave or two
except that when we punctuate our island tale
they swing like sighs across the brutal
sentences, and anger pauses
till they pass away.

*Dennis Scott (Jamaica)*
20th century

# PERSON TO PERSON

## In a Bath Teashop

'Let us not speak, for the love we bear one another –
    Let us hold hands and look.'
She, such a very ordinary little woman;
    He, such a thumping crook;
But both, for a moment, little lower than the angels
    In the teashop's ingle-nook.

*John Betjeman*
*20th century*

# Love

## The Power of Love

It can alter things;
The stormy scowl can become
Suddenly a smile.

The knuckly bunched fist
May open like a flower,
Tender a caress.

Beneath its bright warmth
Black ice of suspicion melts;
Danger is dazzled.

A plain and dull face
Astounds with its radiance
And sudden beauty.

Ordinary things –
Teacups, spoons and sugar-lumps –
Become magical.

The locked door opens;
Inside are leaves and moonlight;
You are welcomed in.

Its delicate strength
Can lift the heaviest heart
And snap hostile steel.

It gives eloquence
To the dumb tongue, makes plain speech
Blaze like poetry.

*Vernon Scannell*
*20th century*

## Friendship

When we were idlers with the loitering rills,
  The need of human love we little noted:
Our love was nature; and the peace that floated
On the white mist, and dwelt upon the hills,
To sweet accord subdued our wayward wills:
  One soul was ours, one mind, one heart devoted,
  That, wisely doting, asked not why it doted,
And ours the unknown joy, which knowing kills.
But now I find how dear thou wert to me;
  That man is more than half of nature's treasure,
Of that fair beauty which no eye can see,
  Of that sweet music which no ear can measure;
  And now the streams may sing for others' pleasure,
The hills sleep on in their eternity.

*Hartley Coleridge*
*1796–1849*

## To Grimold, Abbot of St Gall

Then live, my strength, anchor of weary ships,
  Safe shore and land at last, thou, for my wreck,
My honour, thou, and my abiding rest,
  My city safe for a bewildered heart.
What though the plains and mountains and the sea
  Between us are, that which no earth can hold
Still follows thee, and love's own singing follows,
  Longing that all things may be well with thee.
Christ who first gave thee for a friend to me,
Christ keep thee well, where'er thou art, for me.
  Earth's self shall go and the swift wheel of heaven
Perish and pass, before our love shall cease.
  Do but remember me, as I do thee,
And God, who brought us on this earth together,
  Bring us together in his house of heaven.

*Hrabanus Maurus*
*776–856*
translated from Latin by Helen Waddell

# Sheepstor
## *For Bob Groves*, 1946–78

'WE KNOW THAT THE WHOLE CREATION GROANETH
AND TRAVAILETH IN PAIN TOGETHER UNTIL NOW.'

God's intrusion, upthrust granite
offshoulders layers of sediment,
mantle weathered by God's weather.

The grey creature, lichen, adheres
to tor and tower, to raw and tooled
stone, creation or man's good work.

Granite, a crown not won, but worn
by abraded hills; men made out shapes
in the rock's deeps, holy stone or cross.

This was your place, *Dartmoor mountain;*
you trekked roads and mineral tracks,
mapped its toils, endured its terrors.

A piece of mist bleats and stumbles
away. Sometimes in your spirit
we could make out God's shy image.

Your marrow's fire, all that your bones
suffered, weathered your flesh, stripped you
down to something stubborn, exposed,

your igneous love. At Sheepstor,
above the church, by a large stone
plush with lichen, we scatter ash

and our prayers, all that's left of your
physical mess; grains of clinker
speckle the moor, the rain greets them.

But in memory they persist
like grey wethers grazing the air
to be sold to the credulous.

Credulous, I see the granite,
God's intrusion. One flock, lying
in wait for the resurrection.

*Paul Hyland*
*20th century*

# Wisdom

On a night like this I could wish for wisdom,
To sit outside my kitchen door
In the long twilight hours, draining my glass
And offering my companions more.
What could be better...?
The breeze in our light summer clothing
And blowing the pages of our open Bibles,
Speaking of this world that came from nothing.

*Peter Marshall*
*20th century*

# LOVE BETWEEN MAN AND WOMAN

## True Love

Let me not to the marriage of true minds
Admit impediments. Love is not love
Which alters when it alteration finds,
Or bends with the remover to remove: –
O no! it is an ever-fixèd mark
That looks on tempests, and is never shaken;
It is the star to every wandering bark,
Whose worth's unknown, although his height be taken.
Love's not Time's fool, though rosy lips and cheeks
Within his bending sickle's compass come;
Love alters not with his brief hours and weeks,
But bears it out ev'n to the edge of doom.
If this be error, and upon me proved,
I never writ, nor no man ever loved.

*William Shakespeare*
*1564–1616*

# A Woman's Love

Nothing is to man so dear
As woman's love in good manère.
A good woman is man's bliss
Where her love right and steadfast is.

There is no solace under heaven
Of all that a man may nevene*
That should a man so much glew*
As a good woman that loveth true.
None is dearer in God's herd
Than a chaste woman with lovely word.

*Robert Mannying of Brunne*
*about 1325*

* *nevene*: name; *glew*: gladden

# Contradictions of Love

As fragile as an eggshell bauble
    On a Christmas tree,
But durable as gleaming steel
    Of knife, or sword, or key.

Sweet as the fragrance of the rose
    Or honey from the bee,
But cold and scentless as the snow,
    And salty as the sea.

As gentle as a summer breeze
    Or mother's lullaby,
But burly as a hurricane
    Or thunder in the sky.

As magical as witches' spells
    Or blackbirds in a pie,
But plain and simple as good bread,
    Without which we would die.

*Vernon Scannell*
*20th century*

# The Way They Live Now

You make love and you live together now
Where we were shy and made love by degrees.
By kiss and invitation we learnt how
Our love was growing. You know few of these

Tokens and little gifts, the gaze of eye
To eye, the hand shared with another hand.
You know of few frustrations, seldom cry
With passion's stress, yet do you understand

The little gestures that would mean so much,
The surging hope to be asked to a dance?
You take the whole of love. We lived by touch

And doubt and by the purposes of chance
And yet I think our slow ways carried much
That you have missed – the guess, the wish, the glance.

*Elizabeth Jennings*
*20th century*

# Love Song

I see the pattern of stars and sun
And while they remain
You are fixed in my mind

And the course of the fox and the rabbit
A lad and his lady
The way of a woman with child.

While the waves run onto the beach
And the whale ploughs his road through the ocean
My love reaches out.

As long as the deer runs his race;
Until you can measure the edges of space
I will keep you.

*Cathy Anderson*
*20th century*

# Winter Song

Ask me no more, my truth to prove,
What I would suffer for my love.
With thee I would in exile go
To regions of eternal snow,
O'er floods by solid ice confined,
Through forest bare with northern wind:
While all around my eyes I cast,
Where all is wild and all is waste.
If there the tim'rous stag you chase,
Or rouse to fight a fiercer race,
Undaunted I thy arms would bear,
And give thy hand the hunter's spear.
When the low sun withdraws his light,
And menaces an half-year's night,
The conscious moon and stars above
Shall guide me with my wandering love.
Beneath the mountain's hollow brow,
Or in its rocky cells below,
Thy rural feast I would provide,
Nor envy palaces their pride.
The softest moss should dress thy bed,
With savage spoils about thee spread:
While faithful love the watch should keep,
To banish danger from thy sleep.

*Elizabeth Tollett*
*1694–1754*

# A Marriage Ring

The ring, so worn as you behold,
So thin, so pale, is yet of gold:
The passion such it was to prove –
Worn with life's care, love yet was love.

*George Crabbe*
*1754–1832*

# A Wife to a Husband

(SONNETS FROM THE PORTUGUESE)

How do I love thee? Let me count the ways.
I love thee to the depth and breadth and height
My soul can reach, when feeling out of sight
For the end of Being and ideal Grace.
I love thee to the level of everyday's
Most quiet need, by sun and candlelight.
I love thee freely, as men strive for right;
I love thee purely, as they turn from praise.
I love thee with the passion put to use
In my old griefs, and with my childhood's faith.
I love thee with a love I seemed to lose
With my lost saints, – I love thee with the breath,
Smiles, tears, of all my life! – and, if God choose,
I shall but love thee better after death.

*Elizabeth Barrett Browning*
*1806–61*

# Epithalamion

All our love is deeply (as a folk
tale in the memory of once upon
a time the golden-haired princess awoke
from spellbound slumbers to a carillon
of kisses) grounded in the depth of his
own dying. For the risk of love we dare
(the peasant boy with rustic pleasantries
courted the princess of the golden hair)
because the tale is told (how she was brought
a virgin victim to the dragon's lair,
a bride self-bartered for her people's weal)
of love as strong as death (our hero fought
with death's dark reptile) that our hearts may bear
his true love as an everlasting seal.

*Richard Bauckham*
*20th century*

# Civilisation

Saturday afternoon. Professor Paterson
walks in his garden, bends on his daffodils
looks fond yet stern. His brain, unoccupied, idles.
He hums. Half-heartedly, the watery sun
attempts to gild him, like a saint. He moves
away, deeply ponders a hole in the fence,
reproves a dangling creeper.

   His wife, in the kitchen,
scours the pans. The radio chatters calamity.
Civilisation is teetering to a fall.
Music erupts, with thud and boom and crash
– the mangonels* of the last assault? She sluices
water around the sink. She drops a cup.
It shatters.

   Professor Paterson
sits in his usual chair, and reads. Daffodils
stand in a vase behind him. He looks kindly
over his spectacles. The world settles
back on its base.
   Civilisation, it seems,
is with us yet. She goes to make him tea.

*Evangeline Paterson*
*20th century*

* *mangonel:* a military engine for casting stones

# To my Dear and Loving Husband

If ever two were one, then surely we.
If ever man were loved by wife, then thee;
If ever wife was happy in a man,
Compare me with ye women if you can.
I prize thy love more than whole mines of gold,
Or all the riches that the East doth hold.
My love is such that rivers cannot quench,
Nor aught but love from thee, give recompense.
Thy love is such I can no way repay,
The heavens reward thee manifold, I pray.
Then while we live, in love let's so persever
That when we live no more, we may live ever.

*Anne Bradstreet*
*1612–72*

# The Gate

When they moved into the house he said
'I'll fix that creaking gate one day.'
In later years he changed his tune –
'Creaking gates hang longest – look at me!'
She came to love the gate, it told her things,
told her when he was coming home.

   After the funeral her son said
   'I'll get that gate replaced, Dad
   never got round to it.'

The new gate is silent, swings smooth
on oiled hinges, closes
with a well-ordered click,
but the music has gone out of her life
and she is left with a feeling of betrayal.

*R.P. Fenwick*
*20th century*

# A Marriage

We met
   under a shower
of bird-notes.
   Fifty years passed,
love's moment
   in a world in
servitude to time.
   She was young;
I kissed with my eyes
   closed and opened
them on her wrinkles.
   'Come' said death,
choosing her as his
   partner for
the last dance. And she,
   who in life
had done everything
   with a bird's grace,
opened her bill now
   for the shedding
of one sigh no
   heavier than a feather.

*R.S. Thomas*
20th century

# An Epitaph upon Husband and Wife

To those whom death again did wed
This grave's the second marriage-bed.
For though the hand of Fate could force
'Twixt soul and body a divorce,
It could not sever man and wife,
Because they both lived but one life.
Peace, good reader, do not weep;
Peace; the lovers are asleep.
They, sweet turtles, folded lie
In the last knot that love could tie.
Let them sleep, let them sleep on,
Till the stormy night be gone,
And the eternal morrow dawn;
Then the curtains will be drawn,
And they wake into a light
Whose day shall never die in night.

*Richard Crashaw*
*1613–49*

# On the Death of Sir Albert Morton's Wife

He first deceased – she, for a little tried
To live without him, liked it not and died.

*Sir Henry Wotton*
*1568–1639*

# Introspective

## Alone

*'When I'm alone'* – the words tripped off his tongue
As though to be alone were nothing strange.
*'When I was young,'* he said; *'when I was young...'*

I thought of age, and loneliness, and change.
I thought how strange we grow when we're alone,
And how unlike the selves that meet and talk,
And blow the candle out, and say good night.
*Alone...* The word is life endured and known.
It is the stillness where our spirits walk
And all but inmost faith is overthrown.

*Siegfried Sassoon*
*1886–1967*

## Gold Leaves

Lo! I am come to autumn,
    When all the leaves are gold;
Grey hairs and golden leaves cry out
    The year and I are old.

In youth I sought the prince of men,
    Captain in cosmic wars,
Our Titan, even the weeds would show
    Defiant, to the stars.

But now a great thing in the street
    Seems any human nod,
Where shift in strange democracy
    The million masks of God.

In youth I sought the golden flower
    Hidden in wood or wold,
But I am come to autumn,
    When all the leaves are gold.

*G.K. Chesterton*
*1874–1936*

# Who Shall Deliver Me?

God strengthen me to bear myself;
That heaviest weight of all to bear,
Inalienable weight of care.

All others are outside myself;
I lock my door and bar them out,
The turmoil, tedium, gad-about.

I lock my door upon myself,
And start self-purged upon the race
That all must run! Death runs apace.

If I could set aside myself,
And start with lightened heart upon
The road by all men overgone!

God harden me against myself,
This coward with pathetic voice
Who craves for ease, and rest, and joys:

Myself, arch-traitor to myself;
My hollowest friend, my deadliest foe,
My clog whatever road I go.

Yet one there is can curb myself,
Can roll the strangling load from me,
Break off the yoke and set me free.

*Christina Rossetti*
*1830–94*

# Epitaph

Even such is Time, which takes in trust
Our youth, our joys, and all we have,
And pays us but with age and dust;
Who in the dark and silent grave,
When we have wandered all our ways,
Shuts up the story of our days:
And from which earth, and grave, and dust,
The Lord shall raise me up, I trust.

*Sir Walter Ralegh*
*about 1552–1618*

# Self Ease

My own heart let me more have pity on; let
Me live to my sad self hereafter kind,
Charitable; not live this tormented mind
With this tormented mind tormenting yet.

I cast for comfort I can no more get
By groping round my comfortless, than blind
Eyes in their dark can day or thirst can find
Thirst's all-in-all in all a world of wet.

Soul, self; come, poor Jackself, I do advise
You, jaded, let be; call off thoughts awhile
Elsewhere; leave comfort root-room; let joy size

At God knows when to God knows what; whose smile
's not wrung, see you; unforeseen times rather – as skies
Betweenpie mountains – lights a lovely mile.

*Gerard Manley Hopkins*
*1844–89*

# Thou Shalt Not Kill

I had grown weary of him; of his breath
And hands and features I was sick to death.
Each day I heard the same dull voice and tread;
I did not hate him: but I wished him dead.
And he must with his blank face fill my life –
Then my brain blackened, and I snatched a knife.

But ere I struck, my soul's grey deserts through
A voice cried, 'Know at least what thing you do.
This is a common man: knowest thou, O soul,
What this thing is? somewhere where seasons roll
There is some living thing for whom this man
Is as seven heavens girt into a span,
For some one soul you take the world away –
Now know you well your deed and purpose. Slay!'
Then I cast down the knife upon the ground
And saw that mean man for one moment crowned.
I turned and laughed: for there was no one by –
The man that I had sought to slay was I.

*G.K. Chesterton*
*1874–1936*

# Cock Crow

Wanting to be myself, alone,
Between the lit house and the town
I took the road, and at the bridge
Turned back and walked the way I'd come.

Three times I took that lonely stretch,
Three times the dark trees closed me round,
The night absolved me of my bonds
Only my footsteps held the ground.

My mother and my daughter slept,
One life behind and one before,
And I that stood between denied
Their needs in shutting-to the door.

And walking up and down the road
Knew myself, separate and alone,
Cut off from human cries, from pain,
And love that grows about the bone.

Too brief illusion! Thrice for me
I heard the cock crow on the hill,
And turned the handle of the door
Thinking I knew his meaning well.

*Rosemary Dobson*
*20th century*

# Epitaph

Don't give the children
my ash,
to turn them to dust
when I'm dead.
I lie in
the grain of a star,
safe in earth's crust;
God's bread.

*Isobel Thrilling*
*20th century*

# Sonnet CXLVI

Poor soul, the centre of my sinful earth,
Fooled by these rebel powers that thee array,
Why dost thou pine within and suffer dearth,
Painting thy outward walls so costly gay?
Why so large cost, having so short a lease,
Dost thou upon thy fading mansion spend?
Shall worms, inheritors of this excess,
Eat up thy charge? Is this thy body's end?
Then, soul, live thou upon thy servant's loss,
And let that pine to aggravate thy store;
Buy terms divine in selling hours of dross;
Within be fed, without be rich no more:
   So shalt thou feed on Death, that feeds on men,
   And Death once dead, there's no more dying then.

*William Shakespeare*
*1564–1616*

# Radbod's Epitaph

Hunger and thirst, O Christ, for sight of thee
Came between me and all the feasts of earth.
Give thou thyself the bread, thyself the wine,
Thou, sole provision for the unknown way.
Long hunger wasted the world wanderer,
With sight of thee may he be satisfied.

*Radbod*
*died 917*
*translated by Helen Waddell*

# Samuel Taylor Coleridge

EPITAPH ON HIMSELF

Stop, Christian passer-by! – Stop, child of God,
And read with gentle breast. Beneath this sod
A poet lies, or that which once seem'd he.
O lift one thought in prayer for S.T.C.;
That he who many a year with toil of breath
Found death in life, may here find life in death!
Mercy for praise – to be forgiven for fame
He asked, and hoped, through Christ. Do thou the same!

*Samuel Taylor Coleridge*
*1772–1834*

# Parents and Children

## ABOUT PARENTS

### Obedience

Were my parents right or wrong
not to mow the ripe oats that Sunday morning
with the rainstorm threatening?

I reminded them that the Sabbath was made for man
and of the ox fallen into the pit.
Without an oats crop, I argued,
the cattle would need to survive on town-bought oats
and then it wouldn't pay to keep them.
Isn't selling cattle at a loss like an ox in a pit?

My parents did not argue.
We went to church.
We sang the psalms louder than usual –
we, and the others whose harvests were at stake:

> Jerusalem, where blessing waits,
> Our feet are standing in thy gates.

> God, be merciful to me;
> On thy grace I rest my plea.

Dominie's spur-of-the-moment concession:
'He rides on the clouds, the wings of the storm;
The lightnings and wind his missions perform.'

Dominie made no concessions on sermon length:
'Five Good Reasons for Infant Baptism,'
though we heard little of it,

for more floods came and more winds blew and beat upon that
House than we had figured on, even,
more lightning and thunder
and hail the size of pullet eggs.
Falling branches snapped the electric wires.
We sang the closing psalm without the organ and in the dark

> Ye seed from Abraham descended,
> God's covenant love is never ended.

Afterward we rode by our oat field,
flattened.
'We still will mow it,' Dad said.
'Ten bushels to the acre, maybe, what would have been fifty
if I had mowed right after milking
and if the whole family had shocked.
We could have had it weatherproof before the storm.'

Later at dinner Dad said,
'God was testing us. I'm glad we went.'
'Those psalms never gave me such a lift as this morning.'
Mother said, 'I wouldn't have missed it.' And even I thought
but did not say,
How guilty we would feel if we had saved the harvest!

My father once asked why I live in a black neighbourhood,
and I reminded him of that Sunday morning thirty years ago.
If my sons ever ask me why we live in a black
neighbourhood,
I shall sing my favourite psalm in answer:

> *The Moor, with the Philistine and the Tyrian,*
> *Shall soon, O Zion, throng thy holy gates.*

And I hope my sons will forgive me
(who knows exactly what for?)
as they will hope their sons will forgive them
(who knows exactly what for?)
as I have long ago forgiven my father
(who knows exactly what for?)

Fathers inevitably fail to pass on to sons
their harvest customs
for harvesting grain or real estate or any crop.
But Christian fathers pass on to sons
another more important pattern
defined as absolutely as muddlers like us can manage:
obedience.

*Sietze Buning*
*20th century*

# For my Mother

V

SUDDEN REMEMBRANCE

Orphaned and elderly and yet a child,
For so I am when thoughts of you return,
Return and batter me and I'm not mild
But close to tears and scarred for these tears burn.
You tamed me when most wild,

You comforted my nightmares, came and sat
Beside my bed when sleep was far away.
You were a healing presence. More than that,
You were a joy, a treasure, could display
High spirits when the flat

Dull mood took charge of me. You always were
Busy and quick and swift to suffer too,
But only now and then did I know fear
When I could see a troubled look on you.
Tonight you feel so dear.

It is a cold wet June, the flowers are blown
In tangled throngs, the charcoal clouds hang near
The tousled tree-tops. Had we ever known
So dull a June? I doubt it. How I care
For you. Where have you gone?

My faith speaks of another life and I
Find your nature a right proof of that.
A child, I'd have you crowned up in the sky,
And growing old I see your star well set.
O your death will not die.

*Elizabeth Jennings*
*20th century*

# PARENTS AND CHILDREN

## Having Our Tea

There's something religious in the way we sit
At the tea table, a tidy family of three.
You, my love, slicing the bread and butter, and she,
The red-cheeked tot a smear of blackberry jam, and me...
A new creation is established, a true presence.
And talking to each other, breaking words over food
Is somehow different from customary chatting.

*Bobi Jones (originally in Welsh)*
*20th century*

## The Catalyst

Long after the birth,
she held up the X-ray
of her second-born son
in the womb.

There he hung
against the light,
head-down to the lintel,
translucent
as wax in a glass.

What she saw
was not simply
the curve of the spine,
the seal at the cervix,

but sacrament brightly stilled;
an angelical stone
that cannot be weighed;

the catalyst
of sun through wax –
the ghostly body –
at the casual supper
Christ eating the honeycomb.

*Pauline Stainer*
*20th century*

# Enigma

O Lord support
all the day long
him whom you have
builded wrong.
Squirrel of the children he
hoarding to himself the map
of his singularity.

Through his half eyes
in thrust back head
what he sees
he has not said.
His squirrel fingers do not well
clutch the things he loves and still
unsprung his tongue his loves to tell.

O Lord a lark
trapped in his breast
that beats
and will not give him rest.
Inside his mouth it beats its wings
And stops his lips and makes him cry
and quivering in him it sings.

Lord, loose the lark
that here is trapped
and trace the maze
that you have mapped.
Squirrel light yet lead with weight
what you mismade do not desert
speak to the inarticulate.

*Patience Tuckwell*
*20th century*

# Three a.m. – A Mother Waits

Nuns keep vigil with psalm and measured voice;
nurses manoeuvre amidst groans and snores.
Rocked against the long-drawn ticking night,
dry-mouthed, driven from sleep, I wait,
imagine in each bang and engine noise
the overdue return, the rasping key.
Get up, grope for his empty bed and pray
no less devoutly than the devoted soeurs,
as anxiously as nurses watch for day.
Morning is now four short hours away.
The wind blows litter over silent streets.
Dossers and drunks find huddled brief respite
and junkies dream gaunt nightmares. My fears
fuse with relief and fury – the boy appears.

*Jenny Robertson*
*20th century*

# Two Women

Two women meet each morning to pray
One is a mother, the other her daughter
They belong to different religions
Only blood binds them together

Stephen is the object of their prayer
He is the grandson of one, the son of the other
He lives abroad
He does not want to come home
He wants to be left alone

So the women pray silently – each in her own way
Their words do not cross
They rise and converge
Stephen will be safe for another day.

*Neville Braybrooke*
*20th century*

# A Wish for my Children

On this doorstep I stand
year after year
and watch you leaving

and think: May you not
skin your knees. May you
not catch your fingers
in car doors. May
your hearts not break.

May tide and weather
wait for your coming

and may you grow strong
to break
all webs of my weaving.

*Evangeline Paterson*
*20th century*

## CRADLE SONGS

## *From:* A Cradle Song

Hush! my dear, lie still and slumber,
   Holy Angels guard thy bed!
Heavenly blessings without number
   Gently falling on thy head.

Sleep, my babe; thy food and raiment,
   House and home, thy friends provide;
All without thy care or payment,
   All thy wants are well supplied.

How much better thou'rt attended
   Than the Son of God could be,
When from heaven he descended,
   And became a child like thee!

Soft and easy is thy cradle:
   Coarse and hard thy Saviour lay:
When his birthplace was a stable,
   And his softest bed was hay...

Lo, he slumbers in his manger,
    Where the hornèd oxen fed;
– Peace, my darling, here's no danger;
    Here's no ox a-near thy bed!

May'st thou live to know and fear him,
    Trust and love him all thy days;
Then go dwell for ever near him,
    See his face, and sing his praise!

*Isaac Watts*
*1674–1748*

# A Lullaby

Lullee, lullay,
I could not love thee more
If thou wast Christ the King.
Now tell me, how did Mary know
That in her womb should sleep and grow
The Lord of everything?

Lullee, lullay,
An angel stood with her
Who said, 'That which doth stir
Like summer in thy side
Shall save the world from sin.
Then stable, hall and inn
Shall cherish Christmas-tide.'

Lullee, lullay,
And so it was that day.
And did she love him more
Because an angel came
To prophesy his name?
Ah no, not so,
She could not love him more,
But loved him just the same.
Lullee, lullee, lullay.

*Janet Lewis*
*born 1899*

# Youth and Age

## The Old Woman

As a white candle in a holy place
So is the beauty of an agèd face.

As the spent radiance of the winter sun
So is a woman with her travail done.

Her brood gone from her and her thoughts as still
As the waters under a ruined mill.

*Joseph Campbell*
*1879–1944*

## Old Woman to Cat

Cat, smoother soother than a velvet glove,
How can you thus reply to my caress?
In giving, I receive the touch of love
Yet the gnarled knuckle and the brown age-blotch
Are there for those mysterious eyes to watch
And I thought beauty shrank from ugliness.

Queen Cat, to whom I kneel with joints that creak,
There is no grace in my antiquity
But only movements difficult and weak,
Whereas you move with pure fluidity.
Bear with me, lovely one, and though I grow
Unlovelier still, pretend you do not know.

*M. Bond*
*20th century*

# New Every Day

I'd never wish my childhood back to me.
But there at least we knew the laws
that ruled the universe of every day, when we, being tied,
were free.
Poverty, dependency, best friends, go side by side;
we were only children and, for children, someone can decide.

I hope that they still
give this great freedom of the will
to kids who only need to concentrate
upon what's on the plate.
You cannot fight the dragons of tomorrow
till tomorrow comes,
because you don't know what they are....
today is sums.

My early schooling is a parable
of something given before we knew the need.
The blackboard cleaned in chalky clouds,
erasing name and deed;
forgotten was forgiven.

And chairs
stacked on top of little desks,
and prayers...
hands together, eyes not quite closed
and then a chanted spell,
our sing-song farewell.
And then... The Bell.

It burst like dams the classrooms
and corridors, rivers, flowed with us.
Cloakrooms and the clang
of buckets said the rule of school
cleaners had begun.
They swept us out towards the gate,
where our mothers, outlaws,
waited.
Then, long after, very late,
Night, like a caretaker
locked all the doors.

Piecemeal we lived, new every day
and kept no scores.
All our fights were silly little ones.
Battles, not wars.

*Patience Tuckwell*
*20th century*

## 'You Don't Know What to Do When You Get Old'

In the shuffling melancholy
of life's grey haired rituals
where the misplaced pension book
routine becomes habitual
a nation of confused dissenters
huddles in the aftermath
of governmental legislation
video shops and sauna baths

Left to doze in plastic armchairs
nodding in and out of woe
hearts prepared for termination
by a babbling TV show
dignity of fading people
thin anxiety in their walk
some will freeze whilst some will fall
into repetitious talk
Soon the functional undertaker
watches yet one more last kiss
the coffin's sealed as grief consumes
there must be more to death than this.

*Stewart Henderson*
*20th century*

# Old Woman

See where she sits now,
The green-fern twilight
Green-staining her bones
Almost,
The dust motes dancing
Round her who to dust
Is returned,
Almost.
Inside the fragile
Domed head that is
Skull, almost,
And in and out the eyes
Dart fishtail shadows
Of noonday passions
And midnight terrors
That cause no flicker now
In her moonstone stare.
Sunk fathoms deep now
To where lies only
In the green-fern gloom
The enduring bone.

*Evangeline Paterson*
*20th century*

# Four-Square Gospel

Old Uncle Fred could squint along forty-foot beams
And catch the gentlest wayward drift toward a curve
That no one else saw. His calloused, pitch-stained hands
Would tenderly stroke the flush seams of a perfect joint.
We used to see him astride his unwavering rafters,
Tall as the echoing blows of his worshipping arms,
Looking with pride on the loving work of his mitred,
Four-square world. He always looked sharply to see
If some sinning board in somebody's house were off square,
And longed to redeem it with the righteous tongue of his plane.

And then he slumped into arches and curves of age,
Propped up in a bed, looking out at the slanted east
While unseen termites encircled his squared-off house.
Puzzled, he eyed the long, sad arc of the geese,
The easy bend of a tree-limb heavy with fruit,
And then – we knew by the softening line of his mouth –
Saw the curve of a neck swinging free from the beams of a cross.

*Roderick Jellema*
*20th century*

# From: Rabbi Ben Ezra

Grow old along with me!
The best is yet to be,
The last of life, for which the first was made:
    Our times are in his hand
    Who saith 'A whole I planned,
Youth shows but half; trust God: see all nor be afraid!'...

    Not on the vulgar mass
    Called 'work' must sentence pass,
Things done, that took the eye and had the price:
    O'er which, from level stand,
    The low world laid its hand,
Found straightway to its mind, could value in a trice:

    But all, the world's coarse thumb
    And finger failed to plumb,
So passed in making up the main account:
    All instincts immature,
    All purposes unsure,
That weighed not as his work, yet swelled the man's amount:

    Thoughts hardly to be packed
    Into a narrow act,
Fancies that broke through language and escaped;
    All I could never be,
    All, men ignored in me,
This, I was worth to God, whose wheel the pitcher shaped...

    But I need, now as then,
    Thee, God, who mouldest men;
And since, not even while the whirl was worst,
    Did I, – to the wheel of life
    With shapes and colours rife,
Bound dizzily, – mistake my end, to slake thy thirst:

    So, take and use thy work:
    Amend what flaws may lurk,
What strains o' the stuff, what warpings past the aim!
    My times be in thy hand!
    Perfect the cup as planned!
Let age approve of youth, and death complete the same!

*Robert Browning*
*1812–89*

# Communion for the Aged

Hands that steered the tractor,
arranging properly the day's soil,
ploughed autumn toward sundown,
grateful to hear darkness fall,
harvested wheat that read
forty bushels an acre,
talked to cows with milk pails,
filling with a steady swish
the empty bottom, then adding
three gallons more,
sweat tears as they knocked
against locked doors of life,
hungered and held silent communion
with chicken and fried potatoes;
knuckles now gnarled like the old oak
trunks they watered to green the prairies,
useless now except to dream of plough or udder
or of dying, bow and tremble as they take
bread and wine, body and blood
passed from one veined hand to another.

*Elmer F. Suderman*
*20th century*

# Unacceptables

Aged, infirm and incontinent,
They come to Sunday and to prayers
From ward behind recessed ward;
Buttoned to beds and chairs,
Buttoned to stiff upright clothes,
They come, not to see
Not to hear, not to respond;
Yet who knows what offering
Their ills make upon the altars?
Eroded out of the world's way,
They have been folded, closeted
Like old linens, old faces like embroidered linen
Folded in upon themselves, unacceptable
Longer to kin and to community;
Yet who knows in this communion
How they may be adequate
In the sight of one likewise unacceptable
To those he lived among, the outcast
Buttoned to crossed hoists and spat upon?

*Nancy Westerfield*
*20th century*

# Old Age

The maples are burning,
Kindled with a silent flame,
Like russet torches in the forest depths.
I hear no splutter or crackle of resin,
yet they burn and burn.

Does he see them,
Offering this last sacrifice of summer?
Does he see them in a different time,
Flower in fire,
And suddenly put on winter?

For us in exquisite slowness,
They turn in the cool embrace of Autumn.
In silent dance,
The leaves curl, blush, flame out,
In appalling submission,
To bring him this yearly gift of colour,
amid the Autumn drab.

Lord, in my old age grant me
One last passionate flowering –
Let love burn off my summer green,
In sudden, splendid fire.

*Tim Marks*
*20th century*

# Grandparents

## Grannie

I stayed with her when I was six then went
To live elsewhere when I was eight years old.
For ages I remembered her faint scent
Of lavender, the way she'd never scold
No matter what I'd done, and most of all
The way her smile seemed, somehow, to enfold
My whole world like a warm, protective shawl.

I knew that I was safe when she was near,
She was so tall, so wide, so large, she would
Stand mountainous between me and my fear,
Yet oh, so gentle, and she understood
Every hope and dream I ever had.
She praised me lavishly when I was good,
But never punished me when I was bad.

Years later war broke out and I became
A soldier and was wounded while in France.
Back home in hospital, still very lame,
I realized suddenly that circumstance
Had brought me close to that small town where she
Was living still. And so I seized the chance
To write and ask if she could visit me.

She came. And I still vividly recall
The shock that I received when she appeared
That dark cold day. Huge grannie was so small!
A tiny, frail, old lady. It was weird.
She hobbled through the ward to where I lay
And drew quite close and, hesitating, peered.
And then she smiled: and love lit up the day.

*Vernon Scannell*
*20th century*

# Grandmother: Dying

Aged in one stroke
the old woman lies
in silence,
her lips caved in
in unaccustomed severity
around her toothless gums.

Yet she is not without
dignity. The lines
of her life betray
no hidden gall,
no secret sin for years
eating at her conscience.

Others shout and scream,
abuse their nurses, and
their long-dead husbands.
The grace she learned
in childhood
still wears new.

And when she speaks to us
and says, 'I've been
talking with an angel,'
we know that if our eyes
were opened we would see
a company of angels
standing at her wounded side.

*John Leax*
*20th century*

# The Way of All Flesh

You were, till now
When I stepped in, unexpected,
To ask you to do mending,
Never old, just – Grandma.
But today, your hair down,
Flying about your face in aged frizzes,
As you sat facing an evening alone
And talked of the pain returning
(For the first time with a shade of 'Why?')
You suddenly seemed all your eighty years.

I came home to tell you, 'Mother,
Grandma is suddenly old.'
You were on the couch,
Collapsed after another day's work
Slightly harder than yesterday's,
Your second chin appearing
And more new crow's feet,
Facing an evening of ironing.
I choked the words back,
Not sure why.

And you, self in the mirror,
First crow's feet just appearing
(But only when I'm tired),
Frizzes not from age but choice,
Your freshness slightly faded,
Why so wooden?
Had you forgotten
The way of all fall flesh?

*Carol Addink*
*20th century*

# Time and Eternity

## Last Aid

Time's running out,
(as life-blood seeps
out of a mortal wound).
Nothing now,
short of eternity,
shall ever serve to staunch it!

*Grace Westerduin*
*20th century*

## Cool Siloam

By cool Siloam's shady rill
  How sweet the lily grows!
How sweet the breath beneath the hill
  Of Sharon's dewy rose!

Lo, such the child whose early feet
  The paths of peace have trod;
Whose secret heart, with influence sweet,
  Is upward drawn to God.

By cool Siloam's shady rill
  The lily must decay;
The rose that blooms beneath the hill
  Must shortly fade away.

And soon, too soon, the wintry hour
  Of man's maturer age
Will shake the soul with sorrow's power,
  And stormy passion's rage...

Dependent on thy bounteous breath,
  We seek thy grace alone,
In childhood, manhood, age and death,
  To keep us still thine own!

*Reginald Heber*
*1783–1826*

## Give T'anks

Anodda year of love.
Give t'anks. An' pray
dat God-Above
will seh to time, No way,
No way:
de word is love.

*Mervyn Morris*
*20th century*

# Knole

The white hill-side is prickled with antlers
And the deer wade to me through the snow.
From John Donne's church the muffled and galoshed
Patiently to their holy dinners go.

And never do those antlered heads reflect
On the gentle flanks where in autumn they put their seed
Nor Christians on the word which, that very hour,
Their upturned faces or their hearts received.

But spring will bring the heavy doe to bed;
The fawn will wobble and soon after leap.
Those others will die at this or the next year's turn
And find the resurrection encased in sleep.

*C.H. Sisson*
*20th century*

# Change Should Breed Change

New doth the sun appear,
The mountains' snows decay,
Crowned with frail flowers forth comes the baby year.
My soul, time posts away,
And thou yet in that frost
Which flower and fruit hath lost,
As if all here immortal were, dost stay:
For shame! thy powers awake,
Look to that heaven which never night makes black,
And there, at that immortal sun's bright rays,
Deck thee with flowers which fear not rage of days.

*William Drummond of Hawthornden*
*1585–1649*

## From: A Prayer for the Past

All sights and sounds of day and year,
All groups and forms, each leaf and gem,
Are thine, O God, nor will I fear
To talk to thee of them.

Too great thy heart is to despise,
Whose day girds centuries about;
From things which we name small, thine eyes
See great things looking out.

Therefore the prayerful song I sing
May come to thee in ordered words:
Though lowly born, it needs not cling
In terror to its chords.

I think that nothing made is lost;
That not a moon has ever shone,
That not a cloud my eyes hath crossed
But to my soul is gone.

That all the lost years garnered lie
In this thy casket, my dim soul;
And thou wilt, once, the key apply,
And show the shining whole.

*George MacDonald*
*1824–1905*

## To my Watch

Little monitor, by thee
Let me learn what I should be;
Learn the round of life to fill,
Useful and progressive still.
Thou can'st gentle hints impart
How to regulate the heart;
When I wind thee up at night,
Mark each fault and set thee right,
Let me search my bosom too,
And my daily thoughts review;
Mark the movements of my mind,
Nor be easy till I find
Latent errors brought to view,
Till all be regular and true.

*Anne Steele*
*died 1779?*

# On Time

Fly envious Time, till thou run out thy race,
Call on the lazy leaden-stepping hours,
Whose speed is but the heavy plummets pace;
And glut thy self with what thy womb devours,
Which is no more than what is false and vain,
And merely mortal dross;
So little is our loss,
So little is thy gain.
For when as each thing bad thou hast entombed,
And last of all, thy greedy self consumed,
Then long eternity shall greet our bliss
With an individual kiss;
And joy shall overtake us as a flood
When everything that is sincerely good
And perfectly divine,
With truth, and peace, and love shall ever shine
About the supreme throne
Of him, t'whose happy-making sight alone,
When once our heavenly-guided soul shall climb,
Then all this earthy grossness quit,
Attired with stars, we shall for ever sit,
Triumphing over death, and chance, and thee, O Time.

*John Milton*
*1608–74*

# *From:* Contemplations

O Time the fatal wrack of mortal things,
That draws oblivious curtains over kings,
Their sumptuous monuments, men know them not,
Their names without a record are forgot,
Their parts, their ports, their pomp's all laid in th' dust
Nor wit nor gold, nor buildings scape times rust;
But he whose name is graved in the white stone
Shall last and shine when all of these are gone.

*Anne Bradstreet*
*1612–72*

## *From:* Hurrying Time

My glass is half unspent; forbear to arrest
My thriftless day too soon: my poor request
Is, that my glass may run but out the rest.

My time-devourèd minutes will be done
Without thy help; see, see how swift they run:
Cut not my thread before my thread be spun.

The gain's not great I purchase by this stay;
What loss sustain'st thou by so small delay,
To whom ten thousand years are but a day?

My following eye can hardly make a shift
To count my wingèd hours; they fly so swift,
They scarce deserve the bounteous name of gift.

The secret wheels of hurrying time do give
So short a warning, and so fast they drive,
That I am dead before I seem to live.

And what's a life? a weary pilgrimage,
Whose glory in one day doth fill thy stage
With childhood, manhood, and decrepit age...

Read on this dial, how the shades devour
My short-lived winter's day; hour eats up hour;
Alas! the total's but from eight to four...

Shade not that dial, night will blind too soon;
My non-aged day already points to noon;
How simple is my suit! how small my boon!...

I have a world of sins to be lamented;
I have a sea of tears that must be vented:
O spare till then; and then I die contented.

*Francis Quarles*
*1592–1644*

## From: Times Go by Turns

The lopped tree in time may grow again,
  Most naked plants renew both fruit and flower;
The sorriest wight may find release of pain,
  The driest soil suck in some moistening shower.
    Times go by turns, and chances change by course,
    From foul to fair, from better hap to worse.

The sea of fortune doth not ever flow,
  She draws her favours to the lowest ebb;
Her tides hath equal times to come and go,
  Her loom doth weave the fine and coarsest web.
    No joy so great but runneth to an end,
    No hap so hard but may in fine amend.

Not always fall of leaf, nor ever spring,
  No endless night, yet not eternal day;
The saddest birds a season find to sing,
  The roughest storm a calm may soon allay.
    Thus with succeeding turns, God tempereth all,
    That man may hope to rise, yet fear to fall.

A chance may win that by mischance was lost;
The net, that holds no great, takes little fish;
In some things all, in all things none are crossed;
Few all they need, but none have all they wish.
Unmeddled joys here to no man befall;
Who least, hath some; who most, hath never all.

*Robert Southwell*
*1561–95*

# Death and Beyond

## Wait

These are
the good
old days.

Just wait
and see.

*Steve Turner*
*20th century*

## Eternity

Because I could not stop for Death
He kindly stopped for me,
The carriage held but just ourselves –
And immortality.

We slowly drove, he knew no haste,
And I had put away
My labour and my leisure too,
For his civility.

We passed the school, where children strove
At recess, in the ring,
We passed the fields of gazing grain,
We passed the setting sun –

Or rather, he passed us;
The dews drew quivering and chill;
For only gossamer, my gown,
My tippet only tulle.

We paused before a house that seemed
A swelling of the ground,
The roof was scarcely visible,
The cornice in the ground.

Since then 'tis centuries, and yet
Feels shorter than the day
I first surmised the horses' heads
Were towards eternity.

*Emily Dickinson*
*1830–86*

# Eternity

He who bends to himself a joy
Does the wingèd life destroy;
But he who kisses the joy as it flies
Lives in eternity's sunrise.

*William Blake*
*1757–1827*

# Christ in the Universe

With this ambiguous earth
His dealings have been told us. These abide:
The signal to a maid, the human birth,
The lesson, and the young Man crucified.

But not a star of all
The innumerable host of stars has heard
How he administered this terrestrial ball.
Our race have kept their Lord's entrusted Word...

No planet knows that this
Our wayside planet, carrying land and wave,
Love and life multipled, and pain and bliss,
Bears, as chief treasure, one forsaken grave.

Nor, in our little day,
May his devices with the heavens be guessed,
His pilgrimage to thread the Milky Way,
Or his bestowals there be manifest.

But, in the eternities,
Doubtless we shall compare together, hear
A million alien Gospels, in what guise
He trod the Pleiades, the Lyre, the Bear.

O be prepared, my soul!
To tread the inconceivable, to scan
The million forms of God those stars unroll
When, in our turn, we show to them a Man.

*Alice Meynell*
*1847–1922*

# Death

## Death Blessing

May the Father take you
  In his fragrant clasp of love,
When you go across the flooding streams
  And the black river of death

*Traditional Celtic*
*Collected by Alexander Carmichael*
*9th century*

## The Soul's Garment

Great Nature clothes the soul, which is but thin,
With fleshly garments, which the Fates do spin;
And when these garments are grown old and bare,
With sickness torn, Death takes them off with care,
And folds them up in peace and quiet rest,
And lays them safe within an earthly chest:
Then scours them well and makes them sweet and clean,
Fit for the soul to wear those clothes again.

*Margaret Cavendish, Duchess of Newcastle*
*1625–73*

# To Death

Thou bidst me come away,
And I'll no longer stay,
Than for to shed some tears
For faults of former years;
And to repent some crimes,
Done in the present times:
And next, to take a bit
Of bread, and wine with it:
To don my robes of love,
Fit for the place above;
To gird my loins about
With charity throughout;
And so to travail hence
With feet of innocence:
These done, I'll only cry
*God Mercy!* and so die.

*Robert Herrick*
*1591–1674*

# Crossing the Bar

Sunset and evening star,
    And one clear call for me!
And may there be no moaning of the bar,
    When I put out to sea,

But such a tide as moving seems asleep,
    Too full for sound and foam,
When that which drew from out the boundless deep
    Turns again home.

Twilight and evening bell,
    And after that the dark!
And may there be no sadness of farewell,
    When I embark;

For though from out our bourne of Time and Place
    The flood may bear me far,
I hope to see my Pilot face to face
    When I have crossed the bar.

*Alfred Lord Tennyson*
*1809–92*

# Miserere

Miserere, my Maker,
O have mercy on me, wretch, strangely distressèd,
Cast down with sin oppressèd;
Mightily vexed to the soul's bitter anguish,
E'en to the death I languish.
Yet let it please thee
To hear my ceaseless crying:
Miserere, miserere, I am dying.

Miserere, my Saviour,
I, alas, am for my sins fearfully grievèd,
And cannot be relievèd
But by thy death, which thou didst suffer for me,
Wherefore I adore thee.
And do beseech thee
To hear my ceaseless crying:
Miserere, miserere, I am dying.

Holy Spirit, miserere,
Comfort my distressèd soul, grieved for youth's folly,
Purge, cleanse and make it holy;
With thy sweet due of grace and peace inspire me,
How I desire thee.
And strengthen me now
In this, my ceaseless crying:
Miserere, miserere, I am dying.

*Anonymous*
*about 1615*

# Deathbed

Now, when the frail and fine-spun
Web of mortality
Gapes, and lets slip
What we have loved so long
From out our lighted present
Into the trackless dark

We turn, blinded,
Not to the Christ in Glory,
Stars about his feet,

But to the Son of Man,
Back from the tomb,
Who built fires, ate fish,
Spoke with friends, and walked
A dusty road at evening.

Here, in this room, in
This stark and timeless moment,
We hear those footsteps

And
With suddenly lifted hearts
Acknowledge
The irrelevance of death.

*Evangeline Paterson*
*20th century*

# Prospice

Fear death? – to feel the fog in my throat,
   The mist in my face,
When the snows begin, and the blasts denote
   I am nearing the place,
The power of the night, the press of the storm,
   The post of the foe;
Where he stands, the Arch Fear in a visible form,
   Yet the strong man must go:
For the journey is done and the summit attained,
   And the barriers fall,
Though a battle's to fight ere the guerdon be gained,
   The reward of it all.
I was ever a fighter, so – one fight more,
   The best and the last!
I would hate that death bandaged my eyes, and forebore,
   And bade me creep past.
No! let me taste the whole of it, fare like my peers
   The heroes of old,
Bear the brunt, in a minute pay glad life's arrears
   Of pain, darkness and cold.
For sudden the worst turns the best to the brave,
   The black minute's at end,
And the element's rage, the fiend-voices that rave,
   Shall dwindle, shall blend,
Shall change, shall become first a peace out of pain,
   Then a light, then thy breast,
O thou soul of my soul! I shall clasp thee again,
   And with God be the rest!

*Robert Browning*
*1812–89*

# Bede's Death Song

Before he leaves on his fated journey
No man will be so wise that he need not
Reflect while time still remains
Whether his soul will win delight
Or darkness after his death-day.

*From Cuthbert's account of Bede's death*
*about 735*

# The Border

What shall avail me
When I reach the border?
This staff will fail me,
This pass all in order.

These words I have learned
Will not help me then,
These honours hard earned,
And applause of men.

My harp truly set
Will break string by string;
I shall quite forget
That once I could sing.

Absence pure and cold
Of sense and memory
Lightly will hold
All that is me.

All, all will fail me,
Tongue, foot and hand.
Strange I shall hale me
To that strange land.

*Edwin Muir*
*1887–1959*

# Before the Beginning

Before the beginning thou hast foreknown the end,
Before the birthday the death-bed was seen of thee:
Cleanse what I cannot cleanse, mend what I cannot mend,
O Lord, All-Merciful, be merciful to me.

While the end is drawing near I know not mine end;
Birth I recall not, my death I cannot foresee:
O God, arise to defend, arise to befriend,
O Lord All-Merciful, be merciful to me.

*Christina Rossetti*
*1830–94*

# Extreme Unction

Upon the eyes, the lips, the feet,
  On all the passages of sense,
The atoning oil is spread with sweet
  Renewal of lost innocence.

The feet, that lately ran so fast
  To meet desire, are soothly sealed;
The eyes, that were so often cast
  On vanity, are touched and healed.

From troublous sights and sounds set free;
  In such a twilight hour of breath,
Shall one retrace his life, or see,
  Through shadows, the true face of death?

Vials of mercy! Sacring oils!
  I know not where nor when I come,
Nor through what wanderings and toils,
  To crave of you Viaticum.

Yet, when the walls of flesh grow weak,
  In such an hour, it may be,
Through mist and darkness, light will break,
  And each anointed sense will see.

*Ernest Dowson*
*1867–1900*

# Last Verses

The seas are quiet when the winds give o'er;
So calm are we when passions are no more.
For then we know how vain it was to boast
Of fleeting things, so certain to be lost.
Clouds of affection from our younger eyes
Conceal that emptiness which age descries.

The soul's dark cottage, battered and decayed,
Lets in new light through chinks that Time hath made:
Stronger by weakness, wiser, men become
As they draw near to their eternal home.
Leaving the old, both worlds at once they view
That stand upon the threshold of the new.

*Edmund Waller*
*1606–87*

# Death, be not Proud

Death, be not proud, though some have called thee
Mighty and dreadful, for thou art not so;
For those whom thou thinkst thou dost overthrow
Die not, poor Death, nor yet canst thou kill me.
From rest and sleep, which but thy pictures be,
Much pleasure – then, from thee much more must flow;
And soonest our best men with thee do go,
Rest of their bones and soul's delivery.
Thou'rt slave to fate, chance, kings, and desperate men,
And dost with poison, war, and sickness dwell;
And poppy or charms can make us sleep as well,
And better than thy stroke. Why swellst thou then?
One short sleep past, we wake eternally,
And death shall be no more. Death, thou shalt die.

*John Donne*
*1572–1631*

# A Contemplation Upon Flowers

Brave flowers – that I could gallant it like you,
    And be as little vain!
You come abroad, and make a harmless show,
    And to your beds of earth again.
You are not proud: you know your birth:
For your embroidered garments are from earth.

You do obey your months and times, but I
    Would have it ever Spring:
My fate would know no Winter, never die,
    Nor think of such a thing.
O that I could my bed of earth but view
And smile, and look as cheerfully as you!

O teach me to see Death and not to fear,
    But rather to take truce!
How often have I seen you at a bier,
    And there look fresh and spruce!
You fragrant flowers! then teach me, that my breath
Like yours may sweeten and perfume my death.

*Henry King*
*1592–1669*

# Eternity, I'm Coming

A wife at daybreak I shall be,
Sunrise, thou hast a flag for me?
At midnight I am yet a maid –
How short it takes to make it bride!
Then, Midnight, I have passed from thee
Unto the East and Victory.

Midnight, 'Good night'
I hear thee call.
The angels bustle in the hall,
Softly my Future climbs the stair,
I fumble at my childhood's prayer –
So soon to be a child no more!
Eternity, I'm coming, sir –
Master, I've seen that face before.

*Emily Dickinson*
*1830–86*

# Dark Verge of Life

Be near me when my light is low,
    When the blood creeps, and the nerves prick
    And tingle; and the heart is sick
And all the wheels of Being slow.

Be near me when the sensuous frame
    Is racked with pangs that conquer trust;
    And Time, a maniac scattering dust,
And Life, a Fury slinging flame.

Be near me when my faith is dry,
    And men the flies of latter spring,
    That lay their eggs, and sting and sing
And weave their petty cells and die.

Be near me when I fade away,
    To point the term of human strife,
    And on the low dark verge of life
The twilight of eternal day.

*Alfred Lord Tennyson*
*1809–92*

# Come Quickly, Lord, and Take Me

Never weather-beaten sail more willing bent to shore,
  Never tired pilgrim's limbs affected slumber more,
Than my weary spirit now longs to fly out of my troubled breast,
O come quickly, sweetest Lord, and take my soul to rest!

Ever blooming are the joys of heaven's high paradise,
Cold age deafs not there our ears nor vapour dims our eyes:
Glory there the sun outshines; whose beams the blessed only see,
O come quickly, glorious Lord, and raise my sprite to thee!

*Thomas Campion*
*1567–1620*

# A Prayer Before Death

FROM: THE BATTLE OF MALDON
(FOUGHT IN AD 991)

I give you thanks, Lord God of nations,
For all the worldly joys that I have known.
But now, gracious Maker, I have the greatest need
That you grant my spirit to God,
That my soul may set out to you,
Prince of Angels, going in peace
Into your power. I pray
That the hell-fiends may not humiliate me.

*Anonymous*
*written soon after 991*

# Death Prayer

O God, give me of thy wisdom,
O God, give me of thy mercy,
O God, give me of thy fulness,
And of thy guidance in face of every strait.

O God, give me of thy holiness,
O God, give me of thy shielding,
O God, give me of thy surrounding,
And of thy peace in the knot of my death.

O give me of thy surrounding,
  And of thy peace at the hour of my death!

*Traditional Celtic*
*Collected by Alexander Carmichael*
*19th century*

# Mercy in our Time

Let not mistaken mercy
blind my fading sight,
no false euphoria lull me.
I would not unprepared
take this last journey.
Give me a light to guide me
through dark valleys,
a staff to lean upon,
bread to sustain me,
a blessing in my ear
that fear may not assail me.
Then leaving do not hold my hand,
I go to meet a friend –
   that same who traced
   compassion in the sand.

*Nancy Hopkins*
*20th century*

357

# Dominus Illuminatio Mea

In the hour of death, after this life's whim,
When the heart beats low, and the eyes grow dim,
And pain has exhausted every limb –
   The lover of the Lord shall trust in him.

When the will has forgotten the lifelong aim,
And the mind can only disgrace its fame,
And a man is uncertain of his own name –
   The power of the Lord shall fill this frame.

When the last sigh is heaved, and the last tear shed,
And the coffin is waiting beside the bed,
And the widow and child forsake the dead –
   The angel of the Lord shall lift this head.

For even the purest delight may pall,
And power must fail, and the pride must fall,
And the love of the dearest friends grow small –
   But the glory of the Lord is all in all.

*Richard Doddridge Blackmore*
*1825–1900*

# On the Death of Others

## For a Friend Dying

(1 JOHN 4:7–10)

When light broadens behind the curtains, and I wake
    to my peaceful morning,
my thoughts go at once to you, setting out on your slow
    day's business of dying.

In the midst of my life I am living your death, seeing
    with your eyes the shining
of sun on the leaf. All day I am keeping pace
    with your slow journey

and wishing that those you love may be there to send you
    – from love into Love going –
and may you launch out gently into the dark
    like keel into water moving.

*Evangeline Paterson*
*20th century*

## In Memory of my Dear Grandchild

WHO DECEASED JUNE 20 1669, BEING THREE YEARS AND SEVEN MONTHS OLD

With troubled heart and trembling hand I write,
The heavens have changed to sorrow my delight.
How oft with disappointment have I met,
When I on fading things my hopes have set.
Experience might 'fore this have made me wise,
To value things according to their price.
Was ever stable joy yet found below?
Or perfect bliss without mixture of woe?
I knew she was but as a withering flower,
That's here today, perhaps gone in an hour;
Like as a bubble, or the brittle glass,
Or like a shadow turning as it was.
More fool then I to look on that was lent
As if mine own, when thus impermanent.
Farewell dear child, thou ne'er shall come to me,
But yet a while, and I shall go to thee;
Meanwhile my throbbing heart's cheered up with this:
Thou with thy Saviour art in endless bliss.

*Anne Bradstreet*
*1612–72*

# On the Death of Mr William Hervey

It was a dismal, and a fearful night,
Scarce could the Morn drive on the unwilling light,
When Sleep, Death's image, left my troubled breast
   By something like Death possessed.
My eyes with tears did uncommanded flow,
    And on my soul hung the dull weight
    Of some intolerable fate.
What bell was that? Ah me! too much I know!

My sweet companion, and my gentle peer,
Why hast thou left me thus unkindly here,
Thy end for ever, and my life to moan?
   O thou hast left me all alone!
Thy soul and body, when death's agony
    Besieged around thy noble heart,
    Did not with more reluctance part
Than I, my dearest Friend, do part from thee.

My dearest Friend, would I had died for thee!
Life and this world henceforth will tedious be:
Nor shall I know hereafter what to do
   If once my griefs prove tedious too.
Silent and sad I walk about all day,
    As sullen ghosts stalk speechless by
    Where their hid treasures lie;
Alas! my treasure's gone; why do I stay?...

With as much zeal, devotion, piety,
He always lived, as other saints do die.
Still with his soul severe accounts he kept,
   Weeping all debts out ere he slept.
Then down in peace and innocence he lay,
    Like the sun's laborious light,
    Which still in water sets at night,
Unsullied with his journey of the day.

But happy Thou, ta'en from this frantic age,
Where ignorance and hypocrisy does rage!
A fitter time for Heaven no soul e'er chose –
   The place now only free from those.
There 'mong the blest thou dost for ever shine;
    And whereso'er thou casts thy view
    Upon that white and radiant crew,
See'st not a soul clothed with more light than thine.

*Abraham Cowley*
*1618–67*

# The Blessed Dead

They lie at rest, our blessed dead;
The dews drop cool above their head,
They knew not when fleet summer fled.

Together all, yet each alone;
Each laid at rest beneath his own
Smooth turf or white allotted stone.

When shall our slumber sink so deep,
And eyes that wept and eyes that weep
Weep not in the sufficient sleep?

God be with you, our great and small,
Our loves, our best-beloved of all,
Our own beyond the salt sea-wall.

*Christina Rossetti*
*1830–94*

# Safe

Safe where I cannot lie yet,
    Safe where I hope to lie too,
Safe from the fume and fret;
    You, and you,
Whom I never forget.

Safe from the frost and snow,
    Safe from the storm and the sun,
Safe where the seeds wait to grow
    One by one
And to come back in blow.

*Christina Rossetti*
*1830–94*

# Pine Forest

(IN MEMORIAM – K.A.M.W.)

Among the towering pines
of perennial pride,
falling but not fallen,
the mossy path astride,
adding a new dimension,
one leans across the ride.

Caught at sixty degrees,
it makes a special mark
with shafts of angled light
in the criss-cross dark,
dead among the living,
lying bark to bark.

When will it fall completely,
all support withdrawn
by neighbour pines,
their roots outworn,
on a brushwood couch
to be stripped and sawn?

We stand together now,
silent among the trees,
wondering at the limit
of life's harmonies,
as the wind passing over,
another death decrees.

*Randle Manwaring*
20th century

# Dirge

Calm on the bosom of thy God,
    Fair spirit, rest thee now!
E'en while with ours thy footsteps trod,
    His seal was on thy brow.

Dust, to its narrow house beneath!
    Soul, to its place on high!
They that have seen thy look in death
    No more may fear to die.

*Felicia Dorothea Hemans*
1793–1835

# Early Death

She passed away like morning dew
  Before the sun was high;
So brief her time, she scarcely knew
  The meaning of a sigh.

As round the rose its soft perfume,
  Sweet love around her floated;
Admired she grew – while mortal doom
  Crept on, unfeared, unnoted.

Love was her guardian angel here,
  But Love to Death resigned her;
Though Love is kind, why should we fear
  But holy Death is kinder?

*Hartley Coleridge*
*1796–1849*

# Requiem for the Abbess of Gandesheim Who Died Young

Thou hast come safe to port
  I still at sea,
The light is on thy head,
  Darkness in me.

Pluck thou in heaven's field
  Violet and rose,
While I strew flowers that will thy vigil keep
Where thou dost sleep,
Love, in thy last repose.

*Taken from 'Poetry in the Dark Ages', a lecture delivered by Helen Waddell*

# Hereafter

## Fidele's Dirge

Fear no more the heat o' the sun
   Nor the furious winter's rages;
Thou thy worldly task hast done,
   Home art gone, and ta'en thy wages.
Golden lads and girls all must,
As chimney sweepers, come to dust.

Fear no more the frown o' the great,
   Thou art past the tyrant's stroke;
Care no more to clothe and eat,
   To thee the reed is as the oak.
The sceptre, learning, physic must
All follow this and come to dust.

Fear no more the lightning-flash,
   Nor the all-dreaded thunder-stone;
Fear not slander, censure rash;
   Thou hast finished joy and moan.
All lovers young, all lovers must
Consign to thee, and come to dust.

*William Shakespeare*
*1564–1616*

# The Grave Grows Firm with Grasses

(REVELATION 2:17)

The grave grows firm with grasses;
the fevered leaves lie down.
Then even summer withers,
and we are left alone

in that insensate winter
which whitens all the mind
and drives us deep for moments
in hallways underground

to wait the many mansions
where avenues are full
of all the shining people
who loved and wished us well.

Till then, each gravestone naming
each name stands high and glad
and gleams – an April angel
that smiles and shakes his head.

*James E. Warren Jr.*
*20th century*

# Eternity

O years! and age! farewell:
   Behold I go
   Where I do know
Infinity to dwell.

And these mine eyes shall see
   All times, how they
   Are lost i' th' sea
Of vast eternity.

Where never moon shall sway
   The stars; but she,
   And night, shall be
Drowned in one endless day.

*Robert Herrick*
*1591–1674*

# Resurrection

The wintry winds have ceased to blow,
   And trembling leaves appear;
The fairest flowers succeed the snow,
   And hail the infant year.

So, when the world and all its woes
   Are vanished far away,
Fair scenes and wonderful repose
   Shall bless the new-born day, –

When, from the confines of the grave,
   The body too shall rise;
No more precarious passion's slave,
   Nor error's sacrifice.

'Tis but a sleep – and Sion's king
   Will call the many dead:
'Tis but a sleep – and then we sing,
   O'er dreams of sorrow fled.

Yes! – wintry winds have ceased to blow,
   And trembling leaves appear,
And nature has her types to show
   Throughout the varying year.

*George Crabbe*
*1754–1832*

# Presences Unseen

## The Visionary

Silent is the house: all are laid asleep:
One alone looks out o'er the snow-wreaths deep,
Watching every cloud, dreading every breeze
That whirls the wildering drift, and bends the groaning trees.

Cheerful is the hearth, soft the matted floor;
Not one shivering gust creeps through pane or door;
The little lamp burns straight, its rays shoot strong and far:
I trim it well, to be the wanderer's guiding-star.

Frown, my haughty sire! chide, my angry dame;
Set your slaves to spy; threaten me with shame:
But neither sire nor dame, nor prying serf shall know,
What angel nightly tracks that waste of frozen snow.

What I love shall come like visitant of air,
Safe in secret power from lurking human snare;
Who loves me, no word of mine shall e'er betray,
Though for faith unstained my life must forfeit pay.

Burn, then, little lamp; glimmer straight and clear –
Hush! a rustling wing stirs, methinks, the air:
He for whom I wait, thus ever comes to me;
Strange Power! I trust thy might; trust thou my constancy.

*Emily Brontë*
*1818–48*

# Kinship

I am aware,
As I go commonly sweeping the stair,
Doing my part of the everyday care –
Human and simple my lot and share –
  I am aware of a marvellous thing:
  Voices that murmur and ethers that ring
  In the far stellar spaces where cherubim sing;
I am aware of the passion that pours
Down the channels of fire through Infinity's doors;
  Forces terrific, with melody shod,
  Music that mates with the pulses of God.
I am aware of the glory that runs
From the core of myself to the core of the suns,
  Bound to the stars by invisible chains,
  Blaze of eternity now in my veins,
  Seeing the rush of ethereal rains,
Here in the midst of the everyday air –
  I am aware.

I am aware,
As I sit quietly here in my chair,
Sewing or reading or braiding my hair –
Human and simple my lot and my share –
  I am aware of the systems that swing
Through the aisles of creation on heavenly wing,
  I am aware of a marvellous thing,
Trail of the comets in furious flight,
Thunders of beauty that shatter the night,
  Terrible triumph of pageants that march
To the trumpets of time through eternity's arch.
I am aware of the splendour that ties
All the things of the earth to the things of the skies,
  Here in my body the heavenly heat,
  Here in my flesh the melodious beat
  Of the planets that circle Divinity's feet.
As I silently sit here in my chair,
  I am aware.

*Angela Morgan*
*20th century*

# The Barranong Angel Case

You see that bench in front of Meagher's store?
That's where the angel landed.
What? An angel?
Yes. It was just near smoko* time on a sale day.
Town was quite full. He called us all together.
And was he obeyed?
Oh yes. He got a hearing.
Made his announcement, blessed us and took off
Again, straight up.
He had most glorious wings...
What happened then?
There were some tasks he'd set us
Or rather that sort of followed from his message.
And were they carried out?
At first we meant to,
But after a while, when there had been some talk
Most came to think he'd been a bit, well, haughty,
A bit overdone, with those flourishes of wings
And that plummy accent.
Lot of the women liked that.
But the men who'd knelt, off their own bat, mind you,
They were specially crook* on him, as I remember.

Did he come again?
Oh yes. The message was important.
The second time he hired the church hall,
Spoke most politely, called us all by name.
Any result?
Not much. At first we liked him.
But, after all, he'd singled out the Catholics.
It was their hall. And another thing resented
By different ones, he hadn't charged admission.
We weren't all paupers, and any man or angel
With so little regard for local pride, or money,
Ends up distrusted.

Did he give up then?
Oh no. The third time round
He thought he had our measure. Came by car,
Took a room at Morgan's, didn't say a word
About his message for the first two days
And after that dropped hints. Quite clever ones.

He made sure, too, that he spoke to all the Baptists.
I'll bet that worked.
You reckon? Not that I saw.
We didn't like him pandering to our ways
For a start. Some called it mockery, straight out.
He was an angel, after all. And then
There was the way he kept on coming back
Hustling the people.
And when all's said and done
He was a stranger. And he talked religion.

Did he keep on trying?
No. Gave us away.
Would it have helped if he'd settled in the district?
Don't think so, mate. If you follow me, he was
Too keen altogether. He'd have harped on that damn message
All the time – or if he'd stopped, well then
He'd have been despised because he'd given in, like.
He'd just got off on the wrong foot from the start
And you can't fix that up.

But what – Oh Hell! – what if he'd been, say, born here?
Well, that sort of thing's a bit above an angel,
Or a bit below. And he'd grow up too well known.
Who'd pay any heed to a neighbour's boy, I ask you,
Specially if he came out with messages?
Besides, what he told us had to do with love
And people here don't think that's quite – manly.

*Les A. Murray*
*20th century*

* *smoko:* a work-break; *crook on:* hostile to; abusive

# Heaven

## Care in Heaven

And is there care in heaven? and is there love?
In heavenly spirits to these creatures base,
That may compassion of their evils move?
There is: else much more wretched were the case
Of men than beasts. But O th'exceeding grace
Of highest God that loves his creatures so,
And all his works with mercy doth embrace,
That blessed angels he sends to and fro,
To serve to wicked man, to serve his wicked foe.

How oft do they their silver bowers leave,
To come to succour us that succour want!
How oft do they with golden pinions cleave
The flitting skies, like flying Pursuivant,
Against foul fiends to aid us militant!
They for us fight, they watch and duly ward,
And their bright squadrons round about us plant,
And all for love, and nothing for reward:
O why should heavenly God to men have such regard?

*Edmund Spenser*
*1552–99*

# Peace

My soul, there is a country
   Far beyond the stars,
Where stands a winged sentry
   All skilful in the wars:
There, above noise and danger,
   Sweet Peace sits crowned with smiles,
And one born in a manger
   Commands the beauteous files.
He is thy gracious Friend,
   And – O my soul, awake! –
Did in pure love descend
   To die here for thy sake.
If thou canst get but thither,
   There grows the flower of Peace,
The Rose that cannot wither,
   Thy fortress and thy ease.
Leave then thy foolish ranges;
   For none can thee secure
But one who never changes –
   Thy God, thy life, thy cure.

*Henry Vaughan*
*1622–95*

# There

There, in that other world, what waits for me?
What shall I find after that other birth?
No stormy, tossing, foaming, smiling sea,
   But a new earth.

No sun to mark the changing of the days,
No slow, soft falling of the alternate night,
No moon, no star, no light upon my ways,
   Only the Light.

No grey cathedral, wide and wondrous fair,
That I may tread, where all my fathers trod.
Nay, nay, my soul, no house of God is there,
   But only God.

*Mary Coleridge*
*1861–1907*

# A Land of Pure Delight

There is a land of pure delight
    Where saints immortal reign;
Infinite day excludes the night,
    And pleasures banish pain.

There everlasting spring abides,
    And never-withering flowers:
Death like a narrow sea divides
    This heavenly land from ours.

Sweet fields beyond the swelling flood
    Stand dressed in living green:
So to the Jews old Canaan stood,
    While Jordan rolled between.

But timorous mortals start and shrink
    To cross this narrow sea,
And linger shivering on the brink
    And fear to launch away.

O could we make our doubts remove,
    These gloomy doubts that rise,
And see the Canaan that we love,
    With unbeclouded eyes.

Could we but climb where Moses stood,
    And view the landscape o'er,
Not Jordan's stream, nor Death's cold flood,
    Should fright us from the shore.

*Isaac Watts*
*1674–1748*

# *From:* Hierusalem, My Happy Home

Hierusalem, my happy home,
  When shall I come to thee?
When shall my sorrows have an end,
  Thy joys when shall I see?

O happy harbour of the saints,
  O sweet and pleasant soil,
In thee no sorrow may be found
  No grief, no care, no toil...

No dampish mist is seen in thee,
  Nor cold nor darksome night;
There every soul shines as the sun,
  There God himself gives light.

There lust and lucre cannot dwell,
  There envy bears no sway;
There is no hunger, heat, nor cold,
  But pleasure every way.

Hierusalem, Hierusalem,
  God grant I once may see
Thy endless joys, and of the same
  Partaker aye to be.

Thy walls are made of precious stones,
  Thy bulwarks diamonds square;
Thy gates are of right orient pearl,
  Exceeding rich and rare.

Thy turrets and thy pinnacles
  With carbuncles do shine;
The very streets are paved with gold
  Surpassing clear and fine.

The houses are of ivory,
  The windows crystal clear,
Thy tiles are made of beaten gold,
  O God, that I were there.

Within thy gates nothing doth come
  That is not passing clean;
No spider's web, no dirt, no dust,
  No filth may there be seen...

There trees for evermore bear fruit
   And evermore do spring;
There evermore the angels sit
   And evermore do sing...

Our Lady sings *Magnificat*
   With tune surpassing sweet;
And all the virgins bear their parts
   Sitting about her feet...

Hierusalem, my happy home,
   Would God I were in thee!
Would God my woes were at an end,
   Thy joys that I might see!

*Anonymous*
*This version from a Catholic Commonplace Book*
*dated 1616*

## 'And That Will be Heaven'

and that will be heaven

and that will be heaven
at last   the first unclouded
seeing

    to stand like the sunflower
turned full face to the sun   drenched
with light   in the still centre
held   while the circling planets
hum with an utter joy

    seeing and knowing
at last   in every particle
seen and known   and not turning
away

  never turning away
again

*Evangeline Paterson*
*20th century*

# Exile

Yes, it is beautiful country,
the streams in the winding valley,
the knowes and the birches,
and beautiful the mountain's bare shoulder
and the calm brows of the hills,
but it is not my country,
and in my heart there is a hollow place always.

And there is no way to go back –
maybe the miles indeed, but the years never.

Winding are the roads that we choose,
and inexorable is life,
driving us, it seems, like cattle
farther and farther away from what we remember.

But when we shall come at last
to God, who is our home and country,
there will be no more road stretching before us
and no more need to go back.

*Evangeline Paterson*
*20th century*

# I Never Saw a Moor

I never saw a moor
I never saw the sea;
Yet know I how the heather looks
And what a wave must be.

I never spoke with God,
Nor visited in Heaven;
Yet certain am I of the spot
As if the chart were given.

*Emily Dickinson*
*1830–86*

# The Return of Christ
## and the Last Judgment

## The Heavenly Aeroplane

One of these nights about twelve o'clock
The old world's going to reel and rock,
The sinner's going to tremble and cry for pain
And the Lord will come in his aeroplane.

O ye thirsty of every tribe
Get your ticket for an aeroplane ride,
Jesus our Saviour is a-coming to reign
And take you up to glory in his aeroplane.

Talk about your joy-rides in automobiles,
Talk about your fast time on motor wheels,
We'll break all records as we upwards fly
For an aeroplane joy-ride through the sky.

There will be no punctures or muddy roads,
No broken axles from overloads,
No shocks to give trouble or cause delay
As we soon will rapture up the narrow way.

You will have to get ready if you take this ride,
Quit all your sins and humble your pride,
You must furnish a lamp both bright and clean
And a vessel of oil to run the machine.

When our journey is over and we'll all sit down
At the marriage supper with a robe and a crown
We'll blend our voices with the heavenly throng
And praise our Saviour as the years roll on.

*Anonymous*
*about 1935*

# *From:* A Song for St Cecilia's Day 1687

GRAND CHORUS

As from the power of sacred lays
   The spheres began to move,
And sung the great Creator's praise
   To all the blest above;
So when the last and dreadful hour
This crumbling pageant shall devour,
The trumpet shall be heard on high,
The dead shall live, the living die,
And music shall untune the sky!

*John Dryden*
*1631–1700*

# Hymn for Advent

   Lord, come away!
   Why dost thou stay?
Thy road is ready; and thy paths made straight
   With longing expectations wait
The consecration of thy beauteous feet.
   Ride on triumphantly; behold we lay
   Our lusts and proud will in thy way!

Hosanna! Welcome to our hearts! Lord, here
Thou hast a temple too; and full as dear
As that of Sion, and as full of sin:
Nothing but thieves and robbers dwell therein:
Enter, and chase them forth, and cleanse the floor:
Crucify them, that they may never more
   Profane that holy place
  Where thou hast chose to set thy face!
  And then if our stiff tongues shall be
   Mute in the praises of thy deity,
   The stones out of the temple wall
    Shall cry aloud and call
  Hosanna! And thy glorious footsteps greet!

*Jeremy Taylor*
*1613–67*

# The Last Judgement

When rising from the bed of death,
  O'erwhelmed with guilt and fear,
I see my Maker face to face,
  O how shall I appear?

If yet, while pardon may be found,
  And mercy may be sought,
My heart with inward horror shrinks,
  And trembles at the thought;

When thou, O Lord, shalt stand disclosed
  In majesty severe,
And sit in judgement on my soul
  O how shall I appear?

But thou hast told the troubled mind,
  Who does her sins lament,
The timely tribute of her tears
  Shall endless woe prevent.

Then see the sorrows of my heart
  Ere yet it be too late;
And hear my Saviour's dying groans,
  To give those sorrows weight.

For never shall my soul despair
  Her pardon to procure,
Who knows thine only Son has died
  To make her pardon sure.

*Joseph Addison*
*1672–1719*

# Chaff

Chaff.
Sorted and sifted,
good from bad when God brings Judgement.
Sordid and twisted, victims from villains,
when we try to do it for him.

Driving the supposed chaff from us
with our own hot air,
instead of the appointed four winds
of the Revelation,
we often trample the elect-yet-unconfessed
as pearls before swine,
forgetting what pearls look like
from the outside of the oyster.

The silo barn is
filled with fat-bellied wheat,
layer upon layer,
prouder upon proud stacked in pews.
We reach the vantage of the silo top,
yet from greatest to least
we are carpeted wall to wall,
suspended by the chaff that is
pressed into the damp dirt reality...
in every crack chaff fills.

Settled wheat
ground under so much pressure
looks (to us) like any chaff hogs walk on.

*E. Neil Culbertson*
*20th century*

# Dies Irae

That day of wrath, that dreadful day,
When heaven and earth shall pass away,
What power shall be the sinner's stay?
How shall he meet that dreadul day?

When, shrivelling like a parched scroll,
The flaming heavens together roll;
When louder yet, and yet more dread,
Swells the high trump that wakes the dead;

Oh! on that day, that wrathful day,
When man to judgement wakes from clay,
Be THOU the trembling sinner's stay,
Though heaven and earth shall pass away!

*Sir Walter Scott*
*1771–1832*

# Telephone

I am a telephone
I have heard
Many voices in confidence
I ring and they jump,
And pick up
My hand set.
Then they get set
For a talk.
'Hullo, who's speaking?'
'It's me' and they continue
In topics legal and illegal
They indulge in conversation
They think is all secret
But I listen
And wait like a computer
For the day I will be summoned
As witness
To all the dialogues
That transpired
That will be, the day of judgement.

*Mamman J. Vatsa*
*20th century*

# A Hope

And oh! there lives within my heart
   A hope long nursed by me;
(And should its cheering ray depart
   How dark my soul would be!)

That as in Adam all have died,
   In Christ shall all men live;
And ever round his throne abide,
   Eternal praise to give.

That even the wicked shall at last
   Be fitted for the skies;
And when their dreadful doom is past
   To light and life arise.

I ask not how remote the day,
   Nor what the sinner's woe,
Before their dross is purged away;
   Enough for me to know –

That when the cup of wrath is drained,
   The metal purified,
They'll cling to what they once disdained,
   And live by him that died.

*Anne Brontë*
*1820–49*

# PEN PORTRAITS

## To a Lady Saying Grace in a Station Buffet

Step nearer to my canvas gracious traveller
That I may paint a portrait of you
Sitting tranquilly against a backcloth
Of trains and timetables,
As, mindful of Cana, you offer thanks
For lukewarm coffee
And the veiled hostility of slab cake.

*Sheila Nottage*
*20th century*

# Bible Characters

## OLD TESTAMENT

## Forbidden Fruit

They wondered why the fruit had been forbidden;
It taught them nothing new. They hid their pride,
But did not listen much when they were chidden;
They knew exactly what to do outside.

They left: immediately the memory faded
Of all they'd learnt; they could not understand
The dogs now who, before, had always aided;
The stream was dumb with whom they'd always planned.

They wept and quarrelled: freedom was so wild.
In front, maturity, as he ascended,
Retired like a horizon from the child;

The dangers and the punishments grew greater;
And the way back by angels was defended
Against the poet and the legislator.

*W.H. Auden*
*20th century*

## Abraham

The rivulet-loving wanderer Abraham
Through waterless wastes tracing his fields of pasture
Led his Chaldean herds and fattening flocks
With the meandering art of wavering water
That seeks and finds, yet does not know its way.
He came, rested and prospered, and went on,
Scattering behind him little pastoral kingdoms,
And over each one its own particular sky,
Not the great rounded sky through which he journeyed,
That went with him but when he rested changed.
His mind was full of names
Learned from strange peoples speaking alien tongues,
And all that was theirs one day he would inherit.
He died content and full of years, though still
The Promise had not come, and left his bones,
Far from his father's house, in alien Canaan.

*Edwin Muir*
*1887–1959*

# Lot's Wife

## 1

My home, my lovely home, she wept
while God was sharpening his shafts
against the cities of the plain.
My mother too was called at dawn
and for me Lot's wife has her face,
the same companionable hands
touch what they shall not hold again;
it was because it meant her life
that she was loath to leave that place.
And while her daughters were already running
she stayed to look at a familiar sight:
flowers responding to the early sun
– the valley emulated Paradise;
sweet view, she sighed, if I could leave my eyes...
no one will love you after I have gone

## 2

What was she doing, waiting there
with darkness spattering the air;
don't hang your hearts on things, she'd said:
a nomad used to moving on
with only a shabby, a makeshift home
and daughters who still needed her
hurrying ahead?

## 3

I'd be content with yesterday, she thought,
her memories like clothing in her hands:
her daughters small, herself reckless and young,
and Lot her shelter, and their wanderings.
If God must take, she thought, let him take all...
and shivered as the ground began to shake.

*Karen Gershon*
*20th century*

# The Burning Bush

When Moses, musing in the desert, found
The thorn bush spiking up from the hot ground,
And saw the branches, on a sudden, bear
The crackling yellow barberries of fire,

He searched his learning and imagination
For any logical, neat explanation,
And turned to go, but turned again and stayed,
And faced the fire and knew it for his God.

I too have seen the briar alight like coal,
The love that burns, the flesh that's ever whole,
And many times have turned and left it there,
Saying: 'It's prophecy – but metaphor'.

But stinging tongues like John the Baptist shout:
'That this is metaphor is no way out.
It's dogma too, or you make God a liar;
The bush is still a bush, and fire is fire'.

*Norman Nicholson*
*20th century*

# Coming and Going

The word came
and he went
in the other
direction.
God said: Cry
tears of compassion
tears of repentance;
cry against
the reek
of unrighteousness;
cry for
the right turn
the contrite spirit.
And Jonah rose
and fled
in tearless
silence.

*Thomas John Carlisle*
*20th century*

## Saint John Baptist

The last and greatest herald of heaven's King,
Girt with rough skins, hies to the deserts wild,
Among that savage brood the woods forth bring,
Which he than man more harmless found and mild.
His food was locusts, and what young doth spring
With honey that from virgin hives distilled;
Parched body, hollow eyes, some uncouth thing
Made him appear, long since from earth exiled.
There burst he forth: 'All ye, whose hopes rely
On God, with me amidst these deserts mourn;
Repent, repent, and from old errors turn!'
  – Who listened to his voice, obeyed his cry?
    Only the echoes, which he made relent,
      Rung from their marble caves 'Repent! Repent!'

*William Drummond of Hawthornden*
*1585–1649*

## John the Baptist

As the brittle water dripped
from the young man standing
upright again to the waist
I heard, we all felt we heard
I saw, we all thought we saw
a visionary presence, a voice;
but where are they gone?

I staked almost everything
on the truth of that moment.
This is the lamb (I blurted out)
the very lamb (or some such phrase)
this is the lamb of God…but
that was some years ago.

Now in danger of life, I know
that tyranny will take its course,
and neither the lamb of God nor
anyone else will intervene
to save me.

Where is the hope of his coming?
Was not this the one?
Is the kingdom not after all
at hand?

I waited to see the whole
country rising to his name.
I am waiting

The time is ripe, the world ready
to be reborn, but now

What am I is it the end is he

*Simon Baynes*
*20th century*

## O Sapientia

It was from Joseph first I learned
Of love. Like me he was dismayed.
How easily he could have turned
Me from his house; but, unafraid,
He put me not away from him
(O God-sent angel, pray for him).
Thus through his love was Love obeyed.

The Child's first cry came like a bell:
God's word aloud, God's word in deed.
The angel spoke: so it befell,
And Joseph with me in my need.
O Child whose father came from heaven,
To you another gift was given,
Your earthly father chosen well.

With Joseph I was always warmed
And cherished. Even in the stable
I knew that I would not be harmed.
And, though above the angels swarmed,
Man's love it was that made me able
To bear God's love, wild, formidable,
To bear God's will, through me performed.

*Madeleine L'Engle*
*20th century*

387

# Joseph

He wrestles straining flesh
To free the stubborn child
From clutching womb
While whispered grumblings slip
With sweat from trembling lips,
An awful fit
Compared to angled boards
With just right joints
On firm wood bench.
How far from steady here,
Away from home and youth's
Clear questions, answers cleaned
And ready.

These knots once came with looks
Of age, their smiles and frowns
Among wood grains –
Like hill-side grass in fact
Where wheat and barley browns
Joined pasture greens,
Where rough met smooth
And flat reached round
And sun out far kissed stone in close
Quite warmly. There he soared
In pictured thoughts and deeds,
Or slipped between the blades
Quite nimbly.

To frame those thoughts and deeds
He worked with wood from day
To ordered day.
But here the blood-strewn straw
Brought all the gnarls of Mary back
Again. Her screams
Were caught in slimy folds
On babe's dark head from womb
Now pushing through
But how? And how or what
Began these months of mess
And sexless tomb?
Just how then?

But most of all he wished
A simple peace
With her whose life seemed strange
And far from his own skill
To please. Her fears and joys
She had apart.
Elizabeth alone
Might know those dream desires
Of womb, apart from him,
A man of faith but not
Much hope, belief without
Clear vision, ready though
For waiting.

He shared some good times too,
And once her angel came.
But all in all didn't fit
At all since Mary –
There! And Mary smiled.
Joseph looked around
At dumbly staring cows
Then back again
To see the baby out
Against the breast that he
Loved too, a picture good
Enough to frame,

He dried his hands and heard
New sounds. The baby cooed,
Or was it cried?
Joseph smiled, then Mary smiled
Again. 'And didn't I do
Quite well? And didn't I tell
You God was here?
What was it like for *you*? –
It didn't *feel* like God!'
Joseph kissed the child
With Mary's hope and smoothed
Her knotted string-wet hair
Just now then.

*Paul Borgman*
*20th century*

# The Widow's Mites

Two mites, two drops (yet all her house and land).
Falls from a steady heart, though trembling hand.
The other's wanton wealth foams high, and brave,
The other cast away, she only gave.

*Richard Crashaw*
*1613?–49*

# Lazarus

Sister, you placed my heart in its stone room
where no flowers curiously come, and sun's voice
rebuffed, hangs on the stones dumb. What I could not bear
I still must hear. Why do your tears fall?

why does their falling move him, the friend, the
unsuspected lightning: that he walk our garden
with no flowers upon his friend, but a voice splitting
my stone to a dream gone, my sleep

to day? what, what do tears say to him?

what did he say in tears, that his grief fall
scalding my hands, that cold hands sprung
sleep like a manacle, and drew my eyes a space
that had seen God, back to his human face?

*Daniel Berrigan*
*20th century*

# *From:* On Holy Week

PILATE'S WIFE

I dreamt us strolling, arm in loving arm,
along the avenue that skirts the border;
our tender courting days wheeled back.
Just then we heard a yapping,
loud, a pack in full pursuit!

Into our lives he crashed,
a lamb, bleeding and bruised,
and weary with the chase.
I picked him up and cuddled him
in my warm arms, my newest baby boy.

The hounds were yelping louder,
nuzzling the hedge. And then
(but why? but why?) you snatched
the poor thing from my arms,
and with 'We must not interfere,
my love, the dogs demand their prey,'
you tossed their quarry over
the prickly hedge. The ravenous pack
were through him in an instant,
ravaging the body.

That moment, in my dream,
our sweet love died; that afternoon
I sat alone, playing with thorns.
At length I turned to you
to plead forgiveness.
You offered that, and love;
but, broken in simple grief,
I could not take your proffered
bread and wine.

*Mervyn Morris*
*20th century*

## John in Gethsemane

The grass is pleasant here
rains have given the earth a chance to soften
I wonder we have not come to Gethsemane
    more often.

We are worn out from the Temple crowds
I can hardly stay awake
I wish he would join us and get some rest
    for his own sake.

But ever since supper he has seemed strange –
something on his mind –
I expect it will all work out tomorrow
    and we can all unwind.

How drowsy it all seems this evening
    and the earth
        how kind.

*Shirwood E. Wirt*
*20th century*

# The Thief

'Say bold but blessed thief,
That in a trice
Slipped into paradise,
And in plain day
Stol'st heaven away,
What trick couldst thou invent
To compass thy intent?
What arms?
What charms?'
'Love and belief.'

'Say bold but blessed thief,
How couldst thou read
A crown upon that head?
What text, what gloss,
A kingdom on a cross?
How couldst thou come to spy
God in a man to die?
What light?
What sight?'
'The sight of grief –

'I sight to God his pain;
And by that sight
I saw the light;
Thus did my grief
Beget relief.
And take this rule from me,
Pity thou him, he'll pity thee.
Use this,
Ne'er miss,
Heaven may be stol'n again.'

*Anonymous*
*17th century*

# St Stephen's Day

Yesterday the gentle
Story: the summoning star,
Shepherd and beast and King
In their enchanted ring,
The moment still with awe.

Shepherd and beast and King
Wince at a cry:
It is no new born cry
For he is asleep,
But a cry alerting night.

Who saw the hanging star
Shudder and fall?
I, Stephen, saw
Fragments of hot stone
Whistle down, smite the earth.

Stones thud on flesh,
The bestial mob howls,
No Kings are here to witness.
Yesterday birth blood,
Today pulped flesh and death blood

Streaming from broken eyes:
Yet the triumphant cry,
I see my God.
So was the first day
After the gentle birth.

*Patric Dickinson*
*20th century*

# Saints Official –
# and Saints in the Making

## Soeur Marie Emilie

Soeur Marie Emilie
is little and very old:
her eyes are onyx,
and her cheeks vermilion,
her apron wide and kind
and cobalt blue.

She comforts
generations and generations
of children,
who are 'new'
at the convent school.
When they are eight,
they are already up to her shoulder,
they grow up and go into the world,
she remains,
for ever,
always incredibly old,
but incredibly, never older.

Generations of children
sit in turn by her side,
and help her to shell the peas,
her dry and twisted fingers crackle,
snapping the green pods,
generations of children
sit in turn by her side,
helping to stone the plums,
that will be made into jam,
for the greater glory of God.

She has affinity with the hens,
when a hen dies,
she sits down on a bench and cries,
she is the only grown-up, whose tears
are not frightening tears.

Children can weep without shame,
at her side.
She is simple as flax.
She collects the eggs,
they are warm and smooth,
and softly coloured,
ivory, ochre,
and brown and rose.
They fit the palm of her hand.
Her eyes kindle upon them,
the children, watching gravely,
understand
her dumb, untroubled love.

We have grown up,
and gone away,
'into the world'
and grown cold
in the service of God,
but we would love him
even less than we do,
if we had never known
Soeur Marie Emilie,
with the green peas and the plums,
and the hens and the beautiful eggs,
and her apron as wide and kind
as skies on a summer day,
and as clean and blue.

*Caryll Houselander*
20th century

# Sister Bertha

Who would guess that thin-breasted body
has wheezed Christ into three languages?
She walks down aisles to pews, an oddity
of God's redeeming grace; her sober thighs
are shut against all time and place and cause.
Who would guess her brambled hands held skies
matter-of-factly down to earth, spliced lengths
of heathen centuries to ours with their strength.

And who would guess that at night somewhere off in
a room where the loveliest thing is a fly that drones,
lying, her untouched body on a mattressed coffin,
she stares in the nervous dark, mad or blind,
a lover who primps her soul, and thinks whole poems
into a time and place out of mind.

*Jeanne Murray Walker*
*20th century*

# Mould of Castile

(TO ST TERESA)

A streak of Sappho, it is said,
Inflamed you, the painted and imperious
Charmer in velvet robes at Avila;
But soon your withered young bones rattled
On convent stones: gaunt postulant,
You had fled, still dead to God, from a goblin-flare.

No mist or dream had softened
The bold Castilian flint: there was sun-glare
On bull-fights and flashing lizards
And the hot black stems of olives, pungent cistus,
Awaiting the shift and shock, an El Greco storm.

Did you waste thirty years
In fighting the sun, flashing out
With a gay jest between swoons and fears
Of those winged visions? Did election dare
Molest your Spanish pride
To that length, fan a fury of love
That soared, bled in the trap,
Lapped a wilful ease, lastly, in brisk reform?

You were ageing, an enigma still,
When your mules arrived at San Jose,
And a thunder that thrills my flint
In Cornwall now, spread from the wooden waggons,
Filled with your nuns, lurching over calcined plains,
Up primitive mountain tracks, drifting aground
On river ferries. You and they were bound
For new cells in Elisha's shadow:
Traditional rock like that which my poet-soul,
As wasted and adamant,
Split and gay as yours, descried
Beyond sly bramble, misted kiln
And the dried voluptuary veins.

*Jack Clemo*
*20th century*

# Mother Teresa

No revolution will come in time
   to alter this man's life
   except the one
   surprise of being loved.

It is too late to talk of Civil Rights,
   neo-Marxism
   psychiatry
   or any kind of sex.

He has only twelve more hours to live.
   Forget about
   a cure for cancer, smoking, leprosy
   or osteo-arthritis.

Over this dead loss to society
   you pour your precious ointment,
   wash the feet
   that will not walk tomorrow.

Mother Teresa, Mary Magdalene,
   your love is dangerous, your levity
   would contradict
   our local gravity.

But if love cannot do it, then I see
   no future for this dying man or me.
   So blow the world to glory,
   crack the clock. Let love be dangerous.

*Sydney Carter*
*20th century*

# Miss Pettigrew and Tree

In her small single room
   Miss Pettigrew
     – bird bones and parchment skin –
     lives in a leaf world
       made by her pavement tree.

When the wind blows,
   the moving patterns dance
     across her walls
       and lift her heart like music

and when the wind is still
    leaf shadows touch her face
        with Love that never reached her
            through humankind.

In stark-branched winter
    she feels companioned in
        adversity
and buds in April
    bring her a sign
        from that Far Country
            where she will flower, beyond
            this alien world.

Daily Miss Pettigrew
    – shrunk from life's jostling,
        frail essence in
            a birdcage skeleton –
                wonders why she should be
                so recompensed

and lives, content, in shelter
    of Love enough for her
        beneath her tree.

*Evangeline Paterson*
*20th century*

# Christmas Trees

Bonhoeffer in his skylit cell
bleached by the flares' candescent fall,
pacing out his own citadel,

restores the broken themes of praise,
encourages our borrowed days,
by logic of his sacrifice.

Against wild reasons of the state
his words are quiet but not too quiet.
We hear too late or not too late.

*Geoffrey Hill*
*20th century*

# The Misses Norman

The Misses Norman lived on Marine Square
just as you turn from Broadway at the corner
where now a granite bank shines like new coins;
two short white matrons that I remember
like Lord's Prayers on a rosary that joins
a knotted childhood to their acts of care.

To my young mind it seemed a threatening place.
You pierced the wooden gate through its small door
and stepped into a dimness armed with plants,
cringed up the half-gloom to the upper floor
and called good morning nervous in your pants.
But there you spoke with goodness face to face.

With thanks now rising in me like a lake
an image flashes fresh as yesterday:
a slippered sister in Edwardian dress
shuffling to hear each stanza of distress,
bribing the waiting teeth of reefs away.
It is a bonding that time cannot break.

The lifeguards of this heaving world are rare,
the sinking swimmers thick as August rain.
But one whose feet touched safety when that pair
of spinsters anchored themselves to pain
that was not theirs attempts a line of praise
in words like them, as faithful and as plain.

*Cecil Gray*
*20th century*

# On a Portrait of a Deaf Man

The kind old face, the egg-shaped head
   The tie, discreetly loud,
The loosely fitting shooting clothes,
   A closely fitting shroud.

He liked old City dining-rooms,
   Potatoes in their skin,
But now his mouth is wide to let
   The London clay come in.

He took me on long silent walks
   In country lanes when young,
He knew the name of ev'ry bird
   But not the song it sung.

And when he could not hear me speak
   He smiled and looked so wise
That now I do not like to think
   Of maggots in his eyes.

He liked the rain-washed Cornish air
   And smell of ploughed-up soil,
He liked a landscape big and bare
   And painted it in oil.

But least of all he liked that place
   Which hangs on Highgate Hill
Of soaked Carrara-covered earth
   For Londoners to fill.

He would have liked to say goodbye,
   Shake hands with many friends,
In Highgate now his finger-bones
   Stick through his finger-ends.

You, God, who treat him thus and thus,
   Say 'Save his soul and pray.'
You ask me to believe you and
   I only see decay.

*John Betjeman*
*20th century*

# The Country Clergy

I see them working in old rectories
By the sun's light, by candlelight,
Venerable men, their black cloth
A little dusty, a little green
With holy mildew. And yet their skulls,
Ripening over so many prayers,
Toppled into the same grave
With oafs and yokels. They left no books,
Memorial to their lonely thought
In grey parishes; rather they wrote
On men's hearts and in the minds
Of young children sublime words
Too soon forgotten. God in his time
Or out of time will correct this.

*R.S. Thomas*
*20th century*

# *From:* The Prologue to The Canterbury Tales

THE PARSON

A holy-minded man of good renown
There was, and poor, the Parson to a town,
Yet he was rich in holy thought and work.
He also was a learned man, a clerk,
Who truly knew Christ's gospel and would preach it
Devoutly to parishioners, and teach it.
Benign and wonderfully diligent,
And patient when adversity was sent
(For so he proved in great adversity)
He much disliked extorting tithe or fee,
Nay rather he preferred beyond a doubt
Giving to poor parishioners round about
From his own goods and Easter offerings.
He found sufficiency in little things.
Wide was his parish, with houses far asunder,
Yet he neglected not in rain or thunder,
In sickness or in grief, to pay a call
On the remotest whether great or small

Upon his feet, and in his hand a stave.
This noble example to his sheep he gave,
First following the word before he taught it,
And it was from the gospel he had caught it...

His business was to show a fair behaviour
And draw men thus to Heaven and their Saviour,
Unless indeed a man were obstinate;
And such, whether of high or low estate,
He put to sharp rebuke to say the least.
I think there never was a better priest.
He sought no pomp or glory in his dealings,
No scrupulosity had spiced his feelings.
Christ and his Twelve Apostles and their lore
He taught, but followed it himself before.

THE PLOWMAN

There was a Plowman with him there, his brother.
Many a load of dung one time or other
He must have carted through the morning dew.
He was an honest worker, good and true,
Living in peace and perfect charity,
And, as the gospel bade him, so did he,
Loving God best with all his heart and mind
And then his neighbour as himself, repined
At no misfortune, slacked for no content,
For steadily about his work he went
To thrash his corn, to dig or to manure
Or make a ditch; and he would help the poor
For love of Christ and never take a penny
If he could help it, and, as prompt as any,
He paid his tithes in full when they were due
On what he owned, and on his earnings too.
He wore a tabard smock and rode a mare.

*Geoffrey Chaucer*
*1340?–1400*
translated by Nevill Coghill

# From: The Deserted Village

THE VILLAGE PREACHER

Near yonder copse, where once the garden smiled,
And still where many a garden flower grows wild;
There, where a few torn shrubs the place disclose,
The village preacher's modest mansion rose.
A man he was to all the country dear,
And passing rich with forty pounds a year;
Remote from towns he ran his godly race,
Nor e'er had changed, nor wished to change his place;

. . . . . . . . . . . . . . . . . .

At church, with meek and unaffected grace,
His looks adorned the venerable place;
Truth from his lips prevailed with double sway,
And fools, who came to scoff, remained to pray.
The service passed, around the pious man,
With steady zeal, each honest rustic ran;
Even children followed with endearing wile,
And plucked his gown, to share the good man's smile.
His ready smile a parent's warmth expressed,
Their welfare pleased him, and their cares distressed;
To them his heart, his love, his griefs were given,
But all his serious thoughts had rest in Heaven.
As some tall cliff, that lifts its awful form,
Swells from the vale, and midway leaves the storm,
Though round its breast the rolling clouds are spread,
Eternal sunshine settles on its head.

*Oliver Goldsmith*
*1728–74*

# A Conversion (1741)

Nathan Cole quit his plow
& hurry'd to hear Whitefield preach
& found his religion useless ash
before the stern words 1
'election' 'grace'

'Hellfire hellfire
ran Swift in my mind

'And while these thoughts
were in my mind
God appeared unto me
and made me Skringe: …
and I was Shrinked away
into nothing'

And in that nothing
Nathan Cole burst
with light, found
Farmington, Connecticut
ablaze with matter for praise:

all walls & common fences;
weeds, trees,
    and vines in special;
stones he'd earlier envy'd
for lack of soul –
now were new tongues to hymn
Election's glory,
Jehovah's sure salvation.
Selah.

*Eugene Warren*
*20th century*

# A Letter to John Donne

ON 27 JULY 1617, DONNE PREACHED AT THE PARISH CHURCH AT SEVENOAKS, OF WHICH HE WAS RECTOR, AND WAS ENTERTAINED AT KNOLE, THEN THE COUNTRY RESIDENCE OF RICHARD SACKVILLE, THIRD EARL OF DORSET.

I understand you well enough, John Donne
First, that you were a man of ability
Eaten by lust and by the love of God
Then, that you crossed the Sevenoaks High Street
As rector of Saint Nicholas:
I am of that parish.

To be a man of ability is not much
You may see them on the Sevenoaks platform any day
Eager men with despatch cases
Whom ambition drives as they drive the machine
Whom the certainty of meticulous operation
Pleasures as a morbid sex a heart of stone.

That you could have spent your time in the corruption of courts
As these in that of cities, gives you no place among us:
Ability is not even the game of a fool
But the click of a computer operating in a waste
Your cleverness is dismissed from this suit
Bring out your genitals and your theology.

What makes you familiar is this dual obsession;
Lust is not what the rutting stag knows
It is to take Eve's apple and to lose
The stag's paradisal look:
The love of God comes readily
To those who have most need.

You brought body and soul to this church
Walking there through the park alive with deer
But now what animal has climbed into your pulpit?
One whose pretension is that the fear
Of God has heated him into a spirit
An evaporated man no physical ill can hurt.

Well might you hesitate at the Latin gate
Seeing such apes denying the church of God:
I am grateful particularly that you were not a saint
But extravagant whether in bed or in your shroud.
You would understand that in the presence of folly
I am not sanctified but angry.

Come down and speak to the men of ability
On the Sevenoaks platform and tell them
That at your Saint Nicholas the faith
Is not exclusive in the fools it chooses
That the vain, the ambitious and the highly sexed
Are the natural prey of the incarnate Christ.

*C.H. Sisson*
*20th century*

# BIOGRAPHIES OF AUTHORS

**ABELARD, Peter 1079–1142**
French philosopher and scholar best
remembered for his love for Heloise.
He wrote a collection of hymns.

**ADAM, David 20th century**
Vicar of Holy Island, Northumberland,
England, has a deep interest in the Celtic
Christian tradition. His poems and prayers
are in Celtic style.

**ADDINK, Carol (now Von Klompenburg)
20th century**
American poet, graduate of Dordt College
with an MA in drama.

**ADDISON, Joseph 1672–1719**
Essayist and politician, co-founder of the
*Spectator* magazine.

**AGARD, John 20th century**
Guyanan poet, performer and children's
author. He has lived in the United Kingdom
since 1977.

**ANDERSON, Cathy 20th century**
Housewife, living in South Wales.

**ARNOLD, Matthew 1822–88**
Literary critic and leading 19th-century poet,
son of Dr Thomas Arnold, headmaster of
Rugby School.

**ASHWORTH, Anne 20th century**
Librarian who also teaches poetry at a sixth-
form college.

**AUDEN, Wystan Hugh 20th century**
English poet who later lived in the United
States and became an American citizen. He was
Professor of Poetry at the University of Oxford.

**AUDLEY, (AUDELAY) John 1426?**
Priest. In the manuscript of his verses he
describes himself as 'deaf, sick, blind'.

**AUSTIN, William 1587–1634**
Writer and barrister, his religious writings
were published after his death.

**BABBAGE, Humphrey 20th century**
Leading Australian poet. He taught in Papua
New Guinea for four years. Later involved in
Christian work in New South Wales.

**BALDWIN, William 1547?**
A 'corrector of the press' for a printer, later a
schoolmaster, provided theatrical exhibitions
for Queen Mary's court. He wrote metrical
translations of scripture.

**BARENDRECHT, Cor W. 20th century**
American poet, literary editor of *Calvinist-Contact*.

**BAUCKHAM, Richard 20th century**
Poet and university lecturer in theology.

**BAXTER, Richard 1615–91**
Nonconformist clergyman, chaplain to the
Puritan army. Wrote *The Saint's Everlasting
Rest*.

**BAYLEY, Joseph 20th century**
American poet and writer, on the editorial
staff of the David C. Cook publishing
company.

**BAYNES, Simon 20th century**
Vicar of Winkfield, Windsor. He has lived
and worked in Japan.

**BEDE, the Venerable 673?–735**
Anglo-Saxon scholar, theologian and
historian. He studied and taught at the
monastery in Jarrow, Northumberland.
Canonized in 1899.

**BELLERBY, Frances 1899–1975**
Poet, novelist and short story writer,
deeply influenced by the First World War.

**BELLOC, Hilaire 1870–1953**
French-born British writer and Roman
Catholic apologist; close friend of G.K.
Chesterton.

**BENNETT, John 20th century**
American poet, was Professor of English at
St Norbert College, Wisconsin.

**BERRIGAN, Daniel 20th century**
American poet, teacher, priest and apologist,
has taught theology at Fordham University.

**BERRYMAN, John 1914–72**
American poet, biographer, novelist and
academic, won the Pulitzer prize in 1965.
An alcoholic who finally took his own life.

**BETJEMAN, John 1906–84**
Poet, broadcaster and writer on architecture.
Poet Laureate in 1972, knighted in 1969.

**BIDWELL, Joan 20th century**
Poet, born in Devon. She was a design artist
before retirement.

**BINNEY, Thomas 1798–1874**
Born at Newcastle-on-Tyne, England, a
nonconformist minister. He wrote some fifty
books and several hymns.

**BINYON, Laurence 1869–1943**
Poet and art critic, for 20 years in charge of
Oriental prints and paintings at the British
Museum. Professor of Poetry at Harvard
University.

**BLACKMORE, Richard 1825–1900**
Poet and novelist. His best-known book is *Lorna Doone*.

**BLAKE, William 1757–1827**
Poet, artist and mystic. Worked as an engraver. Created his own beliefs from Christianity and various philosophies.

**BORGMAN, Paul 20th century**
American Christian poet and academic.

**BRADSTREET, Anne 1612–72**
English-born American Puritan poet. She emigrated to New England and her husband became governor of Massachusetts. She brought up eight children in conditions of hardship.

**BRAYBROOKE, Neville 20th century**
He has published poems in the *New Statesman*, the *Spectator* and the *Tablet* .

**BRIDGES, Robert 1844–1930**
Medical doctor then poet and amateur musician. He became Poet Laureate in 1913 and received the Order of Merit in 1929.

**BRONTË, Anne 1820–49**
Wrote as Acton Bell for the three Brontë sisters' volume *Poems* . She worked as a governess and wrote two novels.

**BRONTË, Emily 1818–48**
Wrote as Ellis Bell in *Poems* published by the three sisters. Best known for her only novel, *Wuthering Heights* .

**BROWN, George Mackay 20th century**
Leading Scottish poet and writer who lives in Orkney, background to much of his verse and prose.

**BROWN, T.E. 1830–97**
Brilliant scholar, teacher and curate from the Isle of Man. Much of his poetry in Manx. 'Full of Celtic fire and sensitiveness to beauty'.

**BROWNE, Simon 1680–1732**
Minister of an Independent Chapel. Tragedy brought on mental illness. He wrote theological treatises and hymns.

**BROWNE, Sir Thomas 1605–82**
Writer and physician, born in London. His best-known work is his confession of faith, *Religio Medici*.

**BROWNING, Elizabeth Barrett 1806–61**
Poet and author. Her marriage to Robert Browning freed her from her sickroom and a possessive father. They settled in Italy.

**BROWNING, Robert 1812–89**
Leading Victorian poet. His innovative poetry showed great psychological and spiritual insight.

**BUNING, Sietze 20th century**
American poet and academic, born to Reformed Protestant parents in Middleburg, Iowa.

**BUNYAN, John 1622–88**
Puritan preacher and writer, imprisoned for preaching as a nonconformist. The first part of his great allegory, *Pilgrim's Progress*, was written in Bedford gaol.

**BURNS, Robert 1759–96**
National poet of Scotland. Early influenced by ballads and songs, he rescued and renewed the Scottish folk tradition.

**BYROM, John 1692–1763**
Poet and stenographer, studied medicine but invented and patented a new system of

**CAEDMON 7th century**
The earliest Christian English poet known by name. According to Bede, he received a divine call to compose when he was a herdsman and became a monk at Whitby, under the abbess Hilda.

**CAMPION, Thomas 1567–1620**
Poet, musician and physician. His aim: 'to couple words and notes lovingly together'.

**CARLISLE, Thomas 20th century**
American Presbyterian pastor and poet.

**CARMICHAEL, Alexander 19th century**
Scottish Celtic scholar, who spent a lifetime collecting prayers, songs and poetry of the Scottish Hebridean islands.

**CARMICHAEL, Amy 1867–1951**
Writer and missionary in India who founded the Dohnavur Fellowship, a rescue home for children. Housebound after an accident in 1932.

**CARPENTER, Edward 1844–1929**
Priest, social reformer and writer, who left the church and turned to socialism and the craft movement of William Morris.

**CARTER, Sidney 20th century**
Folk singer, performing poet, teacher, hymnwriter and satirist.

**CAUSLEY, Charles 20th century**
Prize-winning poet, educator and anthologist who also compiled poetry collections for children.

**CAVENDISH, Margaret, Duchess of Newcastle 1625–73**
Exiled during the Civil War when she married William Cavendish. She wrote philosophy, poetry and drama.

**CENNICK, John 1718–55**
Prolific hymn-writer, from a Quaker family, brought up in the Church of England, and became a Moravian minister.

**CHAPMAN, Raymond 20th century**
Professor of English at the London School of Economics and Priest in Auxiliary Ministry.

**CHAUCER, Geoffrey 1343?–1400**
Founding English poet, best known for the Canterbury Tales. He travelled abroad widely and later received various crown offices.

**CHESTERTON, Gilbert Keith 1874–1936**
Critic, novelist, poet, studied art at the Slade School. He became a Roman Catholic in 1922. Popular for his Father Brown detective stories.

**CLARE, John 1793–1864**
Worked on his father's farm and had little schooling; He became successful as 'the peasant poet'. Sadly, ended his days in an asylum.

**CLEMO, Jack 1916–74**
Lived many years among the Cornish clay-pits, which inspired his writing. Deaf for forty years and blind for twenty-five, late marriage brought him much happiness.

**CLOUGH, Arthur Hugh 1819–61**
Resigned his fellowship at the University of Oxford when he rejected the dogmas of the Church of England. Commemorated in Matthew Arnold's poem Thyrsis.

**COGHILL, Nevill 20th century**
Irish-born medievalist and university professor, friend of Tolkien and C.S. Lewis. He translated Chaucer's Canterbury Tales into idiomatic modern English verse.

**COLERIDGE, Hartley 1796–1849**
Man of letters, eldest son of Samuel Taylor Coleridge. He was brought up by the poet Southey, and had a very chequered career.

**COLERIDGE, Mary 1861–1907**
Novelist, essayist and poet, a great-great niece of Samuel Coleridge. She taught at the Working Women's College.

**COLERIDGE, Samuel Taylor 1772–1834**
Published Lyrical Ballads with Wordsworth in 1798. Once a revolutionary, he moved to orthodox Christianity.

**COLLIER, Mary 1690?–1762**
Her parents taught her to read, but could not afford schooling. She worked hard at 'washing, brewing and such labour', devoting all her spare time to books.

**CONSTABLE, Henry 1562–1613**
Friend of Sir Philip Sidney, became a Roman Catholic and went to Paris where he was probably employed on secret missions to England and Scotland.

**COSIN, John 1594–1672**
Doctor of Divinity, Vice-Chancellor of Cambridge University. A friend of Archbishop Laud, he contributed to the final revision of the Prayer Book.

**COWLEY, Abraham 1618–67**
Went with Queen Henrietta Maria to Paris on the defeat of Charles I by Cromwell and was sent on Royalist missions. He returned to England at the Restoration.

**COWPER, William 1731–1800**
A great poet dogged by bouts of madness. A friend of John Newton, he contributed to his Olney Hymns . Two women – Mrs Unwin and Lady Austen – helped and encouraged him.

**CRABBE, George 1754–1832**
Son of a violent father and pious mother, he became a successful poet. First a surgeon, he was later ordained priest.

**CRASHAW, Richard 1613?–49**
Son of a noted Puritan divine, he later became a Roman Catholic. He lived in Paris, Rome and Loreto.

**CROSSMAN, Samuel 1624–83**
Preacher, writer and hymn-writer. He was appointed Dean of Bristol Cathedral a few weeks before his death.

**CRUM, J.M.C. 1872–1958**
Ordained and became Canon of Canterbury Cathedral. He wrote on St Mark's Gospel.

**CULBERTSON, E. Neil 20th century**
American poet. He was a chaplain's assistant during the Vietnam War.

**CYNEWULF 820?**
Anglo-Saxon poet and scholar from Mercia or Northumberland. His identity is known only from his own runic inscriptions on texts.

**DAVIE, Donald 20th century**
Distinguished scholar, poet and literary critic, who has published his collected poems and edited several anthologies.

**DAVIES, W.H. 1871–1940**
English poet who emigrated to the USA, returning to England, where he lived as a tramp and pedlar to raise money for his verses to be collected.

**DICKINSON, Barbara  20th century**
Civil servant who edited poetry magazines
and published two collections.

**DICKINSON, Emily  1830–86**
American poet, a recluse who wrote over a
thousand poems – original in thought and
style – most of them discovered and
published after her death.

**DICKINSON, Patric  20th century**
Academic, educator and poet who has won
poetry awards. He was Poetry Editor for the
BBC.

**DOBSON, Rosemary  20th century**
Australian poet, lives in Sydney. She has
compiled anthologies and published
several collections of verse.

**DODDRIDGE, Philip  1702–51**
Nonconformist clergyman, a pastor and
president of a theological college,
who wrote several well-known hymns.

**DOLBEN, Digby Mackworth  1848–67**
Educated at Eton, where he wrote his
devotional poems. He became a Benedictine
monk. He was drowned in a swimming
accident, aged 19.

**DONNE, John  1572–1631**
Metaphysical poet, who sailed with the Earl
of Essex to Cadiz. He was later ordained, and
became Dean of St Paul's and the greatest
preacher of his time.

**DOWDEN, Edward  1843–1913**
Irish writer, critic and poet. Became professor
of English literature at Trinity College,
Dublin, only four years after graduating there.

**DOWDEN, Mrs Edward  19th century**
Probably Dowden's second wife, Elizabeth
Dickinson (née West) who edited her
husband's poems after his death.

**DOWSON, Ernest  1867–1900**
Poet and translator of French classics, friend
of W.B. Yeats. He lived in France, and died
there of tuberculosis and alcoholism.

**DRUMMOND, William, of Hawthornden
1585–1649**
Son of a courtier, who devoted his life to
poetry and mechanical experiments. Friend of
Ben Jonson. His death was hastened by grief
for Charles I's execution.

**DRYDEN, John  1631–1700**
Poet, playwright and political satiririst. He
became a Roman Catholic and lost his
appointments as Poet Laureate and Royal
Historiographer in the revolution of 1688.

**DUNBAR, William  1460?–1520?**
May have graduated from St Andrews
University and become a Franciscan novice.
By 1504 he had taken priest's orders.

**DURIEZ, Colin  20th century**
Brought up in Wales, lived and studied in
Istanbul. Now lives in Northern Ireland.

**EARLE, John Charles  1749–1818**
Roman Catholic, one of the officiating priests at
the Spanish Ambassador's Chapel in London.

**ELIOT T.S.  1888–1965**
Verse playwright and leading poet of the
modern movement. He was born in America
but became a British citizen and joined the
Church of England.

**L'ENGLE, Madeleine  20th century**
American poet and award-winning writer of
children's books, converted from atheism. She
was librarian and writer-in-residence at the
Cathedral of St. John the Divine, New York.

**FANTHORPE, U.A.  20th century poet**
One-time teacher at Cheltenham Ladies
College, who has had several collections of
poems published.

**FARJEON, Eleanor  1881–1965**
Wrote fantasies and children's stories. There
is a Farjeon Award for outstanding work in
children's books.

**FENWICK, R.P.  20th century**
Served in the Second World War and began
writing poetry as a POW. He joined a Roman
Catholic religious order and became a priest
in 1984.

**FIELD, Michael**
The pen name of Katharine Bradley,
1846–1914, and her niece Edith Cooper,
1862–1913 who lived together and wrote
tragedies and volumes of verse. Both became
Roman Catholics. They died of cancer within
a year of each other.

**FLETCHER, Giles  1586–1623**
Brother of Phineas Fletcher and cousin of
John Fletcher, the dramatist. Reader in Greek
at Cambridge. He took a country living, but
his parishioners did not appreciate him.

**FLETCHER, Phineas  1582–1650**
Held a fellowship at King's College,
Cambridge. He was Rector of Hilgay in
Norfolk from 1621 until his death.

**GASCOYNE, David  20th century**
Published his first book of poems at sixteen
and his first novel the following year. In France
he encountered surrealist artists and poets.

**DE GASZTOLD, Carmen 20th century**
Wrote her Prayers from the Ark in a French convent. They were translated into English by the novelist Rumer Godden.

**GERSHON, Karen 20th century**
Poet, novelist and translator, born in Germany and came to England in 1938. Her German parents died in Hitler's concentration camps.

**GILMAN, Charlotte Perkins 1860–1935**
American feminist writer. She lectured on ethics, economics and sociology.

**GODFREY, Jan 20th century**
Freelance writer, married to a clergyman, closely involved with the Fellowship of Christian Writers.

**GOLDSMITH, Oliver 1728–74**
Irish playwright, novelist and poet. Best known for *She Stoops to Conquer*.

**GRAVES, Robert 1895–1985**
Poet, novelist, essayist and critic. Served in the First World War. Best known for his novels *I, Claudius* and *Claudius the God* .

**GRAY, Cecil 20th century**
Poet, anthologist and lecturer from Trinidad and Tobago, who greatly influenced Caribbean students. He now lives in Canada.

**GREENWELL, Dora 1821–82**
Struggled with poverty and ill-health, but published six volumes of poetry. She pleaded for greater work opportunities for educated women.

**HALDEN, Alistair 20th century**
Educated at Glasgow University, he became an English teacher. He has won poetry prizes.

**HALL, John 1627–56**
Poet and pamphleteer from Durham. Wrote rapidly and had a marvellous memory. Cromwell awarded him a pension for his pamphleteering.

**HALSALL, Martyn 20th century**
Teacher, then a journalist with *The Guardian*. He lives in Lancashire, England and is the paper's northern industrial correspondent.

**HANN, Isaac 1690–1778**
The verses in this anthology hang framed in the ancient Loughwood Baptist Meeting House, near Axminster, Devon, England, where Hann was once minister.

**HARDY, Thomas 1840–1928**
Novelist, poet and dramatist. Practised as an architect and church restorer for a time. Not an orthodox believer.

**HATCH, Edwin 1835–89**
Friend of some pre-Raphaelites, including William Morris. He became Professor of Classics at Toronto University and held academic posts at the University of Oxford.

**HAVERGAL, Frances Ridley 1836–79**
Knew Greek and Hebrew as well as several modern languages. Remembered for her hymns, especially 'Take my life and let it be'.

**HAWKER, Robert Stephen 1804–73**
Published poems and hymns. An Anglican priest, he was received into the Roman Catholic church the evening before he died.

**HEANEY, Seamus 20th century**
Irish poet and critic. He lectured at Queen's College, Belfast, before becoming a full-time writer.

**HEATH-STUBBS, John 20th century**
Poet, critic, anthologist and translator. Described as a 'Johnsonian presence with a Miltonic disability' (a reference to his blindness).

**HEBER, Reginald 1783–1826**
Hymn-writer and compiler, who became Bishop of Calcutta. His best-known hymn is 'Holy, holy, holy, Lord God almighty'.

**HECTOR, Rosemary 20th century**
Irish poet, now living in England. She has won the Edinburgh City Poetry Prize.

**HEMANS, Felicia Dorothea 1793–1835**
Published her first volume of poetry at 14 and wrote prolifically for children and adults. She was praised by Shelley and befriended by Scott and Wordsworth.

**HENDERSON, Stewart 20th century**
Writer and performance poet, born in Liverpool, who has introduced poetry to audiences unfamiliar with it.

**HERBERT, George 1593–1632**
Classical scholar, musician and poet of the Metaphysical school.He was a Member of Parliament with good connections at court, but relinquished them to become a parish priest in Devon.

**HERBERT, Mary, Countess of Pembroke 1561–1621**
Sister of Sir Philip Sidney, and patron of poets. She revised Sidney's *Arcadia* after his death.

**HERRICK, Robert 1591–1674**
Parish priest, described as the most pagan of English poets in spite of his religious poetry. He insisted that his life was not to be judged by his verse.

**HILL, Geoffrey 20th century**
Followed an academic career. His poetry is much concerned with death, sex and religion and his poems have won prestigious prizes.

**HINKSON, Katharine Tynan 1861–1931**
Irish poet and novelist, close friend of Alice Meynell and a leading light in the Irish Celtic Revival.

**HODGSON, Ralph 1872–1962**
A journalist in London, he published three volumes of poems about nature and England. After lecturing in Japan (1924–1938) he made his home in Ohio, USA.

**HOGGARD, Trevor 20th century**
Born in Nottinghamshire, he trained for the ministry.

**HOPKINS, Gerard Manley 1844–89**
Life-long friend of Robert Bridges; Jesuit novice then priest. His verse was experimental, using what he called 'sprung rhythm'.

**HOPKINS, Nancy 20th century**
Poet, writer of articles and short stories, born in Ireland. She came to London and lived in Germany for three years.

**HORNE, Frank 20th century**
Caribbean writer.

**HOUGHTON, Frank 1894–1972**
Was ordained and went as a missionary to China. He became Bishop of Eastern Szechwan, then General Director of the China Inland Mission.

**HOUSMAN, A.E. 1859–1936**
Poet and distinguished classical scholar. Best known for his cycle of poems *A Shropshire Lad*.

**HOW, William Walsham 1823–97**
Bishop of Wakefield. He wrote sermons, a Bible commentary and nearly sixty hymns, some still popular today.

**HOWE, Julia Ward 1819–1910**
American poet, married Samuel Howe, an anti-slavery campaigner. She wrote 'The Battle Hymn of the Republic' for the Northern States in the American Civil War.

**HRABANUS MAURUS 776–856**
Born in Mainz, became abbot of the monastery at Tours and later Archbishop of Mainz, where he dealt with heresy and was the greatest archbishop since Boniface'.

**HUGHES, Ted 20th century**
Yorkshire poet and children's writer, married the American writer Sylvia Plath. He studied archaeology and anthropology and worked as

zookeeper, nightwatchman and gardener before teaching. Became Poet Laureate in 1984.

**HULL, Eleanor 1860–1935**
Wrote on Celtic folklore. She wrote 'Be thou my vision' in verse after it had been translated from the original Irish (8th century) by Mary Byrne.

**HYLAND, Paul 20th century**
Writer and poet, many of his poems have been broadcast on BBC radio. A new collection of his poetry has recently been published.

**IMAGE, Selwyn 1849–1930**
Studied under John Ruskin at the Slade School and became Slade Professor of Fine Art. Ordained in the Anglican church, he published carols and poems.

**JELLEMA, Roderick 20th century**
American, grew up in Michigan. Teacher of English at the University of Maryland and co-director of the Washington National Poetry Centre.

**JENNINGS, Elizabeth 20th century**
Acclaimed poet. Her Roman Catholic faith and her poems are the most important things in her life. Once a library assistant and publisher's reader.

**JONSON, Ben 1572?–1637**
Dramatist and poet, who joined an acting company. He killed a fellow player in a duel and escaped execution by appealing to the clerical courts. Shakespeare acted in his play, *Every Man in his Humour*.

**KAVANAGH, Patrick 20th century**
Irish poet and novelist, he farmed before leaving Dublin to work as a writer and journalist.

**KEBLE, John 1792–1866**
Clergyman and poet, a leading light in the high-church Tractarian movement, along with Newman and Pusey. Wrote *The Christian Year* (poems).

**KELLY, Gerard 20th century**
Poet and performer at the Greenbelt Festival and in schools, churches and youth events. He has had a poetry collection published.

**KEN, Thomas 1637–1711**
Clergyman and hymnwriter. A royal chaplain, he refused to give up his house to Nell Gwynne when Charles II visited Winchester. Deprived of the bishopric of Bath and Wells when he refused to take the oath of allegiance in 1688.

**KENNELLY, Brendan  20th century**
Irish poet, playwright, novelist and anthologist of Irish verse. University lecturer living in Dublin.

**KING, Henry  1592–1669**
Bishop of Chichester, and a royal chaplain, suffered loss during the Civil War. He was a friend of Ben Jonson and Izaak Walton and a close friend of John Donne.

**KIPLING, Rudyard  1865–1936**
Journalist, poet and writer also for children. Born in India, and lived there later. His 'Recessional' was written for Queen Victoria's diamond jubilee.

**KIRKUP, James  20th century**
Poet, anthologist and translator. He has been a professor of English in Spain and Japan and poet in residence in the USA.

**KLUG, Ronald  20th century**
American book editor, he has also taught English at the American School, Madagascar.

**LAMB, Mary  1765–1847**
Sister of Charles Lamb. In a fit of insanity she killed her mother with a table knife. She and Charles together wrote *Tales from Shakespeare* and poems and stories for children.

**LANGLAND, William  1330?–1400?**
The allegorical poem *Piers Plowman* has been attributed to him since the 15th century. He lived in a hovel in London for a while, married and had a daughter.

**LANIER, Sidney  1842–81**
American academic, author, poet and musician. He fought with the Confederates in the American Civil War, where he developed tuberculosis, which later caused his death.

**LAWRENCE, D.H.  1885–1930**
Novelist, poet amd essayist. Son of a miner, he became a teacher then full-time writer. He rejected orthodox Christianity but later recognized the importance of spiritual realities.

**LEAX, John  20th century**
American poet, teaches English at Houghton College. He has had a collection published.

**LEE, Laurie  20th century**
Poet, author and scriptwriter. He travelled widely and has written about many parts of the world. *Cider with Rosie* describes his rural childhood.

**LEWIS, Cecil Day  1904–72**
Irish poet, critic and detective story writer, under the pseudonym of Nicholas Blake.

Once associated with left-wing causes, he renounced communism in 1939. Professor of Poetry at the Universities of Oxford and Harvard. Became Poet Laureate.

**LEWIS C.S  1898–1963**
Irish-born professor of English and writer, converted to Christianity. His broadcasts and books made Christian apologetics popular. He wrote children's books about the imaginary land of Narnia and an adult science fiction trilogy.

**LEWIS, Janet  Born 1899**
American writer best known as a novelist, she has also written children's books and opera librettos. She has taught at universities in the United States.

**LLOYD, Cyril  20th century**
Born in Wales, now living in England. He is a minister of religion.

**LONGFELLOW, Henry Wadsworth  1807–82**
American poet and academic. His poetry – which included 'Hiawatha' and 'The Wreck of the Hesperus' – was very popular in his lifetime.

**LONGFELLOW, Samuel  1819–92**
American. Brother of Henry, ordained as a Unitarian minister. Edited hymnbooks and wrote hymns and a biography of his brother.

**LUCAS, Tony  20th century**
Vicar in south London. His poetry has appeared in various English and American anthologies.

**LYDGATE, John  1370?–1450?**
Benedictine monk who may have studied at Oxford and Cambridge. He travelled on the Continent and became a prior in Essex. In spite of a pension as court poet, he died in poverty.

**MACDONALD, George  1824–1905**
Scottish poet and novelist, best known for his children's books. He was a Congregationalist pastor and later a university professor. Admired and revered by C.S. Lewis.

**MANGAN, James Clarence  1803–49**
Irish poet with a life of 'hapless love, poverty and intemperance'. He translated Irish and German poets.

**MANNYNG, Robert, (also known as Robert of Brunne)  1325?**
English poet and chronicler. In 1288 he entered the Gilbertine monastery near his home.

**MANWARING, Randle  20th century**
London-born poet, now lives in Sussex.
Deputy Chairman of Church Society and
Crusaders.

**de la MARE, Walter  1873–1956**
English poet and novelist, retired from work
on a state pension in 1908 to write full-time.
He wrote for children as well as adults.

**MARVELL, Andrew  1621–78**
Son of a Calvinist clergyman, he became
Milton's assistant, and a member of
Parliament. He tolerantly accepted the
Restoration while still admiring Cromwell.

**MASEFIELD, John  1878–1967**
Poet, novelist and journalist. He retired from
the Merchant Navy because of ill-health.
Appointed Poet Laureate in 1930.

**MASON, John  1645–94?**
Priest and hymnwriter, had a vision of Jesus
and preached that the Second Coming was
near. His last words: 'I am full of the loving
kindness of the Lord'.

**MEW, Charlotte  1861–1928**
Poet and short story writer, admired by
Thomas Hardy. Troubled by illness and family
worries, she committed suicide after her
sister's death.

**MEYNELL, Alice  1847–1922**
Poet, essayist, lecturer and journalist. She
became a Roman Catholic, and married
Wilfred Meynell, by whom she had eight
children. They befriended Francis Thompson.

**MILLER, Vassar  20th century**
American poet who has written three volumes
of poetry.

**MILMAN, Henry Hart  1791–1868**
Theologian, church historian, poet and
hymnwriter. Professor of Poetry at Oxford and
Dean of St Paul's. Described as 'the last of
the great conversers'.

**MILTON, John  1608–74**
Great poet and writer of religious and
political pamphlets. He became totally blind
but probably wrote *Paradise Lost, Paradise
Regained* and *Samson Agonistes* at the end of
his life.

**MITCHELL, Susan  1866–1926**
Irish poet, who mixed in Irish literary circles,
wrote for Irish journals and produced several
volumes of religious verse.

**MORE, Sir Thomas  1478–1535**
Statesman, scholar and writer. Tried to retire
as Lord High Chancellor rather than consent

to Henry VIII's divorce and breach with the
Roman Catholic Church. Executed for failing
to take the Oath of Supremacy. Canonized in
1935.

**MORGAN, Angela  Died 1957**
An American poet, she gave readings across
the United States.

**MORRIS, Mervyn  20th century**
Jamaican poet, academic and poetry
prizewinner. He is Reader in West Indian
Literature at the University of the West
Indies.

**MUIR, Edwin  1887–1959**
Born in Orkney, moved to Glasgow when he
was 14, he was self-educated.He came to
Christian faith late in life and wrote no poetry
until he was 35.

**MURRAY, Les A.  20th century**
Australian poet, leading literary figure, author
of five collections of poetry. He worked as a
translator but has been a full-time writer for
some years.

**MYERS, Frederick William Henry
1843–1901**
Became an Inspector of Schools. He was
president of the Society for Psychical
Research. Best known for his poem 'St Paul'.

**NASH, Ogden  20th century**
American light versifier, who used puns,
parody and alliteration to amuse and to
shock. Contributed often to the *New Yorker*
magazine.

**NEILL, William  20th century**
Former airman and teacher, now lives in
Galloway. He writes in Gaelic, Scots and
English and has published at least eight
collections of poetry.

**NELSON, Alice Dunbar  1875–1935**
American writer and teacher. Her husband,
Paul Dunbar, was the first Black poet widely
accepted in America. Together they collected
great Black literature to be performed on stage.

**NEWMAN, John Henry  1801–90**
Priest and theologian, who wrote for the
Tractarian movement of the Church of
England but later joined the Roman Catholic
Church and became a cardinal.

**NEWTON, John  1725–1807**
Went to sea at 11 and later became a slave
trader. Converted during a dangerous storm
at sea. Ordained in 1764. He and William
Cowper wrote the Olney Hymns. He helped
Wilberforce in the anti slave-trade campaign.

**NICHOLS, Grace 20th century**
Novelist, poet and children's writer. Born in Guyana, she came to Britain in 1977. She won the Commonwealth Poetry Prize.

**NICHOLS, Kevin 20th century**
Poet, teacher and student chaplain who has written widely on literature and education. Now a parish priest in County Durham.

**NICHOLSON, Norman 20th century**
Poet, novelist and playwright. He lives near the English Lake District and writes about its landscape.

**OLDENBURG, E. William 20th century**
American poet and professor of English who was killed in a car accident.

**ORFORD, Margaret 20th century**
Born in Harare, Zimbabwe, now lives in England. She has written historical novels and poetry.

**PALGRAVE, Francis Turner 1825–97**
Poet and critic, professor of poetry at Oxford. Best known as editor of the *Golden Treasury of Lyrical Poetry*.

**PALMER, Herbert Edward 1880–1961**
Poet and literary critic, taught English in England, France and Germany before becoming a full-time writer.

**PATERSON, Evangeline 20th century**
Poet, grew up in Dublin, Ireland, Deeply involved in revival of the arts among evangelical Christians. She has won major poetry prizes.

**PATMAN, Keith 20th century**
American, taught English, art and drama in North Carolina and is now working with his wife with Wycliffe Bible Translators.

**PATRICK, patron saint of Ireland 372–466**
According to legend, carried off by pirates at the age of 15 and sold as a slave in Ireland. He escaped, became a monk in France and later returned to Ireland as a missionary.

**PESTEL, Thomas 1584?–1659?**
Chaplain to King Charles I and a rector until removed by the Westminster Assembly of 1646. His hymns and sermons were published just before he died.

**PITMAN, Marion 20th century**
Poet, brought up in London and keeps a bookshop. She has won poetry competitions and published a collection.

**PITTER, Ruth Born 1897**
Wrote verse from an early age, later encouraged by Hilaire Belloc. She won poetry prizes and published collections of poetry.

**PLUNKETT, Joseph Mary 1887–1916**
Born in Dublin and edited the *Irish Review*. He suffered from ill-health and died in Dublin during the Easter Rebellion.

**POLLARD, Velma 20th century**
Jamaican, lecturer at the University of the West Indies. She has edited schools anthologies and published stories and poems.

**POOLE, Peggy 20th century**
Children's writer and poet, also a freelance journalist and broadcaster. She has had several collections of her poetry published.

**POPE, Alexander 1688–1744**
A leading poet of his century, highly satirical, a convinced Roman Catholic. He suffered all his life from ill-health. He was the first English poet to live by his writing.

**POST, Marie J. 20th century**
American poet, wife and mother from Grand Rapids.

**PRIOR, Matthew 1664–1721**
Poet and diplomat, who helped to bring about the Treaty of Utrecht (1713) for which he was imprisoned after Queen Anne's death. Master of light, epigrammatic and satirical verse.

**PRUDENTIUS 348–405?**
Contemporary of Augustine, Jerome and Ambrose, greatest of the Christian Latin poets. After a life in the law-courts he withdrew at 57 to seek the kingdom of God.

**QUARLES, Francis 1592–1644**
A staunch royalist. He married and had eighteen children and was equally prolific in his poetry. His *Emblems* was the most popular book of the century.

**RADBOD Died 917**
Went to the court of Charles the Bald and studied at St Martin's at Tours. He was made Bishop of Utrecht, where he was much loved

**RAINE, Kathleen 20th century**
Poet who has lived and written in Northumberland, England, since her second marriage broke up.

**RALEGH, Sir Walter 1552?–1618**
Explorer, courtier, writer, one-time favourite with Queen Elizabeth. He spent twelve years imprisoned in the Tower of London, where he wrote his *History of the World*. Finally executed

**ROBERTSON, Jenny 20th century**
Century social worker and writer of children novels and poetry. She and her husband encourage support of Christians in Eastern Europe and currently live in St Petersburg.

**ROLLE, Richard, of Hampole 1290?–1349**
About 1290–1349, mystic and poet, became a hermit at 19. He wrote lyrics, meditations and religious works in Latin and English and translated and expounded the Psalms.

**ROONEY, Elizabeth 20th century**
American poet and member of the Society of the Companions of the Holy Cross, an order of Episcopal laywomen. Her husband is an Episcopal priest.

**ROSSETTI, Christina 1830–94**
Prolific poet, daughter of a distinguished Italian political exile, brother of Dante Gabriel Rossetti. She did charitable work but was an invalid for much of her life.

**SANDYS, George 1578–1644**
English colonist and traveller in Europe and the Middle East. Acted as treasurer of Virginia in America. He wrote poetic versions of the Psalms as well as translating Latin authors.

**SASSOON, Siegfried 1886–1967**
Poet of the First World War, who won the Military Cross. He made an official protest against the slaughter on the Western Front. He became a Roman Catholic.

**SCANNELL, Vernon 20th century**
Writer and poet, who has won awards. Once a professional boxer, then an educator and since 1962 a professional writer and broadcaster.

**SCOTT, Dennis 20th century**
Jamaican playwright, actor, dancer, teacher and poet. He has published several poetry collections including the prizewinning *Uncle Time*.

**SCOTT, Sir Walter 1771–1832**
Scottish novelist and poet who became a national figure. He wrote ballads and novels, many historical.

**SEDULIUS, Scottus ?848–74**
Scholar and poet. After his early life in Ireland he went to France and settled at Liege.

**SHAKESPEARE, William 1564–1616**
Greatest English playwright and poet, also actor, joint-manager of a London acting company and part-owner of a theatre. His birthday is celebrated on 23 April, St George's Day.

**SHAW, Luci 20th century**
Poet grew up in England, Australia and Canada, studied in USA and married an American, with whom she ran a publishing firm. She lectures on poetry and creativity and has published five collections of poetry.

**SHERBURNE, Sir Edward 1618–1702**
Roman Catholic and royalist, deprived of his office as clerk of the ordnance during the Civil War. He wrote Latin tragedy and verse.

**SIDNEY, Sir Philip 1554–86**
Courtier, soldier, scholar and poet. He spent two years abroad at foreign courts and later served in Flushing. Died after a wound in battle.

**SISSON, C.H. 20th century**
Poet, served with British Army Intelligence in India then in Parliament (Under Secretary of State).

**SITWELL, Edith 1887–1964**
She and her brothers, Osbert and Sacheverell, were patrons of the arts. She became a Roman Catholic. Her later poetry is concerned with the suffering of the world.

**SKELTON, Philip 1707–87**
Son of an English settler in Ireland, fatherless at 11, grew up in extreme poverty as one of 10 children. When teacher and curate he gave away half his income and cared for others with generosity and compassion.

**SMART, Christopher 1722–71**
Had periods of madness throughout his life. He was confined in Bedlam, where he is said to have written 'Song to David'. He died heavily in debt. 'Rejoice in the Lamb' was not published until 1939.

**SMITH, Joshua 18th century**
American, compiled a book of *Divine Hymns or Spiritual Songs* in New Hampshire in 1784.

**SOUTHWELL, Robert 1561–95**
Poet and Jesuit martyr. Educated at Douai and Rome, he became chaplain to the Countess of Arundel. He was betrayed, thrown into the Tower of London, tortured thirteen times and hanged and quartered.

**de SOUZA, Eunice 20th century**
Born in India and educated at Bombay and Milwaukee Universities. Poet and literary columnist and Head of English at Bombay College.

**SPEED, Samuel Died 1681**
Stationer and bookseller who wrote verse. A contemporary of Samuel Speed, 1631–1681, a priest said to have fled the country for plotting against Cromwell and joined buccaneers in the West Indies.

**SPENSER, Edmund 1552–99**
Great poet, friend of Sir Philip Sidney and leader of a literary circle. His greatest work – unfinished – was The Faerie Queene, a tribute to Queen Elizabeth I.

**STAINER, Pauline 20th century**
Poet and beekeeper. Her first published collection was a Poetry Book Society recommendation.

**STARKEY, Mike 20th century**
Poet, newsreader and reporter on commercial radio. He has performed his poetry at the Greenbelt Festival and on TV, and published a collection.

**STEELE, Anne Died 1779?**
Daughter of a nonconformist preacher, she wrote a metrical version of the Psalms and many hymns, once popular, but no longer in hymn books.

**STEPHENS, James 1882–1950**
Irish poet and writer. Sent to an orphanage as a child, worked as a solicitor's clerk until successful enough to become a full-time writer.

**SUDERMAN, Elmer F. 20th century**
American academic and poet of Mennonite upbringing, now a Methodist lay preacher.

**SYMONDS, John Addington 1840–93**
Author and poet, who also translated from Latin and Italian. He wrote travel sketches and monographs on Shelley, Sidney and Jonson.

**TABB, John Bannister 1845–1909**
American who served in the Confederate Navy during the Civil War and met Sidney Lanier while a prisoner. Ordained, he became blind before he died.

**TAGORE, Rabindranath 1861–1941**
Indian poet, philosopher and Nobel prize winner. He founded a school to blend Eastern and Western philosophy and education.

**TAMPLIN, Ronald 20th century**
Academic and poet, who has translated Langland's poetry into idiomatic modern verse.

**TAYLOR, Edward 1645–1729**
English-born American colonist who became a Puritan pastor and poet.

**TAYLOR, Jeremy 1613–67**
Priest, theologian and writer, imprisoned three times during the English Civil War. Best known for Holy Living and Holy Dying.

**TENNYSON, Alfred, Lord 1809–92**
For many years poor, depressed and insecure before being hailed as the greatest poet of his day. Became Poet Laureate.

**THOMAS, R.S. 20th century**
Welsh poet and priest, living in Wales but widely recognized. Awarded the Queen's Medal for poetry.

**THOMPSON, Francis 1859–1907**
Religious poet, who failed in his attempts to become a priest or a doctor. Rescued from opium addiction by Wilfred and Alice Meynell, who cared for him until he died of tuberculosis.

**THRILLING, Isobel 20th century**
Her poetry has been on radio and television and in anthologies. She began writing after eye operations which saved her sight.

**TOLKIEN, J.R.R. 1892–1973**
South African-born philologist and writer, best-known for his trilogy, The Lord of the Rings. He was one of the 'Inklings', the literary coterie to which C.S.Lewis belonged.

**TOLLETT, Elizabeth 1694–1754**
Grew up in the Tower of London, where her father had a house. Well-educated, she wrote poems in English and Latin and a verse drama.

**TOPLADY, Augustus Montague 1740–78**
Clergyman and hymnwriter, defended Calvinism and argued well. Best remembered for his hymn 'Rock of Ages'.

**TRAHERNE, Thomas 1636?–74**
Poet, author and clergyman, whose main writings were not discovered until 1896 and 1897 and published in the early 20th century.

**TRENCH, Richard Chenevix 1807–86**
Irish priest, philologist and poet, Professor of Theology at London University, later Archbishop of Dublin.

**TUCKWELL, Patience 20th century**
Poet and educational therapist, who has worked in schools in the UK, Nigeria, Israel and America. She is now disabled by multiple sclerosis.

**TURNER, Steve 20th century**
Poet, writer and performer. He has published several collections.

**UNDERHILL, Evelyn 1875–1941**
Poet and mystic, who lectured on the philosophy of religion. She moved from agnosticism to Christianity.

**UPDIKE, John  20th century**
American novelist, poet and critic, once on the staff of the *New Yorker* magazine. His main status is as a major novelist.

**VANDER MEY, Randall  20th century**
American graduate of Calvin college, he studied for a PhD in English at the University of Pennsylvania.

**VATSA, Mamman Jiya  20th century**
Nigerian poet and children's poet. A lietenant colonel in the army, he lives now in Nigeria where he won a poetry award.

**VAUGHAN, Henry  1622–95**
Welsh poet, physician and Royalist supporter. He wrote only religious poetry after a spiritual experience following serious illness.

**VERY, Jones  1830–80**
American mystic and poet, who lived a retired life in Salem. He became a Unitarian minister and was a friend of Ralph Waldo Emerson.

**WADDELL, Helen  1889–1965**
English medievalist, born in Tokyo. She translated medieval Latin poetry into verse,and also translated prose works.

**WALING, Steven  20th century**
Theology graduate who attends Quaker meetings. He launched and edits a magazine.

**WALKER, Jeanne Murray  20th century**
American Professor of Literature and Creative Writing at Haverford College.

**WALLER, Edmund  1606–87**
Poet and politician, cousin of John Hampden. A Member of Parliament, he plotted on behalf of Charles I, was arrested and exiled for a time.

**WALTNER-TOEWS, David  20th century**
Canadian, brought up in a Mennonite Brethren community in Winnipeg.

**WALTON, John  1410?**
An Augustinian canon of Osney Abbey. He translated the works of the Roman philosopher, Boethius, popular in medieval Europe.

**WANLEY, Nathaniel  1634–80**
Poet and parish priest. His poems remained in manuscript until the 20th century.

**WARREN, Eugene  20th century**
American poet, grew up on a Kansas farm and teaches English at the University of Missouri. Has published several collections of poetry.

**WARREN, James E., Jr.  20th century**
American academic and poet, member of the United Methodist Church. He has published at least nine books of poems and many essays.

**WASHBOURNE, Thomas  1606–87**
Canon of Gloucester, published sermons and poems.

**WATT, Jean M.  20th century**
Of Scottish and Welsh parentage. One-time social worker, she has published poetry and prose translations from French and German.

**WATTS, Isaac  1674–1748**
Hymnwriter, dissenting pastor and eminent preacher at an Independent Congregation. He established the place of hymns in English worship.

**WEDDERBRUN, James, John and Robert  1567?**
Three sons of a Scottish merchant who all graduated at St Andrews University. James upset the church authorities by the plays he wrote and fled to France. John became a priest but was accused of heresy and fled to Wittenburg, joining Luther and other reformers. He wrote and translated Psalms, hymns and ballads. Robert became Vicar of Dundee and wrote some 'Gude and Godlie Ballates'.

**WESLEY, Charles  1707–88**
Scholar, clergyman and hymn-writer, younger brother of John Wesley. He joined his brother as an itinerant missionary. He is said to have written over six thousand hymns.

**WESLEY, John  1703–91**
Evangelist and founder of Methodism who travelled and preached in the open air. In over 50 years he covered 25,0000 miles, mainly reaching working-class neighbourhoods.

**WESTERDUIN, Grace  20th century**
Irish born, graduate of Queen's University, Belfast. She taught at Wilson College in Bombay, married a Dutchman working with United Nations and now lives in Belgium.

**WESTERFIELD, Nancy  20th century**
American poet and English teacher.

**WHEATLEY, Jeffery  20th century**
Poet and business economist. He has written several books.

**WHITING, William  1825–78**
Poet and hymnwriter, known now only for 'Eternal Father Strong to Save'.

**WHITTIER, John Greenleaf  1807–92**
American Quaker writer, poet, journalist and abolitionist, highly acclaimed in his lifetime.

**WILD, Robert  1609–79**
Puritan clergyman and poet, son of a shoemaker. He was a satirist with a reputation for wit and a friend of Richard Baxter.

**WILDE, Oscar  1856–1900**
Irish playwright, novelist, essayist, poet and wit. In later life he was prosecuted and imprisoned for his homosexuality.

**WILKINSON, Marguerite  1883–1928**
Born in Canada and grew up in America, she was a lecturer and poetry reviewer,interested in Christian mysticism. She drowned in a swimming accident.

**WILLIAMS, Charles  1886–1945**
Wrote extensively – novels, poetry and criticism. His writing greatly influenced C.S. Lewis.

**WIRT, Sherwood E.  20th century**
American who has written a number of books and was formerly editor of *Decision* magazine.

**WOLCOT, John  1738–1839**
Pseudonym Peter Pindar. He became physician-general of Jamaica. He became ordained but later devoted his time to writing satires in verse.

**WOTTON, Sir Henry  1568–1639**
Traveller, diplomatist, scholar and poet. Sent by James I as ambassador to Venice, he later became provost of Eton.

**YOUNG, Andrew  1885–1971**
Scottish poet, attached to the YMCA in France during World War I. Minister of an English Presbyterian church, he later became an Anglican vicar.

**YOUNG, Edward  1683–1765**
Poet and writer of satirical verses, he was made chaplain to the king. His *Night Thoughts* were very popular.

# Index of Authors

## a

Peter Abelard  226
David Adam  56, 266
Carol Addink  337
Joseph Addison  46, 378
John Agard  267
Cathy Anderson  306
Matthew Arnold  141
Cliff Ashby  14, 143
Anne Ashworth  71
W.H. Auden  202, 383
William Austin  195

## b

Humphrey Babbage  85
William Baldwin  62
Cor W. Barendrecht  58
Richard Bauckham  308
Richard Baxter  178, 188
Joseph Bayley  223
Simon Baynes  387
Frances Bellerby  107
Hilaire Belloc  285
John Bennett  243
Daniel Berrigan  390
John Berryman  288
John Betjeman  168, 300, 401
Joan A. Bidwell  275

Laurence Binyon  118
Richard Doddridge Blackmore  357
William Blake  52, 104, 105, 108, 138, 146, 284, 346
M. Bond  326
Paul Borgman  389
Anne Bradstreet  310, 342, 358
Neville Braybrooke  323
Robert Bridges  132, 195
Anne Brontë  381
Emily Brontë  116, 147, 366
George Mackay Brown  123, 272
T.E. Brown  9
Sir Thomas Browne  280
Elizabeth Barrett Browning  308
Robert Browning  144, 149, 331, 351
Sietze Buning  259, 319
Anna Bunstan  82
John Bunyan  29, 126, 183
Robert Burns  32
John Byrom  16

## c

Caedmon  39
Thomas Campion  36, 128, 356
Thomas John Carlisle  15, 385
Amy Carmichael  86, 177, 185
Edward Carpenter  88
Sydney Carter  398

Charles Causley 220
Margaret Cavendish, Duchess of Newcastle 347
John Cennick 282
Raymond Chapman 179, 274
Geoffrey Chaucer 187, 403
G.K. Chesterton 107, 313, 315
John Clare 77, 112, 173
Jack Clemo 27, 120, 245, 397
Arthur Hugh Clough 157
Hartley Coleridge 302, 362
Mary Coleridge 16, 52, 192, 237, 371
Samuel Taylor Coleridge 317
Mary Collier 261
Abraham Cowley 359
William Cowper 23, 64, 78, 153, 174
George Crabbe 307, 365
Richard Crashaw 54, 312, 390
J.M.C. Crum 235
E. Neil Culbertson 379
Cuthbert 351
Cynewulf 41, 277

d

Donald Davie 251
W.H. Davies 199
Barbara Dickinson 102
Emily Dickinson 50, 71, 76, 151, 172, 175,
    279, 345, 355, 375
Patric Dickinson 393
Rosemary Dobson 316
Philip Doddridge 181
Digby Mackworth Dolben 26
John Donne 20, 30, 34, 166, 229, 354
Edward Dowden 11
Mrs Edward Dowden 136
Diana Downing 98
Ernest Dowson 353
William Drummond of Hawthornden 205, 210,
    340, 386
John Dryden 377
Colin Duriez 110

e

John Charles Earle 51
T.S. Eliot 63, 219, 239
Madeleine L'Engle 32, 55, 387

f

U.A. Fanthorpe 261
R.P. Fenwick 310
Michael Field 145
Giles Fletcher 56
Phineas Fletcher 30
Edith Forrest 137

g

Carmen de Gasztold 98, 101
Karen Gershon 384
Stephanie Gifford 262
Jan Godfrey 94, 113
Oliver Goldsmith 404
Robert Graves 108
Cecil Gray 400
Dora Greenwell 212

h

Alistair Halden 150
John Hall 74
Martyn Halsall 79
Isaac Hann 140
Thomas Hardy 193
Edwin Hatch 242
Frances Ridley Havergal 178
Robert Stephen Hawker 219
Seamus Heaney 97
John Heath-Stubbs 93, 97, 102
Reginald Heber 339
Rosemary A. Hector 263
Felicia Dorothea Hemans 361
Stewart Henderson 89, 242, 290, 328
George Herbert 37, 38, 45, 60, 65, 112, 114,
    171, 184, 248, 265
Mary Herbert, Countess of Pembroke 171
Robert Herrick 12, 27, 47, 165, 212, 271, 348,
    364
Geoffrey Hill 67, 399
Katharine Tynan Hinkson 81
Ralph Hodgson 90
Trevor Hoggard 75
Gerard Manley Hopkins 69, 79, 115, 140, 172,
    315
Nancy Hopkins 357
Frank Horne 209
Frank Houghton 129
Caryll Houselander 395
Julia Ward Howe 161
Ted Hughes 119
Paul Hyland 24, 156, 303

j

Roderick Jellema 330
Elizabeth Jennings 122, 210, 217, 293, 306, 320
Bobi Jones 321
Ben Jonson 35

k

Patrick Kavanagh 18
John Keble 42

Gerard Kelly 73
Thomas Ken 277, 281
G.A. Studdert Kennedy 87, 268
Brendan Kennelly 182
Jean Kenward 206
Henry King 354
Rudyard Kipling 37
James Kirkup 117
Ron Klug 203

## l

Mary Lamb 273
William Langland 61, 91, 155
Sidney Lanier 224
Andrew Lansdown 294
D.H. Lawrence 54, 128, 181
Thelma Laycock 48
John Leax 250, 336
Laurie Lee 215, 232
Anne Lewin 13
C.S. Lewis 106
D.M. Lewis 154
Janet Lewis 325
Cyril Lloyd 114
Henry Wadsworth Longfellow 201, 213, 248
Samuel Longfellow 122
Tony Lucas 88
John Lydgate 127

## m

George MacDonald 10, 24, 49, 143, 341
Robert Mannying of Brunne 305
Randle Manwaring 361
Walter de la Mare 252
Tim Marks 273, 334
Peter Marshall 304
Andrew Marvell 43, 80
John Masefield 29
Eugene Mason 10
John Mason 25
Hrabanus Maurus 302
Randall Vander Mey 236
Alice Meynell 132, 208, 234, 346
Vassar Miller 137
Henry Hart Milman 222
John Milton 134, 170, 182, 197, 342
Susan Mitchell 216
Sir Thomas More 66,
Angela Morgan 367
Mervyn Morris 339, 391
Edwin Muir 190, 352, 383
Les A. Murray 369
Daisy Myrie 256

## n

Ogden Nash 100
William Neill 252
Alice Dunbar Nelson 263
John Henry Newman 44
John Newton 180, 184
Grace Nichols 99
Kevin Nichols 123
Norman Nicholson 385
Sheila Nottage 382

## o

E.W. Oldenburg 253
Margaret Orford 99

## p

Francis Palgrave 246
Herbert Edward Palmer 269
Evangeline Paterson 136, 258, 109, 324, 329,
   350, 358, 374, 375, 399
Keith Patman 208
St Patrick 159
Thomas Pestel 198
Marion Pitman 233
Ruth Pitter 95
Joseph Mary Plunkett 77
Velma Pollard 84
Peggy Poole 292
Alexander Pope 192
Marie J. Post 221, 254
Matthew Prior 29
Prudentius 283

## q

Francis Quarles 36, 343

## r

Radbod 317
Kathleen Raine 74
Sir Walter Ralegh 131, 314
Jenny Robertson 323
Richard Rolle 57
Elizabeth Rooney 217, 230, 232, 264
Christina Rossetti 14, 48, 61, 121, 200, 216,
   241, 314, 352, 360

## s

George Sandys 236
Siegfried Sassoon 145, 313
Vernon Scannell 199, 301, 305, 335
Dennis Scott 299
Sir Walter Scott 380
Sedulius Scottus 169
William Shakespeare 304, 317, 363

Luci Shaw  86, 105, 116, 207, 278
Sir Edward Sherburne  65
Sir Philip Sidney  63
Kamal Singh  70
C.H. Sisson  340, 406
Edith Sitwell  295
Philip Skelton  41
Christopher Smart  39, 92, 103, 109, 255, 279
Robert Southwell  59, 204, 344
Eunice de Souza  285
Edmund Spenser  235, 370
Pauline Stainer  321
Mike Starkey  289
Anne Steele  341
James Stephens  100
Erlene Stetson  286
Elmer F. Suderman  149, 249, 332
John Addington Symonds  17

**t**

John Bannister Tabb  83
Ronald Tamplin  298
John Tatum  135
Edward Taylor  264
Jeremy Taylor  214, 377
Alfred, Lord Tennyson  67, 70, 152, 348, 355
R.S. Thomas  139, 151, 164, 254, 311, 402
Francis Thompson  18, 247
Isobel Thrilling  231, 316
J.R.R. Tolkien  125,
Elizabeth Tollett  307
Thomas Traherne  183
Diane Karay Tripp  33
Richard Chenevix Trench  23
Patience Tuckwell  322, 328
Steve Turner  287, 345

**u**

Evelyn Underhill  75, 241
John Updike  238

**v**

Mamman J. Vatsa  380
Henry Vaughan  51, 234, 371
Jones Very  15

**w**

Jeanne Murray Walker  20, 396
Edmund Waller  353
John Walton  177
Nathaniel Wanley  214
Rodney Ward  93
Eugene Warren  405
James E. Warren Jr.  364
Thomas Washbourne  175
Jean M. Watt  115
Isaac Watts  38, 193, 227, 244, 325, 372
James, John and Robert Wedderburn  202
Charles Wesley  19, 33, 62, 257, 276
John Wesley  21
Grace Westerduin  266, 338
Nancy Westerfield  233
Jeffery Wheatley  216
John Greenleaf Whittier  142, 176
Oscar Wilde  138
Marguerite Wilkinson  73
Shirwood E. Wirt  391
John Wolcot (Peter Pindar)  90
Sir Henry Wotton  186, 312

**y**

Edward Young  250

# Index of First Lines

**a**

A cold coming we had of it  218
A curiously empty day  232
A dinner-party, coffee, tea  274
A dog starved at his master's gate  109
A frosty Christmas Eve  194
A God and yet a man  189
A holy-minded man of good renown  402
A name written in sand  58
A pagan fire to conjure in the spring – 233
A rusted grating in the ancient wall  252
A shell – how small an empty space  86

A streak of Sappho, it is said  397
A trapped bird  182
A wife at daybreak I shall be  355
Adam in the suburban garden  149
after winter rain the enormous sky  113
Aged in one stroke  336
Aged, infirm and incontinent  333
All earthly things that blessed morning  28
All in tune to William's flute  196
All is best, though we oft doubt  1341
All night had shout of men and cry  234
All other love is like the moon  59
All our love is deeply (as a folk  308

All sights and sounds of day and year 341
All that is moulded of iron 269
All that matters is to be at one with the living
    God 54
All this night shrill chanticleer 195
Almighty God, whose justice like a sun 285
Alone to sacrifice thou goest, Lord 226
Always 206
Amazing grace! how sweet the sound 184
Among the towering pines 361
An old woman, sitting among petunias 262
And if to-night my soul may find her peace 124
And if you go up that way, you will meet with a
    man 151
And is there care in heaven? and is there love
    370
And oh! there lives within my heart 381
And so we took him down 230
and that will be heaven 374
Anodda year of love 339
As a white candle in a holy place 326
As fragile as an eggshell bauble 305
As from the power of sacred lays 377
As I in hoary winter's night stood shivering in
    the snow 204
As the brittle water dripped 386
Ask me no more, my truth to prove 307
Astride the colt and claimed as King 221
At the round earth's imagined corners blow 30
Autumn is here and summer will not stay 116
Awake, my soul, and with the sun 277

b

Batter my heart, three-personed God, for you 20
Be near me when my light is low 355
Be thou my vision, O Lord of my heart 160
Because I could not stop for Death 345
Before he leaves on his fated journey 351
Before the beginning thou hast foreknown the
    end 352
Behold the prodigal! To thee I come 29
Birds I saw in bushes made nests 91
Bless, O God, my little cow 256
Bonhoeffer in his skylit cell 399
Both were dwellers 105
Bowing adorers of the gale 112
Brave flowers – that I could gallant it like you
    354
Breathe on me, breath of God 242
Bring me the sunset in a cup 76
But, ah, our sins, our clouds benight the air 36
By all means 267
By cool Siloam's shady rill 339

c

Calm on the bosom of thy God 361
Can I see another's woe 284
Cat, smoother soother than a velvet glove 326
Chaff 379
Christ, as a light 159
Christ of his gentleness 108
Christ, my Beloved, which still doth feed 62
Christ who knows all his sheep 179
Christ, whose glory fills the skies 276
Christmas Eve, and twelve of the clock 193
Citizen Philip Sparrow, who likes 93
Close by the careless worker's side 268
Come down, O Christ, and help me! reach thy
    hand 138
Come, heavy souls, oppressed that are 175
Come, Holy Ghost, our souls inspire 240
Come, O thou Traveller unknown 19
Come with birds' voices when the light grows
    dim 241
Contentment is a sleepy thing 183

d

Death and darkness get you packing 234
Death, be not proud, though some have called
    thee 354
Devil! I tell thee without nubbs or jubbs 140
Disgusting, really, the way it disfigures 294
Do not forget, Lord 98
Don't be a kyatta-pilla 99
Don't give the children 316
Down from the hills, they come 256
Drop, drop, slow tears 30
Drop thy still dews of quietness 176

e

Each time you go, I'm buried and I hear 20
Each wave that breaks upon the strand 83
Enjoy thy stream, O harmless fish; 90
Ere I sleep, for every favour 282
Eternal Father, who didst all create 132
Even such is Time, which takes in trust 314
Every Christmas we feed the poor 285
Everything panicked. Trees shrieked 236
Expecting him, my door was open wide 9

f

Fain would I say, 'Forgive my foul offence 32
Fairest of morning lights appear 198
Fall, leaves, fall; die, flowers, away 116
Fear death? – to feel the fog in my throat 351
Fear no more the heat o' the sun 363
First chestnut tree, the candle master 79

Flawlessly typed, and spaced  261
Flee from the crowd and dwell with truthfulness: 187
Flower in the crannied wall  70.
Fly envious Time, till thou run out thy race  342
For I will consider my cat Jeoffrey  103
Forth in thy name, O Lord, I go  257
From all that dwell below the skies  38

## g

Give me my scallop-shell of quiet  130
Give me to be thy child, and learn for ever at thy knee  139
Given, not lent  208
Glorious things of thee are spoken  180
Glory be to God for dappled things –  79
Glory to thee, my God, this night  281
God be in my head  55
God be with thee in every pass  128
God moves in a mysterious way  153
God of grave nights  73
God stir the soil  168
God strengthen me to bear myself;  314
God to enfold me  50
God's boundless mercy is (to sinful man)  27
God's intrusion, upthrust granite  303
Good and great God! How should I fear  12
Good is an orchard, the saint saith  81
Great Nature clothes the soul, which is but thin  347
Green  293
Grow old along with me!  331

## h

Hail, heavenly beam, brightest of angels thou  277
Hands that steered the tractor  332
Happy choristers of air  74
Hark, my soul! It is the Lord;  64
Hatred and vengeance, my eternal portion  174
He first deceased – she, for a little tried  312
He fumbles at your soul  13
He is so small the stars bow down  210
He seems to come in like the leaves –  48
He that is down needs fear no fall  183
He who bends to himself a joy  346
He wrestles straining flesh  388
Hear me, O God!  35
Henry Vaughan saw eternity  179
Here come I, the death-watch beetle  102
Here I am and forth I must  129
Here on this accustomed table  274
Hierusalem, my happy home  373
High in the steepled church the shining bells  254
His candle shines upon my head  278

'Hold still,'  162
House-proud housewives, listen to the rumble – 266
How do I love thee? Let me count the ways  308
How fresh, O Lord, how sweet and clean  111
How happy is he born and taught  186
How long, O Lord, shall I forgotten be?  171
How shall I find him, who can be my guide?  10
Hunger and thirst, O Christ, for sight of thee  317
Hush! my dear, lie still and slumber  324

## i

I am a telephone  380
I am aware  367
I am the wind which breathes upon the sea  49
I am – yet what I am none cares or knows  173
I asked for Peace –  26
I come in the little things  75
I could not name a single blessing  27
I dream a dig through dust:  24
I dreamt us strolling, arm in loving arm  390
I fled him, down the nights and down the days; 18
I found thee in my heart, O Lord  11
I give you thanks, Lord God of nations  356
I guard myself with this rod and give myself into God's protection  130
I had grown weary of him; of his breath  315
I have always considered  101
I have no wit, no words, no tears;  121
I heard the bells on Christmas day  201
I know not what the future hath  142
I love the sunshine in the kitchen  273
I love the very thought of Heaven:  72
I missed him when the sun began to bend;  10
I never saw a moor  375
I saw a stable, low and very bare  192
I see his blood upon the rose  77
I see the pattern of stars and sun  306
I see them working in old rectories  402
I shall know why, when time is over  175
I share and share and share again  242
I sing of a maiden  191
I sit and sew – a useless task it seems  263
I spoke to the dead, oiled sea-bird  292
I stayed with her when I was six then went  335
I understand you well enough, John Donne  406
I wake and feel the fell of dark, not day  172
I was a stricken deer, that left the herd  23
If ever two were one, then surely we  310
If I could shut the gate against my thoughts  31
If love be strong, hot, mighty and fervènt  66
If there had anywhere appeared in space  23

In her chosen corner she sits. Rivers of knitting 258

In her small single room 398

In March he was buried 118

In the bleak mid-winter 200

In the hour of death, after this life's whim 357

In the hour of my distress 165

In the quiet place 275

In the shuffling melancholy 328

Into the woods my Master went 224

Intolerably sad, profound 167

It can alter things; 301

It doesn't come easy 135

It is a fearful thing to fall into the hands of the living God 181

It is exasperating 155

It was a dismal, and a fearful night 359

It was from Joseph first I learned 387

I'd never wish my childhood back to me 327

I've found the pearl of greatest price 25

## j

January comes with his ice-crown 123

Jesu, I now begin 57

Jesu, since thou me made and bought 57

Joy to the world! the Lord is come 193

## k

King of glory, King of peace 45

## l

Lavinia is polite, but not profane; 250

Leave me, O love, which reachest but to dust; 63

Lent is a tree without blossom, without leaf 115

Let all the world in ev'ry corner sing 38

Let folly praise that fancy love, I praise and love that Child 59

Let man's soul be a sphere, and then, in this 228

Let me not to the marriage of true minds 304

Let not mistaken mercy 357

Let others look for pearl and gold 212

'Let us not speak, for the love we bear one another – 300

Listen! I will describe the best of dreams 228

Little lamb, who made thee 105

Little monitor, by thee 341

Live while you live, the Epicure would say 181

Lo! I am come to autumn 313

Long after the birth 321

Lord 101

Lord, come away! 377

Lord, grant us calm, if calm can set forth thee; 48

Lord, how can man preach thy eternal word? 248

Lord, I am lonely 14

Lord, in thine anger do not reprehend me 170

Lord, it belongs not to my care 188

Lord, make my heart a place where angels sing! 42

Lord of the winds, I cry to thee 16

Lord, thou clepedest me 11

Lord, thou hast given me a cell 270

Lord, what unvalued pleasures crowned 22

Love asks to penetrate 154

Love bade me welcome; yet my soul drew back 65

Love is and was my Lord and King 67

Lullee, lullay 325

## m

Make me, O Lord, thy spinning wheel complete 264

Make no mistake 238

May a strong guardian 272

May the Father take you 347

May the Light of lights come 278

Mercy is hendest where sin is most 31

Mild yoke of Christ, most harsh to me not bearing 137

Mine eyes have seen the glory of the coming of the Lord: 161

Miserere, my Make 349

Mock on, mock on, Voltaire, Rousseau; 138

Most glorious Lord of life, that on this day 235

Mute, with signs I speak: 145

My blood so red 221

'My brethren…' And a bland, elastic smile 251

My glass is half unspent; forbear to arrest 343

My hands are warm to the butterfly 98

My home, my lovely home, she wept 384

My own heart let me more have pity on; let 315

My soul, there is a country 371

My spirit longeth for thee 16

## n

Nathan Cole quit his plow 405

Near yonder copse, where once the garden smiled 404

Never weather-beaten sail more willing bent to shore 356

New doth the sun appear 340

No coward soul is mine 147

No night could be darker than this night 215

No revolution will come in time 398

No war of earth or heaven darkens 250

No worst, there is none. Pitched past pitch of grief 140

Non nobis  37
None other Lamb, none other Name  14
Nothing is so beautiful as spring –  115
Nothing is to man so dear  305
Now come all you who have been brought  177
Now I arise, empowered by thee  255
Now is the time for the burning of the leaves  118
Now the green blade riseth from the buried grain  235
Now we must praise the Guardian of Heaven  39
Now, when the frail and fine-spun  350
Nuns keep vigil with psalm and measured voice  323

O

O all the problems other people face  288
O come, dear Lord, unbind: like Lazarus,  32
O God the Holy Ghost who art Light unto thine elect  241
O God, give me of thy wisdom  356
O heart, be lifted up; O heart be gay  356
O King! thou art the wall-stone  41
O Lord support  322
O Lord, my heart is all a prayer  177
O Lord, seek us, O Lord, find us  61
O my dear heart, young Jesus sweet  202
O never harm the dreaming world  74
O shut your bright eyes that mine must endanger  202
O soul, canst thou not understand  145
O thou not made with hands  246
O thou who camest from above  62
O thou who dost direct my feet  129
O thou, whose eyes were closed in death's pale night  291
O Time the fatal wrack of mortal things  342
O world invisible, we view thee  247
O years! and age! farewell:  364
Of all the creatures both in sea and land  37
Oft have I seen at some cathedral door  248
Often I try  254
Often the wanderer pleads for pity  127
Oh, you gotta get a glory  258
Old Uncle Fred could squint along forty-foot beams  330
On a day sweet with April showers  253
On a night like this I could wish for wisdom  304
On earth there is no man so self-assured  83
On this doorstep I stand  324
One of these nights about twelve o'clock  376
One spirit – his  78
One time of the year  206

Only a gentle swish  84
Orphaned and elderly and yet a child  320
Over the great city  87

P

Paulina the heifer would not stand still  259
Pilgrim remember  26
Poor soul, the centre of my sinful earth  317
Praise above all – for praise prevails  39
Praise to the Holiest in the height  44
Prayer is like watching for the  13

r

Rejoice in God, O ye tongues; give glory to the Lord, and the Lamb  92
Remorse is memory awake  172
Rich man, rich man, who are you?  217
Ride on! Ride on in majesty!  222
Rods of rain piledrive mercilessly into the tarmac  75
Run, shepherds, run, where Bethlem blest appears  210

s

Safe where I cannot lie yet  360
Saint Francis found his way (saints, in a dream  96
Saturday afternoon. Professor Paterson  309
Saviour of mankind, Man, Emmanuel!  236
'Say bold but blessed thief  392
Say not the struggle naught availeth  157
See how the flowers, as at parade  80
See where she sits now  329
Seek the Lord, and in his ways persever  128
Set free thy people, set free thy servants  169
Shadow and coolness, Lord, art thou to me  185
'Shall I bring you wisdom, shall I bring you power?'  217
She passed away like morning dew  362
She sweeps with many-coloured brooms  279
she'd have had her mother's eyes  289
Sick wards. The sailed beds  164
Silent is the house: all are laid asleep:  366
Since I am coming to that holy room  166
Six centuries have gone  252
Sleep now, little one  203
So free, so bright, so beautiful and fair  243
Socks and stockings  263
Soeur Marie Emilie  394
Some creatures of our God and King  98
Some folks can afford  81
Spirit of place. Spirit of time. Re-form  122
Spring  231
Step nearer to my canvas gracious traveller  382

Still falls the Rain – 294
Stop, Christian passer-by! – Stop, child of God 317
'String him up,' some repoman shouted 154
Strong Son of God, immortal Love 152
Sunset and evening star 348
Sunshine let it be or frost 52
Sweet day, so cool, so calm, so bright 114

t

Tarry no longer; toward thine heritage 127
Teach me, my God and King 265
Thank you 216
That day of wrath, that dreadful day 380
That man over there say 286
The angel and the girl are met 190
the cormorants 93
The Council's plywood barricades 88
The dove descending breaks the air 63
The enclosed garden, sensuous and chaste 156
The fool said to the animals 107
The grass is pleasant here 391
The grave grows firm with grasses 364
The kind old face, the egg-shaped head 401
The kingdoms fall in sequence, like the waves on the shore 95
The last and greatest herald of heaven's King 386
The lilac bush puts forth its purple spikes 114
The lopped tree in time may grow again 344
The Lord in his wisdom made the fly 100
The Lord's Prayer 249
The man of Mercy (says the Seer) 109
The maples are burning 334
The Misses Norman lived on Marine Square 400
The night is come like to the day 280
The off'rings of the Eastern kings of old 214
The only news I know 50
The other night 205
The proud Egyptian Queen, her Roman guest 65
The ring, so worn as you behold 307
The rivulet-loving wanderer Abraham 383
The Road goes ever on and on 125
The rooftree of the year is fallen, fallen 123
The sacred Three be over me 266
The Saviour comes! by ancient bards foretold: 192
The sea is calm to-night 141
The seas are quiet when the winds give o'er 353
The sky is low, the clouds are mean 71
The sky was low, the sounding rain was falling dense and dark 106

The South East Asians 287
The star has risen in the heart 216
The sunshine bathes in clouds of many hues 77
The Three Kings rode through the gate and the guard 213
The time to weep is in the heart's winter 110
The toil of day is ebbing 283
The tree of life my soul hath seen 42
The tree waves in the wind 142
The waves run up the shore 139
The white hill-side is prickled with antlers 340
The wintry winds have ceased to blow 365
The wise guys 209
The word came 385
The world is charged with the grandeur of God 69
Then I saw the wild geese flying 18
Then live, my strength, anchor of weary ships 302
There blows a cold wind today, today 158
There have been bombs before 296
There is a land of pure delight 372
There is a tree grows upside down 245
There shall always be the Church and the World 239
Therefore to whom turn I but to thee, the ineffable Name? 144
There, in that other world, what waits for me? 371
There's something religious in the way we sit 321
These are 345
These clothes, of which I now divest 279
They gave to thee 214
They hanged him on a clement morning, swung 299
They lie at rest, our blessed dead; 360
They say there is a hollow, safe and still 178
They were all looking for a king 24
They wondered why the fruit had been forbidden; 383
They, looking back, all the eastern side beheld 133
This is my little town 264
This is the month, and this the happy morn 197
Those – dying then 151
Thou art the peace of all things calm 56
Thou art the Way 132
Thou bidst me come away 348
Thou hast come safe to port 362
Thou hidden love of God, whose height 21
Thou who createdst everything 226
Three ancient men in Bethlehem's cave 219

Throw away thy rod  60
Thrums nor odds of thread  262
Thus far did I come loaden with my sin  29
Thy God was making haste into thy roof  54
Times without number have I prayed  33
Time's running out  338
'Tis winter now; the fallen snow  122
To God, the everlasting, who abides  17
To God, ye choir above, begin  40
To Mercy, Pity, Peace, and Love  52
To see a World in a grain of sand  146
To spread the azure canopy of heaven  205
To those whom death again did wed  312
Tonight  223
True faith matures without discarding  120
Truth proclaims it: love the wonder healer –  61
Tune thy music to thy heart  68
Twice  94
Two mites, two drops (yet all her house and land)  390
Two still-green trees rub together  84
Two women meet each morning to pray  323
'Twould ring the bells of Heaven  90
Tyger! Tyger! burning bright  104

**u**

Under the watchful lights  199
Unto my faith as to a spar, I bring  136
Upon the eyes, the lips, the feet  353
Upon the sandy shore an empty shell  86

**v**

View me, Lord, a work of thine  36

**w**

Wanting to be myself, alone  316
We are a Garden walled around  244
We doubt the Word that tells us: Ask  134
We give thanks for St Thomas  137
We had our ritual too. Down the long glen  150
We know a field  117
We met  311
We stood on the hills, Lady  211
Were my parents right or wrong  318
What a spendthrift you are, sir  71
What attracted us to one another initially  290
What God gives, and what we take  47
What happy, secret fountain  51
What hath man done that man shall not undo  56
What he never thought to consider was whether  136
What is there in my heart that you should sue  67

What shall avail me When I reach the border?  352
When all thy mercies, O my God  46
When all virtue  33
When bright Orion glitters in the skies  260
When fishes flew and forests walked  107
When Francis preached love to the birds  97
When God at first made man  184
When I consider how my light is spent  182
When I survey the wondrous Cross  227
'When I'm alone' - the words tripped off his tongue  313
When Jesus came to Golgotha they hanged him on a tree  87
When light broadens behind the curtains, and I wake  358
When Mary thro' the garden went  237
When Moses, musing in the desert, found  385
When rising from the bed of death  378
When they moved into the house he said  310
When thou turn'st away from ill  49
When we were idlers with the loitering rills  302
Where does the lion, Judah's lion walk?  208
Where the remote Bermudas ride  43
Whether I kneel or stand or sit in prayer  55
Who is at my window? Who? Who?  12
Who knows the name and country now  199
Who would guess that thin-breasted body  396
Who would true valour see  126
Who's that knocking on the window  220
Why first, you don't believe, you don't and can't  148
Wide fields of corn along the valleys spread;  51
Wilt thou forgive that sin where I begun  34
Wilt thou not visit me?  15
Winter wakens all my care  121
With floods and storms thus we be tossed  176
With this ambiguous earth  346
With troubled heart and trembling hand I write  358
Wrapped in his shroud of wax, his swoon of wounds  232

**y**

Yesterday the gentle  393
Yes, it is beautiful country  375
Yet if his Majesty, our sovereign lord  53
You are as inevitable as morning  89
You ever feel  702
You make love and you live together now  306
You see that bench in front of Meagher's store?  368
You were, till now  337

# Acknowledgments

We would like to thank all those who have given us permission to include poems in this anthology. Every effort has been made to trace and contact copyright owners. If there are any inadvertent omissions in the acknowledgments we apologize to those concerned. Each figure refers to the page numbers of a poem.

Abelard, Peter (translated by Helen Waddell): 226, from *Medieval Latin Lyrics*, Constable & Co Ltd 1933; (US) Mary Martin

Adam, David: 56, 266, from *The Edge of Glory*, SPCK/1985. Used by permission of SPCK.

Addink, Carol: 337

Agard, John: 267, by kind permission of John Agard c/o Caroline Sheldon Literary Agency, *By All Means Bless* from *Loveliness for a Goat-Born Lady* published by Serpent's Tail 1990

Anderson, Cathy: 306

Ashby, Cliff: 14, 143, from *Plain Song*, Carcanet Press Ltd, 1985

Ashworth, Anne: 71

Auden, W.H.: 202, from *W.H. Auden: Collected Poems* edited by Edward Mendelson, Faber & Faber 1972, (US) Random House Inc.; 383, from *Collected Shorter Poems*, Faber & Faber, (US) Random House Inc.

Babbage, Humphrey: 85

Barendrecht, Cor W.: 58

Bauckham, Richard: 308

Bayley, Joseph: 223, from *Psalms of my Life*, reprinted by permissions of Chariot Family Publishing

Baynes, Simon: 387

Bellerby, Frances: 107, from *Selected Poems*, Enitharmon Press, used with permission of David Higham Associates

Belloc, Hilaire: 285, reprinted by permission of the Peters Fraser & Dunlop Group Ltd

Bennett, John: 243, from *The Reformed Journal*, Wm. B. Eerdmans Publishing Co

Berrigan, Daniel: 390, The World Publishing Company

Berryman, John: 288, Faber & Faber, (US) Farrar, Straus & Giroux Inc.

Betjeman, John: 168, 300, 401, reprinted by permission of John Murray (Publishers) Ltd

Bidwell, Joan A.: 275

Bond, M.: 326

Borgman, Paul: 389

Braybrooke, Neville: 323

Brown, George Mackay: 123, 272

Buning, Sietze: 259, 319

Caedmon: 39, from *Anglo-Saxon World*, Oxford University Press, 1984, used with permission of Rogers, Coleridge and White Ltd

Carlisle, Thomas John: 15, 385

Carmichael, Amy: 86, Dohnavur Fellowship; 177, from *Rose from Brier*; 185, from *Gold Cord*. Used with permission of Christian Literature Crusade

Carter, Sydney: 398, National Book League

Causley, Charles: 220, from *Collected Poems*, Macmillan, used with permission of David Higham Associates

Chapman, Raymond: 179, 274

Chaucer, Geoffrey: 187, translated by Henry Van Dyke, from *The Man behind the Book*, Charles Scribner's Sons; 403, translated by Nevill Coghill, from *The Canterbury Tales*, Penguin Classics 1951, Fourth revised edition 1977, reproduced by permission of Penguin Books Ltd

Clemo, Jack: 245, used with kind permission of Mrs R, Clemo; 120, 397, reprinted by permission of Bloodaxe Books Ltd, from *Selected Poems*, Bloodaxe books 1988

Crum, J.M.C.:235, from *The Oxford Book of Carols*, used by permission of Oxford University Press

Culbertson, E. Neil: 379

Cynewulf: 277, translated by Sir Israel Gollancz, from *God of a Hundred Names,* reproduced with kind permission of Victor Gollancz Ltd

Davie, Donald: 251, from *Brides of Reason*, Carcanet Press Ltd

Dickinson, Barbara: 102,

Dickinson, Patric: 393, from *The Bearing Beast*, Chatto & Windus Ltd, used with permission of Mrs Sheila Dickinson

Dobson, Rosemary: 316, from *Collected Poems*, by permission of HarperCollins Publishers Australia

Downing, Diane: 98

Duriez, Colin: 110

Earle, John Charles: 51, reproduced by permission of Burns & Oates Ltd

Eliot, T.S,: 63, from *Little Gidding*; 219, from *Ariel Poems*; 239, from *Collected Poems*. Used by permission of Faber & Faber, (US) Harcourt Brace

L'Engle, Madeleine: 32, 387, reprinted from *The Weather of the Heart* by Madeleine L'Engle, © 1978 by Crosswicks, used by permission of Harold Shaw Publishers, Wheaton, Il, USA; 55, from *The Risk of Birth*, Harold Shaw Publishers

Fanthorpe, U. A.:261, from *Selected Poems*, Peterloo Poets

Fenwick, R.P.: 310

Forrest, Edith: 137,

de Gasztold, Carmen (translated by Rumer Godden): 98, 101, from *Prayers from the Ark*, Macmillan Children's Books, (US) Curtis Brown Ltd

Gershon, Karen: 384, from *Coming Back from Babylon*, Victor Gollancz Ltd, literary executor of Karen Gershon

Gifford, Stephanie: 262

Godfrey, Jan: 94, 113

Graves, Robert: 108, from *More Poems*, Cassell and Co. Ltd, 1961

Gray, Cecil: 400

Halden, Alistair: 150

Halsall, Martin: 79

Heaney, Seamus: 97, from *Death of a Naturalist*, Faber & Faber

Heath-Stubbs, John: 93, 97, 102, from *Collected Poems 1943–1987*, Carcanet, reprinted by permission of David Higham Associates

Hector, Rosemary A.,:263

Henderson, Stewart: 89, 242, 290, 328, from *Assembled in Britain – Poems 1972–1986*, Marshall Pickering, reprinted by permission of HarperCollins Publishers

Hill, Geoffrey: 67, 399, from *Collected Poems by Geoffrey Hill*, Penguin Books 1985, copyright © 1978 Geoffrey Hill, used with permission of Penguin Books Ltd, (US) Oxford University Press, New York

Hodgson, Ralph: 90, used by permission of Macmillan London Ltd and the Estate of Ralph Hodgson, (US) Macmillan Publishing Co, New York

Hoggard, Trevor:

Horne, Frank: 209, from *Kid's Stuff*, Simon & Schuster

Houghton, Frank: 129

Houselander, Caryll: 395, from *The Flowering Tree*, Sheed and Ward Ltd

Hughes, Ted: 119, from *Season's Songs*, Faber & Faber, (US) Penguin USA

Hyland, Paul: 24, 156, 303, from *The Stubborn Forest* by Paul Hyland, Bloodaxe Books, 1984

Jellema, Roderick: 330

Jennings, Elizabeth: 122, 210, 293, 306, 320, from *Time and Seasons*, Carcanet Press, reprinted by permission of David Higham Associates; 217, from *Consequently I Rejoice*, Carcanet Press, reprinted by permission of David Higham Assoc

Jones, Bobi (translated by Joseph Clancy): 321, from *Selected Poems*, Christopher Davies Publishers Ltd

Kavanagh, Patrick: 18, by kind permission of the trustees of the Estate of Patrick Kavanagh, c/o Peter Fallon, Literary Agent, Loughcrew, Oldcastle, Co. Meath, Ireland

Kelly, Gerard: 73

Kennelly, Brendan: 182

Kenward, Jean: 206, from *A Book of Faith* by Elizabeth Goudge, Hodder and Stoughton

Kirkup, James: 117

Klug, Ronald: 203, from *Decision*, Billy Graham Evangelistic Assocation

Langland, William: 61, 91, 155, translated by Ronald Tamplin, reprinted with permission of Ronald Tamplin

Laycock, Thelma: 48

Leax, John: 250, 336

Lee, Laurie: 215, 232, Peters, Fraser & Dunlop Group Ltd

Lewin, Ann: 13

Lewis, C.S.: 106, reprinted by permission of HarperCollins Publishers Ltd

Lewis, D.M.: 154

Lewis, Janet: 325, reprinted with permission of Ohio University Press/Swallow Press, Athens, USA

Lloyd, Cyril: 114, reprinted with permission of Mrs Grace Lloyd

Lucas, Tony: 88

Manwaring, Randle: 361

de la Mare, Walter: 252, used by permission of the Literary Trustees of the Estate of Walter de la Mare and The Society of Authors

Marks, Tim: 273, 334

Marshall, Peter: 304

Masefield, John: 29, from *The Everlasting Mercy*, used by permission of The Society of Authors as the literary representatives of the Estate of John Masefield

Maurus, Hrabanus (translated by Helen Waddell): 302, from *Medieval Latin Lyrics*, Constable & Co. Ltd 1933, (US) Mary Martin

Miller, Vassar: 137, from *Wage War on Silence*, © 1960 by Vasar Miller, Wesleyan University Press by permission of the University Press of New England, USA

Morgan, Angela: 367

Morris, Mervyn: 391, from *Shadowboxing* by Mervyn Morris, published by New Beacon Books Ltd 1979, reprinted by permission of New Beacon Books Ltd

Muir, Edwin: 190, 352, 383, from *Collected Poems*, Faber & Faber, (US) Oxford University Press USA

Murray, Les: 369

Myrie, Daisy: Nelson Carribean

Nash, Ogden: 100, Reprinted by permission of Curtis Brown Ltd, New York copyright © 1942 Ogden Nash, renewed; (US) from *Verses from 1942 On* by Ogden Nash, by permission of Little Brown and Co. USA

Neill, William: 252

Nichols, Grace: 99, from *The Fat Black Woman's Poems*, Virago Press, reprinted by permission of Virago Press

Nichols, Kevin: 123

Nicholson, Norman: 385, From *Fiver Rivers*, Faber & Faber

Oldenburg, E.W.: 253, from *Sightseers into Pilgrims*, Harold Shaw Publishers Ltd

Orford, Margaret: 99

Palmer, Herbert: 269, reprinted with permission of Mrs Phoebe Hesketh

Paterson, Evangeline: 136, 258, 309, 329, 350, 358, 374, 375, 399

Patman, Keith: 208

Pitman, Marion: 233

Pitter, Ruth: 95, from *Collected Poems 1926–1960*, Barrie and Jenkins Ltd; from End of Drought, Barrie and Jenkins Ltd

Pollard, Velma: 84

Poole, Peggy: 292

Post, Marie, J.: 221, 254

Prudentius (translated by Helen Waddell): 283, from *Medieval Latin Lyrics*, Constable & Co. Ltd 1933, (US) Mary Martin

Radbod (translated by Helen Waddell): 317, from *Medieval Latin Lyrics*, Constable & Co. Ltd 1933, (US) Mary Martin

Raine, Kathleen: 74

Robertson, Jenny: 323

Rooney, Elizabeth: 217, 230, 232, 264, poems copyright © Elizabeth Rooney and reprinted here with her permission

Sassoon, Siegfried: 145, 313, G.T. Sassoon

Scannell, Vernon: 199, reprinted by permission of Vernon Scannell; 303, 305, 335, from *Love Shouts and Whispers* by Vernon Scannell, published by Random House UK Ltd, reprinted by permission of Random House UK Ltd

Scott, Dennis: 299, reprinted from *Uncle Time* by Dennis Scott, by permission of the University of Pittsburgh Press, © 1973 Dennis Scott

Scottus, Sedelius (translated by Helen Waddell): 169, from *Medieval Latin Lyrics*, Constable & Co. Ltd 1933, (US) Mary Martin

Shaw, Luci: 86, 207, from *The Secret Trees*, reprinted by kind permission of Luci Shaw; 105, 278, from *Listen to the Green*, reprinted by kind permission of Luci Shaw; 116 reprinted from *The Sighting*, © 1981 by Luci Shaw, used by permission of Harold Shaw Publishers, Wheaton, Il, USA

Singh, Kamal: 70

Sisson, C.H: 340, 406, from *Collected Poems*, Carcanet Press Ltd 1984, used by permission of Carcanet Press Ltd

Sitwell, Edith: 295, from *Collected Poems*, Sinclair Steveson, reprinted by permission of David Higham Associates

de Souza, Eunice: 285

Stainer, Pauline: 321, from *The Honeycomb*, Bloodaxe Books 1989, reprinted with permission of Bloodaxe Books

Starkey, Mike: 289

Stephens, James: 100, reprinted with permission of the Society of Authors, on behalf of the copyright owner, Mrs Iris Wise

Suderman, Elmer F.: 149, 249, 332

Tamplin, Ronald: 298

Tatum, John: 135

Thomas, R.S.: 139, 164, 311, from *Mass for Hard Times* by R.S. Thomas, reprinted by permission of Bloodaxe Books Ltd, 151, 254, from *Selected Poems 1946–1968* by R.S. Thomas, reprinted by permission of Bloodaxe Books Ltd, 402, reprinted by permission of R.S. Thomas

Thrilling, Isobel: 231, 316

Tolkien, J.R.R.: 125, from *Lord of the Rings*, reprinted with permission of HarperCollins Publishers Ltd, (US) Houghton Mifflin Company

Tripp, Diane Karay: 33

Tuckwell, Patience: 322, 328

Turner, Steve: 287, 345 Hodder and Stoughton

Updike, John: 238, from *Collected Poems 1953–1993* by John Updike, Hamish Hamilton 1993 (first published by Alfred A Knopf,), copyright © John Updike 1960, 1993, reproduced by permission of Hamish Hamilton Ltd, (US) Alfred A Knopf

Vander Meym Randall: 236

Vatsa, Mamman J.: 380

Walker, Jeanne Murray: 20, 396

Ward, Rodney: 136

Warren, Eugene: 405

Warren, James E. Jr.: 364

Watt, Jean M.: 115

Westerduin, Grace: 266, 338

Westerfield, Nancy: 233, *Christianity Today*

Wheatley, Jeffery: 216

Wirt, Sherwood E.: 391, from *Decision*, Billy Graham Evangelistic Association